Occupied with Crime

Sir Richard Jackson, C.B.E.

Occupied
with Crime

1967
DOUBLEDAY & COMPANY, INC.
GARDEN CITY, NEW YORK

LIBRARY OF CONGRESS CATALOG CARD NUMBER 66–17426
COPYRIGHT © 1967 by Sir Richard Jackson
ALL RIGHTS RESERVED
PRINTED IN THE UNITED STATES OF AMERICA
FIRST EDITION IN THE UNITED STATES OF AMERICA

CONTENTS

6

Occupied with Crime

CHAPTER 1

A Small Room, Overlooking the Thames

When I was young, I thought of Scotland Yard, like the wild West, as a place of romantic adventure. I was not alone in this agreeable delusion; it was, and is, shared by half the world. The Assistant Commissioner himself has always been a favourite character in detective fiction. Later I found out that there are four Assistant Commissioners at Scotland Yard, but in the stories there was only one—the Assistant Commissioner in charge of criminal investigation. Sometimes he was a master mind, a spider at the centre of his web, controlling a small army of detectives. Sometimes, as I now realise, he grossly neglected his real duties to go out detecting on his own.

Alas for youthful dreams. When I came eventually to hold this position myself, I had long ceased to see the job in detective story terms or to feel at all like the hero of a thriller. After twelve years in the office of the Director of Public Prosecutions, working closely with the C.I.D., and seven years as Secretary at the Yard itself, I had few illusions of that sort left. I knew what the Assistant Commissioner's job would be like. I was faced, in the event, with two developments, both ominous for the future health of this country, which I did not expect and which I think no one could have predicted; but of those more in due course.

When people ask me about Scotland Yard, I often find that the first thing I must do is to explain what it isn't.* It is not,

* Or rather wasn't. In 1967 the Metropolitan Police moved their headquarters to an expensive new building some quarter of a mile away, larger and more streamlined but less distinctive.

9

for instance, a National Department for the investigation of crime.

New Scotland Yard is a rather ugly building on the Embankment. Within this building were the headquarters of the Metropolitan Police who are responsible for guarding the lives and property of more than 8,000,000 people in an area of more than 736 square miles. The official name for these headquarters is the Commissioner's Office. The Assistant Commissioner "C" is in charge of both the Criminal Investigation Department and the Special Branch. The great majority of the detective officers serving under him, however, are not at Scotland Yard at all but based on the twenty-four Divisions which make up the Metropolitan Police District. They don't get much publicity and they rarely feature in thrillers but they have to handle almost all crimes in the Metropolitan Police area, and supervising them is an important part of the A.C.C.'s job.

All high level administrative jobs doubtless have much in common. Some of my duties were, however, slightly different from those which the director of a business might be called upon to undertake. For instance I had to authorise payments to informants. Each authority was signed by me personally. I allowed payments only for information which had actually led to a conviction. The amounts were carefully considered. They were just large enough—or so we hoped—to keep the flow of information going.

The informant's real names were never given. In most cases only the officer to whom an informant talked knew his real name. "This informant," I remember writing on one chit, "must be advised to change his pseudonym." The name he had chosen was "Joe Jackson" (and Joe I should explain is what most people call me).

"C" Department's whole purpose is to fight criminals. No Assistant Commissioner, however competent an administrator, would be much good if he didn't throw himself enthusiastically had acquired a great deal of knowledge about criminals and about the police.

Authors nowadays tend to be more scrupulous, or at least more wary, about accuracy of background. Many of those who used policemen in their stories came to see me when I was at the Yard. I was able to give some guidance to the television companies too. In the original opening to "No Hiding Place," an otherwise accurate and agreeable series, Superintendent Lockhart was provided with a pair of motorcycle outriders whenever he drove forth in splendour from Scotland Yard: an escort which, I pointed out, was not used in real life even by the Commissioner.

In my room at the Yard I had a number of detective stories and books about crime, which their authors had sent me; together with several volumes of the Notable British Trials series, an admirable compilation which I have collected ever since my university days.

It was a small room, overlooking the Thames; much less impressive than the grandiose office which television and film producers generally imagine for the Assistant Commissioner. Small, but, I think, the right size. For conferences it would just hold fifteen or sixteen people sitting intimately in chairs round the desk, an arrangement I much prefer to the rather pompous atmosphere which inevitably arises when people are formally seated at a long table. Once a month we had a Superintendents' Conference attended by about sixty, but that was held in the main conference room. The most I ever needed to assemble in my office were the Chief Superintendents of the various Branches of the Department plus the Commander and two Deputy Commanders.

When I first saw that room, visiting my friend Ronald Howe, it was painted dark green and mustard yellow. The furniture was heavy and dark. The chimneypiece was decorated, if that's the right word, with a pair of opium pipes and three death masks borrowed from the Black Museum. This was rather too melodramatic for my taste.

I sent back the opium pipes and the death masks, and replaced them with a large bronze tiger which had been given to my father by his friends in India when he retired from the Bar. I also had a portrait of my great-grandfather, Sir Thomas Turton, who became Advocate General of Bengal.

From the crime writer's point of view, my desk was perhaps more satisfactory. Beside the three telephones, it bore what might have been described in an old-fashioned thriller as "strangely wrought Oriental daggers." They were, in fact, two Malay krises, the workmanship of their wavy blades as delicate as watered silk, which I had acquired on a visit to Malaya in 1949.

Because I never felt that being Assistant Commissioner was a romantic job, I saw no necessity to surround myself with romantic or dramatic trappings. But, if it wasn't romantic, it was of course fascinating. Directing any important organisation is a satisfying thing to do, and the C.I.D. is, by any standards, a very important organisation indeed. If Scotland Yard isn't quite what outsiders suppose, it is nevertheless justly world-famous, and I was proud to be connected with it. And since my own work was concerned not primarily with techniques or machines but with people, it was endlessly varied and interesting.

Had I continued in practice, I suppose I might have made a success at the criminal Bar and perhaps ended as a Metropolitan Magistrate or even one of the Judges at the Old Bailey or London Sessions. I would probably have enjoyed myself in any of these roles, but no more than I enjoyed being head of criminal investigation at New Scotland Yard—and probably not as much.

Never for a moment have I regretted my decision to enter that curious Victorian building with its famous arch and turrets; a decision I took in the autumn of 1945.

On that November afternoon, I was in the West London Magistrates Court, appearing before Mr. Paul Bennett, V.C. I represented the Director of Public Prosecutions, in whose department I had then worked for twelve years. My job that day was to open proceedings against two Polish deserters, Marian Grondkowski and Henryk Malinowski, who were charged with murder.

The police officer in charge of the case was Detective Chief Inspector Somerset, to whom, many years later, I gave command of the Detective Training School. I remember being once again struck, as I read his report and the accompanying statements, with the speed and thoroughness of the C.I.D.'s work.

The body had been found, shortly after 6:30 A.M. on November 1, by a police constable walking his beat through Chepstow Place, Kensington. The corpse lay slumped on the rear seat of an Opel motorcar. A felt hat had been placed over the face, which was covered in blood. The man had evidently been shot through the head from behind at close range. There were some fragments of glass on his clothes, apparently from the light in the roof, which had been smashed.

A post-mortem examination, carried out within a few hours by Dr. Donald Teare, showed that the bullet had entered at the nape of the neck, passed through the brain and emerged above the right eye. Dr. Teare put the time of death as between 2 and 4 A.M. and estimated that the victim had lived about twenty minutes after being shot, though unconscious and incapable of movement.

Meanwhile, an examination of the victim's clothes revealed the probable motive. All but one of his pockets had been turned inside out. The exception was his left trouser pocket, on which his body had been lying; this contained £6:10:0 in notes, the only property of any value found on him.

More fragments of glass from the interior light were found on the floor and on the seat at the rear. A .32 nickel-plated bullet and an empty cartridge case lay on the floor beside the driver's seat. Just above and to the front of this seat, there was a dent in the metal roof of the car, apparently caused by the bullet. The man had obviously been shot while in the driver's seat and then carried to the rear and robbed.

Bloodstained fingerprints appeared quite clearly on the off-side pillar of the windscreen. The Fingerprint Branch failed to identify them, which suggested that the murderer was not a convicted criminal. But the victim was known to the police. He was a man called Ruben Martirosoff, about whom the files of the Criminal Record Office at Scotland Yard offered a good deal of information. A stateless Armenian, known as "Russian Robert," he had five convictions in England and five more in France and Germany, and had been living for years as a thief and a receiver of stolen property. During and after the war he had been active on the Black Market, dealing mainly in foreign currency and gold.

Martirosoff's widow was brought to Kensington Mortuary and identified his body. She told Chief Inspector Somerset that her husband always carried large sums of money on him in connection with his business. On the night of his death he had left home, just after eleven o'clock, to meet a Polish naval officer whose identity she did not know. She did know, however, that they were to meet at Edgware Road underground station.

A wartime constable of "F" Division reported that he had seen the car stationary in Kensington Park Road at 1 A.M. on the night of the murder. He had observed three men walking away from it, one of them dressed in the uniform of a foreign naval officer with two gold rings on his sleeve. About twenty minutes later he had seen the same three men return to the car and drive away.

The police enquiries at first met little success. Officers visited clubs, public houses, and other places in and around the West

End where gentlemen in Martirosoff's line of business were known to resort. They heard several times that "Russian Robert" had been seen in the company of a Polish naval officer and a taller civilian, also believed to be a Pole. They even found a club where the three men had called at about 11:15 on the night of the murder and left perhaps half an hour later. Several people knew Martirosoff at least by name and sight, but nobody could give any more information about his companions.

Eventually, however, a club waitress told the police that she had recognised one of the men with Martirosoff as a Pole who was in business, together with a Spaniard, making handbags in a flat at Notting Hill. This was the taller man, the civilian, and he answered, she said, to the name of Marian. She was able to point out the flat—but Somerset found that it had been empty for two months.

The next step forward was made by a young woman detective, Shirley Jennings, who had been in the C.I.D. just a week. (She is now Chief Superintendent in command of all the Metropolitan Women Police.) She brought word of a foreigner said to be making handbags at a flat in Maida Vale. Somerset promptly called there on the pretext of looking for lodgings, and he heard from the landlady that again the bird had flown. But he learned too that the handbag-maker was Spanish, had been in the habit of receiving foreign visitors, and had left the flat on November 1, the day Martirosoff was murdered.

A watch was put on the building, and at 2:30 the same afternoon a Polish seaman called at the flat. He was stopped and questioned. He said he had come to deliver a suitcase to the Spaniard, sent by a Polish civilian named Marian. Somerset questioned the Pole very thoroughly for an hour. At last the man revealed that he was to meet Marian in the East India Dock Road at 4 P.M. As the time was already 3:30, he was driven to the East End as quickly as possible in a police car.

The detectives followed him to his street-corner rendezvous, and challenged the man to whom he spoke.

This man said his name was Marian Grondkowski and gave an Ilford address. He was cautioned and searched. In his pockets the police found a wallet and a lighter, and on his wrist a watch, all of which Mrs. Martirosoff subsequently identified as her husband's property. At Grondkowski's lodgings in Ilford they also found a naval officer's uniform, a signet ring, and two more watches that had belonged to "Russian Robert," a small suitcase containing two unused boxes of matches of a brand called "Punch," and two automatic pistols—a .38 Luger and a .32 Walther with a loaded magazine.

By this time, Grondkowski had told the police that his friend Henryk Malinowski, who shared his lodgings, had shot "Russian Robert." Somerset followed the trail to the house of a widow, who told him that her two daughters were friendly with a Polish naval officer named Henry. And Henry, she added, was at that moment upstairs with the two girls.

Malinowski was in civilian clothes when the police took him. "I saw you pick up Grondkowski," he said. He was cautioned, but went on: "I was there but I do not shoot. Grondkowski kill him." They searched Malinowski and found four £5 notes in a wallet which Mrs. Martirosoff later identified.

Both men in due course made written statements through an interpreter. Their stories agreed in most respects. Both denied that they had planned the crime but admitted that after the murder they robbed Martirosoff and shared the loot. They differed on just one detail: each insisted that the other fired the shot.

It was still less than forty-eight hours since Martirosoff met his death: and the men responsible had been traced and arrested, with ample evidence to charge them both with murder. They were brought before the magistrate, Mr. Bennett, on November 5, and remanded until November 20.

When a few days later Vincent Evans, the Assistant Director of Public Prosecutions, handed me the papers in the case, the evidence had become stronger still. The bloodstained fingerprints in the car had been identified as Grondkowski's: and a ballistics test showed that the fatal bullet had been fired from the Walther .32 which was found at Ilford. And, to tie the final knot, the Polish seaman who had led Chief Inspector Somerset to the rendezvous with Grondkowski now recalled a conversation in which he had overheard the two men planning to kill and rob Martirosoff and afterwards to rob his wife.

This was the case I had been presenting when I returned, that afternoon, from the West London Magistrate's Court to my office. I found a message saying that Mr. Howe wanted to see me. He would like me to call at Scotland Yard on my way home.

Earlier that same year my old friend Ronald Howe had succeeded Sir Norman Kendal as A.C.C. My first thought was that some unexpected snag must have arisen in the Martirosoff case. But this seemed unlikely because the evidence was so strong.

I made my way to Whitehall and went up in the lift to the room which was one day to become so familiar. Ronnie made no reference to the murder or any other case. He wanted to talk about something quite different. He told me that the Secretary of the Commissioner's Office was about to retire, and asked if I would like to be considered for the vacancy.

My knowledge of the Secretary and his duties was sketchy, to say the least. I knew only that such an official existed, because, hanging in every room at Devonshire House, the wartime home of the Directors Office, was the Metropolitan Police List, an enormous printed document which sets out the details of the Districts and Divisions of the Force, and of the Headquarters Departments at New Scotland Yard. Among these latter appeared "S" Department, with the Secretary as its head.

I asked what the Secretary did and what he got for doing it. Succinct as ever, Ronnie outlined the job and mentioned a salary considerably larger than I was earning. The work sounded interesting and the increase in salary attractive.

I spoke to the Director next day. He was in favour of my putting in for the post, and in fact did everything he could to help me get it. A few days later I was summoned to an interview with Mr. Howgrave-Graham, the retiring Secretary, a small, rather fragile-looking man in his early sixties, with piercing blue eyes, a crisp forceful manner, and a sardonic sense of humour.

"Can you be ruthless?" he asked suddenly in the middle of our conversation.

I said I thought I could be ruthless if necessary, and remarked that some people considered it a qualification required in the department where I was currently working. I added that they were wrong. He gave me another of his piercing looks, and then, relaxing a little, began to ask questions about my work at the Director's office and about my previous experience. Then he turned to sport, particularly boxing. At that point Howgrave-Graham showed that he certainly could be ruthless when necessary. I heard someone open the door behind me. The Secretary glared at the intruder (I still don't know who he was) and snapped: "I told you I wasn't to be disturbed. *Go away!*" The door closed and the Secretary calmly resumed his questions.

The interview must have gone all right, because a day or two later I was sent for by the Commissioner, Sir Harold Scott. He sat at his desk, leaning back in a curiously stiff posture; I heard afterwards that he had been injured by a fall from a horse and was wearing a sort of plaster cuirass beneath his uniform. This interview didn't take very long. Scott impressed me, not only as an able and clever man, but as being modest, genial, and broadminded; someone with whom it would be a pleasure to work. In the years which followed I never had any reason to change my opinion.

During the next few weeks, while I waited for a decision, my colleagues in the Director's office suggested that, at a mere forty-three, I might be considered by officialdom too young for the job. One day towards the end of December, however, Vincent Evans summoned me and showed me a letter from the Home Office saying that I had been appointed Secretary and was to take up my duties on January 14, 1946.

I managed to complete most of the cases on hand. On January 1, Grondkowski and Malinowski were committed for trial to the Old Bailey, and my official interest in that affair was over. On January 14, I walked into the Secretary's office at Scotland Yard and began what really was, for me, a new life. I wondered whether I should ever see the Old Bailey again; even such a grim place takes a nostalgic hold on the affections, when one has worked there for so long in company with many good friends. In the event, I saw it again much sooner than I expected.

In February the United Nations Organisation held its first meeting in London. Among the numerous visitors to Scotland Yard was a small group of American lawyers, one of whom expressed a wish to see the Old Bailey in action. I am no great admirer of the United Nations nowadays, but hopes were higher then: and, more to the point, the attorney in question was a very charming lady. So I volunteered to be her guide.

Next Wednesday afternoon we slipped into the seats immediately behind Counsel in Court No. 1. Mr. Justice Croom-Johnson was on the Bench. We arrived just in time to hear Anthony Hawke (who later became Recorder of London) opening a charge of murder in some case about which I knew nothing. Before he had gone very far, there was a stir in Court and the jury from the previous case filed in. At the same time, into the dock came Grondkowski and Malinowski.

They had both stuck to their stories, and it was never determined whose finger actually pulled the trigger. The question was academic, for in the eyes of the law they were equally responsible. The jury had not taken long to find them guilty.

Following ancient custom, the Usher called upon all present to be silent under pain of imprisonment while sentence of death was passed. It was an unnecessary admonition. I stole a glance at my guest, sitting beside me in the City Lands, and noticed with some apprehension that she had gone rather pale. I hoped she wouldn't faint and have to be carried out. Mr. Justice Croom-Johnson was not a man who welcomed unconventional behaviour in Court.

The black cap was put on and sentence of death passed in the full grim formula which was then still used. My guest grew visibly paler, but survived the ordeal. Grondkowski and Malinowski appeared quite unmoved. Malinowski turned round and gave a smile and a bow to someone at the back of the Court before he was taken down.

Both men appealed, mainly on the ground that their trials ought to have been separate. Their appeals were dismissed by the Court of Criminal Appeal, over which Lord Goddard, the newly appointed Lord Chief Justice of England, was presiding. On April 2, 1946, they were hanged.

Among the many vicious criminals I saw during my years at the Old Bailey, I reckon these two as callous and brutal as any. They were cold-hearted killers. They wanted money, and decided that the simplest way to get it was by shooting an acquaintance from behind and robbing him as he lay dying. They carried out this plan with no more compunction than they would have shown in shooting a rabbit.

Moreover, although it never came out in public, the police had good reason to believe that at least one of them had murdered another man, in very similar circumstances, only fourteen days before they killed Martirosoff.

22

Shortly after dawn on October 18, the body of a large thick-set man had been found crammed into one of the two small National Fire Service shelters which in those days stood on Lambeth Bridge. He had been robbed. Most of his pockets had been turned inside out, but a few notes in an inner pocket had been overlooked. He had been shot through the head from behind at point-blank range, the bullet entering behind the left ear, passing through the brain and emerging beside the right eye. When the body was found, his face was covered by his own raincoat.

The dead man was identified as Frank Everett, a London taxi driver. His cab was found abandoned a few miles away in Notting Hill; embedded in the framework was a .32-calibre bullet. Reconstructing the crime, the police decided that Everett had been shot from behind while he sat at the driving wheel, and then been dragged to the rear of the vehicle and robbed. The electric light leads had been ripped out, apparently to extinguish the interior light. A mottled-coloured fountain pen cap was discovered on the floor at the rear of the cab.

Detective Chief Inspector Chapman, who was in charge of the case, carefully investigated the murdered man's background and personal life. It emerged that Everett had himself been an officer in the Metropolitan Police for sixteen years, retiring with the rank of sergeant. During the First World War he served in the Grenadier Guards. He had been a cabby for fifteen years and was fifty-six years old when he was murdered. An honest man with no known enemies, his fellow taxi drivers called him "The Duke," because he was accustomed to work nightly for several weeks and then take a week's leave at his home in Gloucester, his "country seat."

The publicity which this murder received brought the usual collection of crackpots and exhibitionists eager to "confess." Eliminating them gave Chapman and his team a lot of extra work in what was already a difficult investigation.

The detectives established that Everett did not own a mottled-coloured fountain pen, so it could well have been dropped by someone pulling the body in or out of the cab: but it was a popular make and impossible to trace. They pieced together Everett's movements on the night of his death: but could get no further than two hours before the estimated time of the murder. The last person to see him alive was another cabby who remembered having given Everett two boxes of matches to take home to Gloucester; a worthwhile gift, because matches were in short supply after the war. These matches were not found either on Everett's body or in the taxi. The cabby said that they had been a brand called "Punch"; a detail which was noted, though it seemed unimportant at the time.

The case had not been solved when Martirosoff's body was found; and the similarity between the two murders was immediately obvious.

Both men had been shot through the head from behind while seated at the driving wheel of a car. Both crimes were committed in the early hours of the morning. The motive in both cases was robbery and the weapon a .32 automatic. In both cases the victim's body had been dragged to the rear of the car before being searched. In both, the victim's pockets were turned inside out but some paper money had been overlooked. Both men's faces were covered, Martirosoff's with his hat, Everett's with his coat. The interior lights of both cars had been violently extinguished, the leads torn away in Everett's taxi, the light itself smashed in Martirosoff's car. Both vehicles had been abandoned in Notting Hill within a mile of each other and within easy walking distance of the place where Grondkowski and Malinowski usually slept.

The difference in the way the bodies had been disposed of seemed at first glance to spoil the pattern. But Malinowski said, after his arrest, that he and Grondkowski had meant to drive the Opel into the country and dump "Russian Robert's" body. The only reason why they failed to do so was that they couldn't start the car; just the sort of unpredictable mishap which not infrequently spoils a well-planned crime.

Following this suggestive parallel, Chapman discovered another link: the "Punch" matches which had been found in the suitcase together with the gun which killed Martirosoff.

The two men both denied knowing anything about the murder of Everett. But Malinowski, eager to help the police build a case against Grondkowski, said that on the night Everett was killed Grondkowski did not return to their lodgings until 4 A.M. He also said, when asked about the fountain pen cap, that Grondkowski had owned a mottled pen and matching pencil, and, about the time of Everett's murder, had lost the pen. After the killing of Martirosoff, when they were both in funds, Malinowski had actually been present when Grondkowski bought a new fountain pen. Grondkowski confirmed most of this story—everything which didn't matter—but said the pen had been stolen from him while he was drinking in a pub.

The Walther .32 which killed Martirosoff could not, a ballistic comparison showed, have fired the bullet which killed Everett. The gun which did so was never found. One London newspaper suggested that the murderer had probably thrown it into the Thames. Chapman, when he next saw the reporter, observed with some vigour that if the murderer hadn't already thrown the gun into the Thames before reading the story, he certainly would do afterwards.

The evidence would perhaps never have been strong enough to support a conviction for Everett's murder, but it justified the police in regarding the case as cleared up. Personally I never had any doubt that Grondkowski murdered Everett, probably with the help of another man. This accomplice was not, I think, Malinowski. As far as I know the man whom the police suspected—on good grounds but with no proof—is still alive and at liberty.

This case has stayed in my mind, and seemed worth recording at some length, for several reasons. It illustrates good police work, and the way in which chance often decides whether criminals will be caught or not. It introduces a pair of ruthless murderers whose viciousness and utter worthlessness seem to me a strong argument for capital punishment. It marks in the criminal history of Great Britain a turning point, the high tide of wartime and postwar crime with its human flotsam and sleazy undertow of black market and illegal currency dealings; afterwards the tide retreated, until in the mid-1950s it turned again, and began flooding forward in new and more formidable waves.

And in my own life too this case marked a turning point. When I stood up to prosecute Grondkowski and Malinowski I was still an advocate as I had been for nearly twenty years. When I watched them disappear down the steps at the Old Bailey, I already belonged to Scotland Yard.

CHAPTER 2
The Larger Gentleman

I was born in India in 1902, when my father was already sixty-one and at the height of a very successful career at the Calcutta Bar.

He was influenced, I think, to try his luck there by memories of his mother's father, Sir Thomas Turton, who, as the portrait in my office at the Yard testified, had been Advocate-General of Bengal. In a book called *Reminiscences and Recollections* by Captain Gronow this great-grandfather of mine is said to have been highly regarded as a classical scholar by Dr. Goodall, the Headmaster of Eton, and by his schoolfellows "as a determined poacher whose daring led him to exert his abilities in Windsor Park itself." On one such occasion, according to Gronow, he escaped by swimming the Thames with a hare in his teeth, leaving the royal keepers frustrated on the river bank. I wish I could claim that it was a desire to emulate this feat which encouraged me to win the Junior and School swimming cups when I was at Eton: but, to be honest, I hadn't read Gronow's book in those days.

My father was called to the Bar at the Middle Temple in 1865, and sailed for India the following year. He settled down to practice in Calcutta. His forceful advocacy soon attracted work, both civil and criminal, and, backed by a fiery temper, brought him the nickname by which he was to be universally known for the next half-century: "Tiger." He always considered himself a man of mild and equable temperament, occasionally and reluctantly driven by the aggressiveness of others to fight

27

back. I remember his telling me, soon after I was called to the Bar, that it didn't pay to be rude to anybody in Court. I must have looked a little surprised at receiving such advice from him, for the old man added "—unless he starts it, of course."

He was not pompous himself, and pomposity in others never failed to irritate him. Among those who regarded him with less than the affection felt by his large circle of friends were some of the Judges before whom he practiced. One in particular was always trying to score off him. It was this Judge who, turning to the other members of the Appellate Court before whom my father had been developing some argument, said in a voice just loud enough to be heard: "I've listened to this fellow for half the morning and I still don't know what he's talking about."

My father said: "I beg your Lordship's pardon. Did you address some remark to me?"

"I was addressing my brethren, Mr. Jackson," replied the Judge coldly. "Observations on the Bench are not necessarily intended for the Bar."

Turning to his Junior, my father said in an undertone which was also just audible: "The trouble with this case, Chaudhuri, is that we can supply the law and the facts but we can't supply the intelligence to understand them."

The Judge flushed angrily. "Mr. Jackson, did you make some observation to the Court?"

"My Lord," said my father blandly, "I spoke to my learned friend Mr. Chaudhuri. As your Lordship will be the first to appreciate, observations made at the Bar are not necessarily intended for the Bench."

Another relationship was soured without even a confrontation in Court. My father and a friend were returning to India in a P. and O. liner and had seated themselves in two of a row of deck chairs, when a bulky and important-looking gentleman bustled up to them and said: "You're sitting in my chairs—you, sir—you and your friend."

"Oh, are we?" replied my father, getting up. "Well, I don't suppose we've done them any harm."

"That, sir," said the large gentleman, "is beside the point. The chairs are *mine*."

"And who are you?" asked my father.

"If you look at the back of the chairs, you can see for yourself."

My father looked, and saw that both chairs and three others were labelled *Lady* ——

"Judging by the evidence available," he observed, "I should think you were Henry VIII."

It was an unfortunate first encounter between the leader of the Calcutta Bar, which my father was by that time, and the newly appointed Chief Justice of Bengal.

In the early 1880s my father decided to retire and return to England for the life of ease which he could now well afford. But a few years later there was a *cause célèbre* in India; a case of fraud by certain officials of the Chartered Bank. He was offered a handsome fee to come out of retirement and defend one of them. It wasn't the money which lured him, though. It was the realisation that a life of ease was no compensation for the excitement and interest of his practice. He went back to Calcutta: and, when the case was over, his client, alone of the defendants, had been acquitted. He gladly forgot about retirement, continued in full practice until 1926 when he was in his eighties; and even after that, he remained a familiar figure in the precincts of the court and in the Bar Library.

In 1895 he met a lady whom he hadn't seen since she was a child, the only daughter of his old friend Henry Wansbrough Stevens, a civil engineer in the East India Company's public works department. They were married two years later.

We had a happy childhood—my two elder brothers, my sister, and I. Until I was seven, we all lived in India. We had a house in Calcutta and another, called Sebastopol, in the hills at Mussoorie, and the family moved from one to the other at the appropriate seasons.

Life in India, where there were so many servants and everything was made so easy, might, I suppose, have been bad for older children: but, for young children, it was an exciting and enriching place. Everything was bigger. Instead of sparrows and robins, we had kites and the pugnacious little "King Crows." Our ayah told us magnificent stories of ghosts and princes. There were snake charmers, and marvellous puppet shows at the Hill Station, and an old blind flute player . . . all sorts of things you remember when everything else is forgotten. Our houseguard, or darwan, had been a sergeant in the Gurkhas and wore a kukri at his waist. He was, I think, a more effective crime-preventer than any I've met since. When I went out to India in 1928, I found his grandson still guarding my father's house.

My surviving brother lives quietly in the country today. On the rare occasions when he comes to London we dine nostalgically at an Indian restaurant, and remember India as it was then; a vanished world, and in some ways, I believe, a better one.

In 1909 we were brought home to England, though my father remained, to the end of his life, officially domiciled in India. He rented a house at West Tarring, then a semi-rural village near Worthing, but now long-since submerged by the tide of building which, between the wars, flowed over it and beyond it.

This village had once been a place of some importance. Among its earliest Rectors, according to the local legend, was Thomas à Becket; which is why, we were told, West Tarring belongs to the See of Canterbury, not Chichester. There was a fig garden in the village, where for a few pence you could buy a paper bag full of green figs and be shown the withered tree stump described as Thomas à Becket's Fig Tree. Alas, this legend, like many legends, seems to have been untrue. Thomas à Becket was never the Rector of Tarring and the parish church has always been part of the See of Chichester. It is, however, in the Archbishop of Canterbury's gift and has been ever since (in the words of Dugdale's *Monasticum Anglicanum*) "King Athelstan gave the vill of Terring situate upon the sea in Sussex to the Church of Christ in Canterbury" —which must have been in or about the year 941. But the legend was a pleasant one, and we would have been no better off for knowing the truth.

Our arrival in the village caused quite a sensation, because we brought with us a staff of Indian servants: and, if servants were more common in 1910 than they are today, Indians in the Sussex countryside were considerably less so. They came for a three-year period, eight at a time. The division of labour required by the caste system wouldn't have permitted a smaller staff. We had a butler, an under butler, a cook and a cook's mate, two bearers and two sweepers. I remember in particular Kulbi, the odd-job man. Small boys used to follow him round whenever he went into Worthing. Indeed, he was a side show in himself, six feet three inches tall, with a black beard down to his waist. When my mother rashly gave him some round dish covers to polish, he took them in his great hands and they became oval.

From 1909 until 1914 my father spent November to January with us, and returned to Calcutta for the rest of the year. After the outbreak of war, we didn't see him again until 1919, though he wrote regularly to every member of the family—and expected regular replies. My mother was therefore responsible for our bringing up. She kept us in order intermittently, spoiled us, and generally behaved as a good Edwardian mother was supposed to. Frank Benson, the actor-manager, was a friend of hers, and she used to take us to Stratford for the Shakespeare Festival, which in those days only lasted a fortnight. I remember one of Benson's company whose moving delivery of some great speech had provoked the audience to tears, being asked afterwards exactly what certain lines meant. "I have no idea, laddie," he replied, with a modesty which I'm afraid one would be hard put to it to find among modern Shakespearean actors.

In February 1916 my father's colleagues in Calcutta gave him a dinner to celebrate what the menu described as "Fifty Years' Splendid Advocacy." Thirty barristers, as many Indians as Englishmen, acted as hosts, and they seem to have done themselves well. According to that yellowed menu, which I have in front of me now, they ate *Caviare, Potage Fausse Tortue, Becktie* (which is a delicious Indian fish) with *Sauce Homard, Filet de boeuf Rossini, Dinde et Jambon, Selle de Mouton Rôti, Cailles, Tortue des Abricots, Byculla Club Soufflé, Laitance de Harengs aû Crouton, Crême de Nougat, Dessert* and coffee: and to wash it down, Milk Punch, Manzanilla Sherry, Roxheimer Riesling 1904, Louis Roederer 1906, Old Tawny Port, East India Madeira, and Liqueurs.

Eardley Norton, my father's old friend and chief rival at the Bar, wrote some verses for the occasion, which are also printed on the menu. They may not be high poetry but they pleased the old man. They ended:

> Men strive for stars and kindred chaff,
>   Men built on microscopic plan,
> Your's is a nobler epitaph,
>   "Here lies the larger gentleman."
>
> Still at injustice all aflame
>   As though a boy with your first brief,
> We rise to toast your honoured name,
>   Impulsive, generous, dear old Chief.

"The larger gentleman . . ." It's a pleasant thought.

Almost to the very end of his long life, my father's power of

32

recall was strong and exact. When he was eighty-seven, he had a bet with a friend about the precise words used by a long-dead Judge in a case nineteen years before. I went, as umpire, to the library of the Bengal Club and looked up the bound copies of the newspapers for that date. And there it was, word for word, as my father had said it would be.

When he left England in 1914, I was only twelve. I was seventeen before I saw him again, and I'd been at Eton for three years. He had mellowed considerably. I found him a kindly old gentleman with a keen interest in the world around him and a dry sense of humour. He was delighted when I told him that I intended going to the Bar. We had long talks about the lessons he had learned in his practice, and he told me innumerable stories about the Judges and advocates whom he had admired—and about the equally large number of Judges and advocates whom he had not admired.

A favourite character, who appeared in many of his anecdotes, was Mr. Justice Maule, a mid-Victorian Judge, notorious for his mordant and often macabre sense of humour. A friend of Maule's (obviously one of those "damned good natured friends" to whom Sheridan so rightly objected) once told the Judge that a certain Sergeant-at-Law disliked him intensely. "Does he?" replied Maule. "I cannot think why. I have never done him a favour."

My father believed that champagne was the best, and indeed the only genuine, medicine for most human ills, whereas I have always put my faith in Scotch whisky. He loved the poetry of Dryden and Pope, whereas my first love was given to such ringing declamatory pieces as *Lepanto* and later, thanks to Cyril Alington, to Shakespeare's Sonnets. He was fond of racing and boxing. He took great pride in being, for many years, the senior member of the Calcutta Turf Club; and boasted that his height, weight, and general measurements as a young man had been exactly those of the great Tom Sayers, the Champion of England. Sayers was a bricklayer's labourer and the constant throwing of bricks had given him tremendous muscles and a right-hand punch called "the auctioneer" (going . . . going . . . *gone*). In April 1860 he fought Heenan, the "Benicia Boy," a much heavier man, round after round, until Sayers' right arm was broken and Heenan's eyes were so puffed that he could scarcely see. One certain way of rousing my father's ire was even to suggest that Heenan might have been winning this epic battle when it was finally stopped by the police.

As he grew older, he limited his meals virtually to dinner at night. But he liked his dinner ceremoniously served, and invariably accompanied it with a bottle of Moet et Chandon; a habit he continued until the evening before his death at the age of nearly ninety-one.

In January 1912 my brothers and I went to Cheam School, which was at Cheam in those days, and not, as it is now, at Newbury; nor had it acquired popular fame through the patronage of royalty. Compared with our cosseted life in India, its discipline seemed austere indeed. We each had, I remember, a round wicker basket into which our clothes were to be folded at night. And we played a game called "Dibs" with the knucklebones of sheep. Both baskets and knucklebones are, I'm told, still used at Cheam today. Academically it was very highpowered; an advantage largely wasted on me, like putting a second-class racehorse under a first-class trainer. Nevertheless, I only just missed being an Oppidan Scholar at Eton and began my career in Upper Remove, which was I think my last academic achievement of any note.

The Headmaster of Cheam, Arthur Tabor, was a formidable gentleman, of whom we stood in much awe. He had, I believe, played cricket for Eton and Cambridge, so cricket was taken very seriously at Cheam. He used to place his deck chair in a strategic position from which he could watch three games at once and apportion praise or blame through a megaphone. It may have been reaction from his enthusiasm which made me choose to be a Wet Bob at Eton; for I was, if anything, even less effective in a boat than at cricket. The only memorable incident in my nautical career occurred when I was detailed, by a character known as "Froggy," for exercise in a long narrow boat of the kind called a "whiff." This one happened to have a hole in it and sank under me, to the undisguised amusement of a small crowd watching from Windsor Bridge.

Fortunately, as I soon discovered, all that was required of us at Eton was that we should take a stipulated amount of physical exercise every week. In winter there was football, including the Wall Game and Rugby, at which I played for the school in a rough and ready sort of way with considerable enjoyment. And there were, I found, two outstandingly good teachers of boxing, George Howson and George Pape. Howson was one of the most remarkable all-rounders I've ever met. He had been middleweight boxing and wrestling champion of the Royal Navy, wore a Black Sash at Judo and had been a Services' champion with sabre, foil, and épée.

During the summer halves, I spent many hours learning boxing and wrestling from these two, and in 1920, much to my father's joy, I was able not only to win the school heavyweight contest but to reach the finals of the Public Schools Boxing Championship. It was then that a sportswriter on, I think, the *Daily Mail* remarked that Eton had produced another Beckett, referring, I regret to say, not to the saintly Archbishop and legendary Rector of Tarring, but to the ponderous, beetle-browed gentleman who was currently the heavyweight champion of England. And so I acquired the nickname "Joe," which has stayed with me ever since. (I have heard it slanderously suggested that I am called Joe because that was the name of Mr. Wardle's servant, the Fat Boy, in *Pickwick Papers*. This explanation I reject.)

When I went up to Cambridge the following year, I was

lucky enough to find another superb teacher of boxing, Bill Child. He trained us rigorously, and taught us how to hit hard with either hand and not to signal our punches. I got my half-blue and succeeded in stopping my Oxford opponent, F. B. Carter of Balliol, who is now a very distinguished doctor in the United States, during the first round of our bout.

Some schools, I believe, have now dropped boxing altogether, and substituted optional Judo. This strikes me as a pity, and unnecessary. Except in a freak accident, which is just as likely to occur on the football field, boys do not injure each other when fighting under amateur rules and using large boxing gloves. I should have thought that Judo was potentially at least as dangerous. My views on such matters are doubtless unfashionable, just as it is unfashionable to admit having enjoyed one's life at a public school. I enjoyed my five years at Eton very much. I have no complaints about the public school system. I only wish that all schools maintained and instilled a similar discipline.

I must have been at Eton shortly before Evelyn Waugh was at Lancing, which from the engaging first volume of his memoirs he seems to have hated. We had wartime shortages at Eton too, of course, but I don't remember that they troubled as much, whereas, from Mr. Waugh's account of it, Lancing seems to have been a meagrely run place.

My tutor was a short square man with a grey moustache. His name was Matthew Davenport Hill, but he was known to us as "Piggy" Hill: and we liked him very much. He controlled the House with a quiet sub-acid wit. During the latter years of the war, we were badly off for fuel, and one morning Library—that is, the House Prefects—decided, as a form of protest to wear their overcoats at breakfast. Piggy came in, said "The tropical heat in here is overpowering," removed his jacket and sat in his shirtsleeves throughout breakfast.

His was the art which conceals art. I'm sure his effects were always calculated, but he preferred that they should seem not to be.

I remember mentioning to him once that an Australian boy called Reid would shortly be going home. "Fortunate fellow," said Piggy, "he will see Stringops in his native haunts."

"Who will he be able to see?" I asked.

"He will see Stringops in his native haunts." I continued to look blank. "R. L. Jackson," said Piggy briskly (he always addressed us by our full names), "do not pretend to an ignorance you cannot really possess. Even you must know that Stringops is the burrowing parrot of Australia." Though I have visited Australia I have never been fortunate enough to see Stringops in his native haunts; but I have never forgotten his name.

For some reason it was the tradition of the house that the Captain of the House read prayers in the evening. In other houses I believe the housemaster did. I sat at the head of the long table and everyone else knelt down along its two sides, including Piggy who was immediately on my right. One evening some small boy, who had bolted his supper, gave vent to a mild belch. Piggy's head rose. Looking at no one in particular, he said sternly, "I trust that nauseating sound was unintentional." He then resumed his devout position, leaving me to continue with prayers.

I achieved membership of Pop, that supreme schoolboy glory. Five or six years ago at the Pop dinner in London I heard Sir Alec Douglas Home give the gay and graceful speech which became famous, in the circles where such things are discussed, as an example of how effective he can be on intimate private occasions.

He was equally effective on a much less important occasion. He did me the honour of attending a dinner given me by friends when I retired, and of proposing my health. His description of our life at school was very amusing if not wholly accurate.

37

I can't pretend I worked particularly hard at Eton or at Cambridge, but, whether as a gift inherited from my father or thanks to the custom at Cheam whereby we each had to memorise a passage of verse or prose every day and repeat it to the headmaster next morning on the way to breakfast, I have always had an excellent visual memory. By its aid I scraped through the necessary exams with moderate success: and I can still draw on that pre-breakfast repertoire for suitable quotations with which to impress the assembled company on convivial occasions.

If my time at Eton was happy, my time at Trinity was happier. We led a gay life then. My tutor was an American with a pronounced English accent, named Gaillard Lapsley. He gave splendid luncheon parties and mixed the best dry martinis in Cambridge. Once when I had been absent for an excessive number of nights during the term, he felt obliged to gate me for a fortnight. "You will find it an extremely expensive punishment," he said, "because all your friends will arrive every night, just before the door closes, expecting to be entertained." He was right.

My friends were mostly reading law, as I was. My closest and oldest friend, Stanhope Joel, the son of Sol Joel, the diamond millionaire, read law because I persuaded him to—and proceeded to get a much better degree than I did. Others who became litelong friends were C. L. ("Bruce") Burgess, now Clerk of the Inner London Sessions; Edward Robey, the son of George Robey the great comedian of the English music halls, now a Metropolitan Magistrate; and the late Derek Curtis-Bennett.

We were all members of the Alibi Club, a dining club to which we invited well-known members of the Criminal Bar. Sir Edward Marshall Hall, Q.C., came and told us how he secured an acquittal in a celebrated murder trial—adding that he could have done as much for Dr. Crippen had he been briefed in that case.

On another occasion, Derek's father, Sir Henry Curtis-Bennett, K.C., spoke about his unsuccessful defence of Major Armstrong, the dapper little solicitor at Hay-on-Wye who poisoned his wife. Sir Henry said that in his experience poisoners never confessed, and, if successful, would always turn to poison again when the need arose. He was a great burly man with a deep resonant voice and a jovial manner which went down well with juries. I had already discovered how paralysing stage-fright can be, and I was comforted to hear Sir Henry say that he still felt a touch of it whenever he stood up in an important case. He remarked that most good advocates did.

Among his useful apophthegms was that one should never despair when defending in a case which involved indecency. "Six of the jury won't believe that such things happen," he said, "and the other six do it themselves."

I heard my first murder trial when I was an undergraduate. Stan Joel and I spent a day at the Cambridge Assizes, where Mr. Justice Bray was presiding over the trial of a man charged with murdering his wife by neglect. It was a grim enough tale, but it has remained in my mind because of a single phrase. The woman who found the body was being cross-examined.

"What was the condition of the room?" counsel asked her.

"Filthy and deplorable like the woman herself," the witness replied.

"Did you look at the bed?"

"I did."

"And what was its condition?"

"Filthy and deplorable like the woman herself."

"And this unfortunate lady's clothing—"

"Filthy and deplorable like the woman herself."

The witness was hypnotised by her own phrase and went on repeating it like a gramophone record. Counsel tried desperately and vainly to get her to say something else. And Stan and I almost collapsed in a fit of most unsuitable giggles.

39

Forty years later, I spent part of my retirement leave from the Yard cruising the Aegean in Stan's yacht. After lunch one day at a Greek *taverna*, he vanished to a rather primitive lavatory, and, when he returned, I asked what it was like.

"Filthy and deplorable like the woman herself," he replied.

So do the lessons we learn at the university remain with us throughout life.

CHAPTER 3
The Absence of Mr. J. G. Reeder

I came down from Cambridge in 1924, and spent the next two years reading for the Bar and eating the required number of dinners in Hall—that pleasant survival from the days when the Inns of Court were almost a residential university. In 1926 I began my pupillage with St. John Micklethwaite, who had a busy practice both in London and on the Oxford Circuit. And in May 1927, in the beautiful Hall of the Middle Temple, I was called to the Bar on the same evening as my Cambridge friends, Stanhope Joel and "Bruce" Burgess.

When my year as a pupil was over, I went into Chambers headed by John Douglas Young, who soon afterwards went out to India and became Chief Justice of Lahore. I shared a room with Stan Joel and another Cambridge friend, Gerald Paul.

Life was very agreeable. Stan's father owned the Drury Lane Theatre, so we generally had the run of the Royal Box; there was a convenient private room behind, and we always found a bottle of champagne on ice and some caviare sandwiches waiting for us. Night clubs, as I remember, were not dark and mucky but much more elegantly appointed than they are now. Ciro's Victors, Rectors, and the Embassy were favourites. London was full of friends whom I'd known at school or at Cambridge. Was life really gayer in those days? It's hard to tell. Perhaps the truth is that to enjoy life as we did you have to be young.

41

I wasn't earning much money. In the 1960s, for various reasons (including the great increase in crime, for it is indeed an ill wind which blows nobody any good), the Bar has been enjoying an unprecedented boom: but when I started in practice very few could hope to earn a proper living in much less than five or six years. After paying his clerk's fee and the rent of his chambers, a young barrister's income was likely to be a minus quantity. As someone observed dryly, when asked about the financial advantages of being at the Bar, "One can always save £300 a year by giving it up."

Gerald Paul and I joined the South Eastern Circuit and the Sussex Sessions. Lewes, Chichester, and Brighton were conveniently close to my home, and I picked up a few cases before the local Justices and at Quarter Sessions. Always at the back of my mind, however, was the idea of following my father's example and going out to India. When I spoke to him about it, he very wisely made no attempt to dissuade me but suggested I went with him, to have a look round, when he returned at the end of the year. In the event, the whole family made the trip together.

My father's many friends, almost all of whom were a generation younger than he, welcomed us warmly. I discussed my idea of practising in India with a lot of them, some on the Bench, some at the Bar. From what they said, and from what I could see for myself, I was forced to realise that the days when an Englishman could build up and maintain a really big practice in Calcutta were numbered. There were already a large number of excellent Indian lawyers, and, perhaps more important, the political trouble had started. My father came to India only nine years after the East India Company handed over to the British Raj. Now Nehru and Gandhi were active. The clouds were building up. My father said it had been a mistake to move the capital from Calcutta to Delhi, for the Indians, remembering the fall of previous dynasties, believed that an empire ruled from Delhi, as so many had been, was inevitably doomed. They were right.

Reluctantly, therefore, I abandoned my idea. All that remained was to enjoy the rest of my stay. My sister and I were invited by Sir Victor Sassoon to stay with him for the week of the Delhi Horse Show. A Miss Mary Pooley came from Bombay to join the house party; her father, like my mother's father, was a civil engineer working for the Indian government. She was nineteen, I was twenty-seven. We spent only four days together in India, and we were both engaged to someone else at the time. Without consulting one another, we both subsequently broke off our engagements. She returned to England at the end of 1929. We became engaged, and in July 1930 we were married.

I had moved, meanwhile, into new Chambers. They had the advantage of being smaller, and connected with the South-Eastern, rather than the Oxford, Circuit. Their disadvantage was that a lot of the work concerned tax, rating and local government; which, with the best will in the world, I could never find very interesting. There were only four of us in Chambers: E. M. Konstam, K.C., who became a County Court Judge; Michael Rowe, who is now a Q.C. and Deputy Chairman of the Local Government Commission, received a knighthood on the same day as I did, and to whose youngest daughter I am god-father; and E. H. Tindal Atkinson. Tindal Atkinson was a good deal older than Michael Rowe and me, and he had a well-established general practice. This brought work into Chambers, and was therefore helpful: but the really important thing about him, from my point of view, was that two years later he became Director of Public Prosecutions.

I came to realise, quite soon, that my primary interest was in the criminal law. Michael, who was already beginning to build up a very successful practice, kindly passed on to me as many as possible of the criminal cases which were sent to him.

43

On one occasion, he even passed on a Chancery case, a branch of work about which I knew, and know, nothing. All it involved, fortunately, was my appearance, together with five other barristers, in front of Mr. Justice Clauson. We were applying, I gathered, for the release of some trust funds. As one man, we rose and bowed to him. He looked up from what he was writing, and said, "I assume there is consent in this case?" We bowed again, and sat down. For this short, though doubtless impressive, performance I received no less than eleven guineas; a tolerable sum in those days.

I was also picking up a certain amount of work at Magistrates' Courts both in London and in Sussex, mostly for the defence in driving cases. Such cases were prevalent even then. No one, of course, is ever at fault when driving a motorcar, and to be accused when one is not at fault is an outrage: so people are usually indignant and keen to defend. At that time, too, the insurance companies were starting to fight the criminal charges in order to strengthen their hands in subsequent civil proceedings. I was lucky enough to score several good wins; which brought more briefs of the same kind.

Sometimes I appeared in the County Courts, where, I found, the Judges varied considerably in their attitude to young and inexperienced counsel. It was a pleasure, for instance, to appear before Sir Mordaunt Snagge at Marylebone, but less pleasant to be in front of His Honour Judge Hill-Kelly at Bloomsbury. Austere and learned with a keen sense of his own importance he found it impossible to disguise his contempt for what he regarded, no doubt rightly, as the incompetence of immature advocates.

There was one County Court Judge, however, whom I remember with great affection; at least, I remember everything about him except his name. It was a cold day and he appeared on the Bench wearing an overcoat on top of his robes, which struck me as eminently sensible. My case came on second, and

44

I had hardly begun when His Honour rose and disappeared behind a screen which concealed the door leading off the Bench. Assuming that he had left for reasons beyond his control, I stopped speaking: whereupon, his voice came from behind the screen, "Go on, Mr. Jackson, I can hear you very well from here." So on I went. Suddenly a cloud of smoke rose like a redskin signal, above the screen. As I was then a heavy smoker, getting through about forty cigarettes a day, I only wished I could join him.

Meanwhile, my private life was settling into its new shape. Among my close friends was Oliver Barnett, a *bon vivant* with a deceptively quiet manner, who is today Judge Advocate General. He served as best man at my wedding. Afterwards, Mary and I took a flat in Hyde Park Mansions, where we lived until 1941.

Among my neighbours in that block of flats was a gentleman well known to the police. He was eventually arrested and charged with conspiracy, and I was concerned with his prosecution.

Every morning for about a week we travelled to the Old Bailey, he in his large car and I by underground. I knew him by sight but I don't think he recognised me. After his trial he did not return to his flat for some months.

In August 1931 my father died, two months before his ninety-first birthday. I don't think I'd ever realised, until I read his obituaries, quite how distinguished his career had been and how deeply he had impressed several generations of lawyers in India.

It was a bad time for realising assets. The houses in India which in 1921 had been valued at nearly seven lakhs (or about £48,000) were now worth only one and a half lakhs (about £10,000). My mother moved from Worthing to a smaller house near Woking.

Oliver Barnett had joined the staff of the Director of Public

Prosecutions soon after Tindal Atkinson was appointed. He was followed, a few months later, by Ted Robey. I gathered from what they told me that life in the Director's office was rather like being in a very large set of barristers' chambers. I began to think that I might do worse than follow their example. Mary and I discussed the idea with Oliver, and I decided to apply for the next vacancy which arose.

Like Oliver and myself, Ted Robey eventually left the Director's office. He went back into practice for a couple of years, because he wanted to be a Magistrate and thought, rightly, that a member of the Director's staff had little chance of being appointed straight to the Bench. In the ordinary way, however, going into the Director's office meant permanently abandoning a career at the Bar and the glittering prizes which that profession still holds out to its successful members. On the other hand, it also meant a regular salary and the complete disappearance of the expenses entailed in practising at the Bar. I can't pretend that my decision was any kind of conscious dedication to the fight against crime: but it did involve a certain commitment. It meant, after all, that my efforts from then on would be concentrated wholly on the prosecution of criminals. This would hardly have been an acceptable prospect if I hadn't already decided that, with the exception of a few engaging rogues, I didn't like criminals. They tend—at least, the big fish among them—to be tough, intelligent, ruthless men assailing victims who are less tough, intelligent, and ruthless than they are. Crime causes suffering. There are worse ways of spending one's life than in fighting it. So I had no moral qualms about becoming a whole-time prosecutor.

Early in 1933 I was given a "noting" brief in what became a *cause célèbre*: the trial of Leopold Harris. Harris was an insurance assessor. Not content with assessing damage, he had apparently helped to cause it. The technique was to fill the insured pemises with goods damaged in some other fire, then burn the place down and claim as though the lost goods had been new. Harris appeared with sixteen other defendants in the dock of Court No. 1 at the Old Bailey; the charges were conspiracy, arson, and fraud.

The scene remains clear in my mind, not only because the trial attracted a great deal of publicity, but because, like the Grondkowski-Malinowski case, it marked a watershed in my own life, and because the *dramatis personae* included so many people who were, or were to become, significant in my career.

There was a formidable array of barristers. I was led by Norman Birkett, then at the height of his fame, and by "Khaki" Roberts, then Senior Treasury Counsel at the Old Bailey. The other defence counsel included Sir Henry Curtis-Bennett and Walter Monckton. Against us were Roland Oliver, K.C., H. D. Samuels, K.C., and L. A. Byrne. It was rumoured that Oliver had turned down all other work to concentrate on this one case. The Junior, Laurie Byrne, was among the most able members of the Criminal Bar. One of the defending Counsel, I remember, leaned across to me and whispered: "No human being can be capable of the restrained intelligence that appears on Byrne's face." It was scarcely an exaggeration. Byrne, so reserved and so effective, was influential in quietening down the whole style of advocacy. The old full-blooded style already survived only in a form which was hardly more, I suspect, than a parody of what it had been in the hands of the great masters. The tradition of emotional pleading had passed to the United States where it remains popular to this day.

Prosecutors especially have accepted that they ought to be unemotional and objective. It wasn't always so. Sir Charles Mathews, for example, the first real Director of Public Prosecutions, felt no such inhibitions. I remember the late Sir Seymour Hicks, the famous English stage star, describing how Mathews, prosecuting some minor official for embezzlement, lifted his arms like a little black-gowned raven and addressed the jury:

47

"I must explain this indictment to you. What would you think, gentlemen of the jury, if I were to tell you that this man had wrongfully appropriated £5000 of public money—that is, of your money and mine?" He paused to let the enormity of the crime sink in. "But what would you think if I told you that he had taken, not £5000, but £7000?" Another pause. "And what if he had taken, not £7000, but £10,000?" He leaned forward, his voice vibrant with indignation. "Gentlemen of the jury, I have to tell you that he took, not £5000, not £7000, not £10,000, but no less than £15,000 of your money and mine." By which time the jury would gladly have seen the prisoner hanged, drawn and quartered. Of course there was no story which that fine actor, Seymour Hicks, could not improve . . .

Such histrionics, as I say, were already a thing of the past when I was at the Bar. Perhaps they died with Marshall Hall. Pat Hastings (I remember him sitting like a brooding eagle, waiting to pounce) was forceful and ironic rather than dramatic. My friend "Khaki" Roberts was a tremendous tank of a man, and his style as an advocate matched his physique. Birkett, on the other hand, was calm, eloquent, and immensely persuasive. I loved listening to him because his command of the English tongue was so precise and literate. It had been rounded and enriched by his experience as a lay preacher. The Bible and Shakespeare were still part of the fabric of educated minds and speech, to an extent which is, I'm afraid, no longer true. Arnold Lawson-Walton, who was a colleague of mine in the D.P.P.'s office, once showed me a volume of Shakespeare which had belonged to his father, Sir John, who had been Attorney-General. It was annotated throughout in tiny neat writing, and, looking closely, I saw that each entry gave the date and place at which Sir John had used a quotation. He was scrupulous, Lawson told me, never to repeat a quotation to the same audience. Men like that were trying, as very few advocates do today, to raise oratory to the level of literature and drama.

The Harris trial lasted from July 4 to August 18, and all the defendants were found guilty, including Adam John Loughborough Ball, the insurance assessor for whom Birkett, Roberts, and I were appearing. One of the key witnesses for the prosecution was a man named Camillo Capsoni. He had himself played a prominant role in the conspiracy, and the only reason he wasn't in the dock was that he had "shopped" his confederates. Roland Oliver explained Capsoni's position to the jury, assured them that his story would be corroborated, and warned them not to allow their natural contempt for such a man to prejudice them against his evidence. Oliver concluded these remarks with a very sapient observation. "It is not expedient in the public interest," he said, "that there should be honour among thieves."

The truth of this remark was constantly borne in on me at Scotland Yard. Informers are like earthworms, ugly but necessary: and the police cultivate and protect them with the greatest care. We are all conditioned from our schooldays to dislike people who tell tales, but it is the crooks who dislike informers most. Every professional criminal knows that the "grass," "snout," or "nark" is the greatest threat to his safety, more insidious and dangerous than any security device, or any method of scientific detection, yet invented. Informers are therefore treated as the scum of the underworld, and great efforts are made to neutralise them. They are not as likely to be murdered here as their equivalents are in America, but there are various ways, some not pretty, of ensuring that they can't or won't talk. Fortunately, there are usually some who can and do.

Another feature of the Harris case which impressed me was the care and industry with which the police had built it up. While it wound its serpentine way towards the verdict of guilty,

49

I met a number of C.I.D. officers whom I was afterwards to know well. Among them was a certain Detective Sergeant Hatherill. Many years later I recommended that he should be transferred from the uniform branch and promoted to be Commander of the C.I.D.; and he was my first lieutenant all the time I was Assistant Commissioner.

Halfway through the trial, and before Birkett had even opened Ball's defence, I left the Old Bailey for an hour or so to appear before a Selection Board for the appointment of a "Professional Legal Clerk" in the D.P.P.'s department. Two months later, I learned that I had got the job. Knowing Tindal Atkinson doubtless helped, for I believe there were between sixty and seventy applicants for three vacancies. Be that as it may, towards the end of October I walked up the steps of No. 1, Richmond Terrace, in Whitehall, where the Director's office was in those days situated.

Edgar Wallace provided the D.P.P.'s department with a delightful investigator, Mr. J. G. Reeder. Alas, there is no such personage in real life. The Director and his assistants never take any part in the investigation of crimes, as, for example, District Attorneys do in the United States. His functions are strictly limited and often misunderstood. He cannot properly be called, as the newspapers do sometimes call him, "the Public Prosecutor." England has no Public Prosecutor in the sense of an official whose department is responsible for prosecuting anyone who is charged with any sort of crime. The Director is responsible for prosecuting only in those comparatively few cases which are deemed important enough, or difficult enough, to justify his adopting them as "public prosecutions." For the rest, every citizen in England and Wales has an absolute right, except in a few cases which require the Attorney-General's permission, to institute criminal proceedings. This right is not very often exercised by private persons, because most people find it easier to complain to the police and let them prosecute: but the right does still exist and is, in fact, sometimes used. On at least two occasions in recent years major criminal proceedings—one a charge of murder—were instituted privately after the police had decided no charge would stick. The police were proved right: both prosecutions failed at an early stage. There are more frequent occasions when, on grounds of policy or economy or mere convenience, the police deliberately leave the prosecution of certain offences to private complainants. Some Chief Constables, for instance, have taken the view that, since supermarkets make pilfering so easy, the prosecution of shoplifters must be the management's responsibility. A comparable situation may arise between the police and the D.P.P. I've known cases in which the Director declined to prosecute, usually because he thought the chances of success too slim, but with which the police were determined to continue on their own. And, since all prosecutions are, to some extent, a gamble, the police sometimes won where the Director feared to tread. The Commissioner of Metropolitan Police has, thanks to Lord Trenchard, a solicitor's department of his own, quite capable both of advising and prosecuting; only the major cases, as I say, ever go to the D.P.P.'s department at all.

Small cases used to be sent out to an ordinary firm of private solicitors. Serious crimes, such as murder, were, until 1879, reported by the police to the Home Office, which then instructed the Treasury Solicitor to prosecute. In that year the new post of Director of Public Prosecutions was created, but its first incumbent was a rather dim old gentleman, who did little more than advise the Treasury Solicitor. The two offices were merged in 1884, but separated again in 1908. When this separation occurred, the solicitor's side of the work in public prosecutions was left with the Director, who became, in effect, the Crown's solicitor for criminal matters. The anomalous situation resulted that the Director and his staff, though they may be barristers, have to act as Solicitors. The staff currently includes both branches of the legal profession and, as far as I know, always has. The system, like many historical anomalies in this country, works well enough.

The Director is appointed by the Home Secretary after consultation with the Attorney-General. Though a civil servant, however, he is not a Home Office official nor is his work controlled by the Home Secretary. Theoretically he comes under the Attorney-General: in practice he enjoys a considerable measure of independence.

He is obliged to prosecute in any case where the offence is (or, I suppose, since hanging for murder has been abolished, one must now say "was") punishable with death; in any case sent to him by a government department if he considers a prosecution justified; and in any other case where, on grounds of public importance or complexity, he thinks it desirable to intervene. There are also a number of offences which the police are obliged to report to him, so that he can decide whether or not to take over the prosecution: and he has a general duty to give advice, whether asked or unasked, to government departments, Justices' Clerks and Chief Officers of Police.

The first Director under the Act of 1908 was Sir Charles "Willie" Mathews, Q.C., the son of a well-known stage comedian of mid-Victorian days. His style of advocacy, as I have already suggested, was theatrical but scarcely comic—at least, to his victims. It seems to have been effective. He continued as Director until his death in January 1920, but, by the time I joined the Department, he was a legendary figure. One of the things chiefly remembered about him was his habit, in the good leisurely days before 1914, of departing in a hansom cab at around 12:30 for luncheon at the Garrick Club, calling in at a matinee on most afternoons and only then returning to the office to deal with any matters which might have arisen needing his attention.

Very different was the daily routine of his successor, Sir

Archibald Bodkin, who had been Senior Treasury Counsel at the Old Bailey and prosecuted, among many others, George Joseph Smith, the "Brides in the Bath" murderer. He was famous, not only for his profound knowledge of criminal law and for his tenacity as an advocate, but for his immense capacity for work. It was his custom every evening to take half a dozen files home, and to read them and carefully note them after dinner. This onerous habit, I should explain, is by no means unusual at the Bar, though my own practice was never large enough to require it: but civil servants, even civil servants of so specialised a kind, do not normally behave like practising barristers, whose incomes are dependent on the amount of work they get through. Hence the awe—not untinged, I dare say, by resentment—which Sir Archibald's labours provoked.

Among the changes he made in the Department's routine was to increase the number of cases which his own professional staff undertook in the Magistrates' Courts. Previously they had been conducted in most cases by Treasury Counsel, but Sir Archibald regarded this as an extravagance. Since advocacy therefore became more important, he recruited a number of young barristers to his staff. Tindal Atkinson followed the same policy. The six appointments to the professional staff between 1930 and 1939 were all from the Bar; a policy not wholly approved by the older members of the staff, most of whom were solicitors.

The office was divided into two "sides," one dealing exclusively with cases which arose in the Metropolitan Police District and the City of London, the other with cases in the rest of England and Wales. My entire service was on the London Side; which, as things turned out, proved very helpful, because I met a great many people, including a lot of policemen, who were to be important to me when I moved to the Yard.

My immediate chief was a solicitor called C. R. V. Wallace. We had much in common, including a fondness for good food and for poker, no aversion to alcohol, and a keen dislike of violent criminals. We became good friends. At our first meeting, however, he stared morosely at me for a moment, and said: "You're another of these bloody young barristers, are you?"

"Well, that's one way of putting it," I replied.

This seemed to cheer him up. "Sit down, my lad, sit down," he said, and proceeded to explain the rules which guided the conduct of the London Side. These consisted mainly of not pestering him on Monday mornings or between luncheon and four o'clock any afternoon. He then gave me the papers in a motor manslaughter case, and I went off to read them.

Charles Wallace ran the London Side autocratically, not to say idiosyncratically, but with complete efficiency. Provided our work was done properly, he never worried about such trifles as the time we reached or left the office. His opinions were blunt and sometimes expressed in colourful language, but he was liked, as well as respected, by most of the C.I.D. officers who brought their cases to him.

I was told by one of them about an occasion before the First World War when Charles had been running the Director's work at the Old Bailey. He was in Court when two powerful thugs, who, having given evidence against each other, had just been convicted, came to blows in the dock. The prison officers joined in, and for some minutes there was complete pandemonium. High above the noise of battle could be heard the voice of young Mr. Wallace urging the warders to "pitch the bastards down the steps."

Relations between the police and the D.P.P.'s Department have always, at least in my time, been extremely good: and indeed it's most important that they should be. When I was offered the job at Scotland Yard, Sir Theobald Mathew, the Director, was quite pleased. "It's a good advertisement for us," he said. The very fact that two successive A.C.C.s came from

54

his Department presumably shows that the police hold it in some regard.

During my first few months, I appeared two or three times a week in Magistrates' Courts, conducting cases which ranged from coining to attempted murder.

Coinage offences were much more common then than they are today. Inflation has rendered them scarcely worth while. In those days a counterfeit half-crown, easy enough to make with a Syphon-top and a plaster of Paris mould, could be exchanged for a packet of cheap cigarettes and 2s. 2½d. change. Uttering the false coins was usually a two-man operation. One would enter the shop, carrying only a single counterfeit piece: the rest were held by his confederate, who kept a look-out and could decamp rapidly if necessary. The man in the shop could always pretend that he didn't know the coin was false. This excuse would have looked thin, however, if the police had searched him and found his pockets full of cheap cigarettes and a mass of change.

Long ago there was a Commissioner at the Old Bailey who used an invariable formula when sentencing coiners with any previous convictions. "Once a smasher, always a smasher," he said. "Seven years!" (The word "smasher," at least in this connotation, has, I suppose, become as uncommon as the offence.) Though I deprecate so wholesale a formula, it is true, in my experience, that coiners usually stuck to their own specialised brand of crime. I remember one cheerful rogue whom I prosecuted three times for coinage offences. His first conviction was quashed because of a technical slip by the Judge. At our subsequent encounters he used to greet me from the dock, "Morning, Mr. Jackson. They've made another mistake 'ere." But they hadn't.

When I was A.C.C., only about a dozen counterfeit coins used to turn up in six months. Notes were still forged of course; the Black Museum at Scotland Yard contains a hand-drawn ten shilling note of exquisite workmanship which must have taken days to manufacture. But even forgery is growing less common. It requires more effort and skill and pays less well than bashing some weaker person with an iron bar and stealing genuine money.

Most of our indictable cases were tried at the Old Bailey and one member of the London Side was responsible for instructing the Treasury Counsel who were briefed in almost all of them. Nomination of Counsel for the Director's Cases is a matter for the Attorney-General. On the Country Side he nominated members of the circuit concerned but at the Old Bailey he appointed a panel of six barristers known as Treasury Counsel. Some public bodies retained their own counsel. One was the Post Office. Another was the Mint; and its prosecuting counsel from 1931 until 1939 was a young man called Patrick Devlin. In those days, at almost every session of the Old Bailey, he and I spent a day or two before the Common Sergeant, Cecil Whitely, who tried most of the coinage cases. He relinquished the Mint post in 1939 and I saw little of him for some years, but I followed his brilliant career with pleasure and no surprise at all. Long afterwards he paid me the compliment of consulting me when he was revising for publication his Sherrill Lectures at Yale University in 1957 on *The Criminal Prosecution in England*. Still later, when he was a Lord of Appeal, he lectured to the Detective Training school much to the benefit of the police officers then being trained there.

In May 1934 I took over the Old Bailey work, which meant spending perhaps a fortnight in every month at the Central Criminal Court. During the other fortnight I still had to prosecute or conduct committal proceedings in the Magistrates Courts, but I was given as far as possible only those cases which could be completed in a single hearing.

By no means all our work could be dealt with so expeditiously. The London Side inevitably had a high proportion of fraud cases, some of them exceedingly complex. It was not un-common to wait half the morning, while the Magistrate dealt with his daily ration of drunks, prostitutes, and remands, and then to be left with only just enough time to open the case and call the first witness before being remanded for a week. Seven days later the whole thing would happen again, until, weeks after the first hearing, one's man would be committed for trial. In one case, which I remember all too clearly, we had seventeen witnesses and a mass of documentary evidence, and I had to come back nine times.

I soon became very familiar with the various Magistrates and the different ways in which they liked to hear a case pre-sented. One Chief Metropolitan Magistrate in those days was Sir Rollo Graham Campbell, who was famous for his polite-ness to everyone in Court. After watching him at Bow Street, the American writer, Alexander Woollcott, was asked what seemed most different from the United States. He replied: "The old-world courtesy with which your magistrates treat your whores."

In July 1934 I appeared before Graham Campbell to prose-cute a foolish young solicitor, charged with having made a false statement to help a girl get a passport. She wanted the passport so that she could go to Malta and marry a Maltese whom she'd met in London. I've always remembered the case because it introduced me to three people—or rather two and a name—which were to become very familiar.

One was the defending solicitor, Thompson Halsall, who re-mained a close friend of mine until the day of his death. An-other was the police officer in charge of the case, Divisional Detective Inspector Leonard Burt. As Commander of the Special Branch, Burt became, and deserved to be, famous. As a number of spies and traitors discovered, he was a most able interrogator, combining a pleasant manner with utter ruth-lessness. He always maintained, in dead-pan style, that he had

57

joined the police by mistake. He had been looking, he said, for Great Scotland Yard, which was the headquarters for Army recruiting.

He told the Chief Magistrate, that day in 1934, that there was strong reason to believe this was a case of attempted procuring, but that the solicitor had been unaware of it. The solicitor was fined £50 with ten guineas costs. But the memorable thing was the name of the Maltese gentleman whose matrimonial hopes had been so cruelly disappointed: Eugene Messina.* Many years were to pass before the sinister and sordid activities of the Messina brothers were finally brought to an end.

* The Messina family, Giuseppe and his five sons, were deported first from Malta, then from Egypt. The father died soon after they arrived in England. Under cover of an export-import business, involving frequent trips to the Continent, the sons built up an impressive chain of prostitutes, "clubs" and gaming houses. Subsequent investigation identified thirty-two prostitutes working for the Messinas—one of them had earned £2368 in six weeks. The brothers carried guns, and inevitably there were clashes with other gangs. Eventually they transferred their headquarters to Brussels, and in 1955 two of them were picked up by the Belgian police after a fracas with some French terrorists. They were found to be carrying false passports and loaded automatics. Belgian detectives, working with Interpol, began unravelling the threads . . . and the Messina empire collapsed.

CHAPTER 4
The Bad Bargain

For a barrister to find himself acting as a solicitor is, in the British legal system, a distinctly odd position. Barristers are like surgeons, called in to do a particular job and comfortably isolated from most of the preparations and arrangements. A solicitor, on the other hand, must be a man of affairs; he has to interview witnesses, collect statements, answer questions, deal with costs. My work as an instructing solicitor at the Old Bailey was different from anything I'd done before. I thought how wise Derek Curtis-Bennett's father had been to insist that he spend six months in a solicitor's office before being called to the Bar.

However, I soon got into the swing of my new job, thanks very largely to the help of another member of the Director's staff, Hayward King, who acted as my assistant and dealt imperturbably with every crisis. He was the best kind of civil servant. I remember waiting in the Director's office at the Old Bailey for the jury to come back with their verdict in a long and complicated fraud case. I was playing Whisky Poker with my friend Henry Elam, one of the Treasury Counsel, and we invited King to join us. "No, thank you," he said. "It looks rather a chancey game." King was not a man who took chances in any part of his life.

In those days, as I've said, the Bar was not as prosperous as it is now. A number of elderly Counsel haunted the Old Bailey, collecting the briefs which are known as "soups"—Court prosecutions handed out by the Clerk's office like dole from a

59

soup kitchen. Some of them were decidedly eccentric. The one I recall most clearly was St. John Macdonald, generally called Bob or "Fighting Mac." I remember being told of his remark to an enthusiastic young solicitor who started to expound the facts in his client's favour. "Never mind about that," interrupted Bob. "What did the bloody fool say to the police?"

On another occasion he told the Court of Criminal Appeal: "My Lord, the Chairman of Quarter Sessions in this case was a most extraordinary man. He looked like Harry Tate."

Mr. Justice Avory interposed, in his usual acid tones: "Is that your only ground of appeal?"

"My Lord," Macdonald replied, "I also threatened him with this Court, but he had the cheek to say that he'd never heard of Mr. Justice Avory."

A suspicion of a smile crossed the Judge's iron features. "Come along, Mr. Macdonald," he said quite mildly. "Don't let's waste time."

There were six Treasury Counsel in my day, three Juniors and three Seniors, though as a matter of policy, to save the extra expense, none was in fact a silk.

The Senior Treasury Counsel, when I arrived at the Old Bailey in March 1934, were Eustace Fulton, "Khaki" Roberts, and Gerald Dodson; the Juniors were G. B. McClure, L. A. Byrne, and Anthony Hawke. I soon got to know them all extremely well. Before long, however, Dodson left to become a Judge, McClure became a Senior, and Christmas Humphreys joined the team.

Eustace Fulton was a remarkable man, tall and thin, with a harsh corn-crake voice and constantly twitching fingers. Sir Henry Curtis-Bennett told me that Fulton had once been considered the likeliest of all his contemporaries to have a brilliant career. But something went wrong. Perhaps he had *too* quick a mind. When he became Chairman of London Sessions, he would sometimes decide very early that the case against the accused ought to be stopped, and, because he hated to waste time, would give the jury a hint to that effect. But the jury, unfortunately, being rather less quick at grasping the situation, might blithely return a verdict of guilty—and clearing the matter up would waste a great deal more time.

He had a nice dry sense of humour, and I became genuinely fond of him. His tactical skill was outstanding. During a conference about a case in which the Solicitor-General would be appearing for the Crown and Sir Patrick Hastings for the defence, he said: "We must at all costs prevent Pat from seizing some red herring and dashing off across country with the Solicitor-General pounding along behind him." Which was about as accurate and succinct an estimate of the relative performances of those two eminent Counsel as one could have wished to meet.

In his day, Fulton was one of the deadliest cross-examiners I ever heard at the Old Bailey. His technique, unlike that of some Counsel, did not consist merely of repeating, or contradicting, the evidence in the form of questions beginning, "I put it to you . . .": nor did he subscribe to the fallacy admirably described by a judge who said, "The art of cross-examination does not consist of asking questions in a cross voice."

I heard him in a murder trial at the Old Bailey in 1936 which is perhaps worth recalling both as an example of his effectiveness and for the broader moral of the case. It was a curious enough story, anyway.

It began three, or even five, years earlier. In September 1933, just a month before I joined the D.P.P.'s office, a man named Frederick Field was tried at the Old Bailey for the murder, two years before, of Norah Upchurch, a prostitute.

Field had been employed, at the time, as a fitter by a firm of sign writers. He had been given the keys to an empty shop in Shaftesbury Avenue, and told to go there and remove a To Let board. Two days later, he hadn't returned the keys and was asked where they were. He said he had handed them over to a man whose name he didn't know but who had shown him a letter of authority. Since no such letter had been issued, the foreman accompanied Field to the shop next day and forced an entry. They found the body of Norah Upchurch. Her skirt had been removed, part of her white jumper had been used as a gag, and she had been strangled with the belt from her jacket. She had been dead for three or four days.

Field, of course, was the prime suspect, but there was no real evidence. The police pigeonholed the case, and probably no more would ever have been heard of it had not Field walked into a newspaper office two years later and calmly informed a couple of journalists that he was the murderer of Norah Upchurch. He offered to tell them the whole story if they paid him for it.

They spent all day going over the story with him, and finally, after nine hours, told the police. Field was detained, and made a statement confessing to the crime. He had strangled the girl in a fit of temper, he said, and had afterwards stolen her handbag and then discarded it. The police made a careful search but never found the handbag. Too much time had elapsed. There was nothing to corroborate Field's statement.

Confessions, as every detective knows, are very far from being the best evidence. They are generally repudiated at the trial, and, in the present climate of opinion, seem more apt to bring suspicion on the police than on their authors. Much safer and more valuable is a detailed statement which can be proved, by external evidence, to be false.

At his trial Field admitted making the confession but said it had been untrue. He had given himself up, he explained, so that he could have an opportunity of proving he hadn't committed the murder. For lack of any corroborating evidence, Mr. Justice Swift directed the jury to acquit him, and the Judge had some crisp things to say, in passing, about the journalists.

Two and a half years later, another London prostitute, Beatrice Vilna Sutton, was found strangled to death. She was lying on the bed in her flat at Clapham, seemingly prepared for sexual intercourse. Death was due to manual strangulation. When her body was found at 11:30 on a Sunday morning, she had already been dead for twelve hours—and for eleven of them her murderer had been in police custody, though the police had no idea that he was a murderer. He had been arrested at Tooting as an absentee from the RAF when nobody except the man who murdered her could have known then that Beatrice Sutton was dead.

He was detained in custody until the Monday morning, and then taken by an RAF escort to his station at Hendon Aerodrome. That evening, a Metropolitan Police officer arrived to charge him with the theft of four cheques, and was told by the RAF guards that their prisoner had just confessed to a murder in Clapham. The aircraftman repeated his confession to the police. His name, which rang loud bells at Scotland Yard, was Frederick Field.

He said he had killed Beatrice Sutton, whom he'd never seen before, because he was tired of being broke and wanted to end his own life. "I hadn't got the guts," he went on, "so I thought I'd stick myself in a position where somebody else would have to do it. I went into her place and she got ready to let me have intercourse with her, but I never meant to do that. I then done her in and, as you might say, put myself on the spot."

Divisional Detective Inspector Halliday, who was in charge of the case, saw Field, and, finding him in a voluble mood, encouraged him to go into as much detail as he liked—where he bought some doughnuts, the appearance of other prostitutes in the street, the position of an ashtray in which he had stubbed out his cigarette, the contents of the room and the position of the body when he left. This statement proved fatal to his defence, not, on this occasion, because the details were false, but because they were all true.

Field was committed for trial, and the papers joined the other Old Bailey cases on my table. Halliday had been able to corroborate Field's statement at almost every point. He had even persuaded the streetwalkers to give evidence; which is usually a difficult thing to do.

I discussed the case with Fulton and Byrne, who would be prosecuting. None of us doubted that Field would again admit to having made the confession but would again say it was untrue. We were right.

Field seemed bursting with confidence. As he walked from the dock to the witness box, I saw him wink at a friend. His story this time was that he had heard a quarrel going on in Beatrice Sutton's flat, and had seen a man rush out. He had then gone in to see if anything was wrong. He found a woman lying there just as he had described her in his statement. "For a moment I didn't know what to do. If I called the police, they would ask me what I was doing there. Then it occurred to me that, if I were to take the blame, I could accomplish what I hadn't the courage to do myself—that is, commit suicide. I knew it would be no good saying I'd done something unless I gave pretty full details to the police." He had therefore taken careful stock of things in the room, he said, so as to strengthen his confession. He hadn't turned on the light, but could see enough in the glow of a big fire.

When Beatrice Sutton's body was found, her head and neck were covered with a pillow. For some reason—consistent comprehensive lies are difficult to tell—Field denied having lifted the pillow during his inspection of the room.

Fulton rose to cross-examine. As usual, he was short and to the point. After dealing with a few minor discrepancies, he asked: "When you got inside and saw the woman dead, did it occur to you to assist her?"

"It did," replied Field, "but I knew she was dead."

"How did you know that?"

"I listened to her heart."

"Did it not occur to you to call the police?"

"Yes, but I knew that if I did, they'd discover I was a deserter. Also," he added, "it occurred to me to confess to the murder myself."

"If you wanted to confess to a murder you had not committed, what could have been more convincing than to put your head out of the window and call the police?"

"At that time I hadn't definitely decided to confess to the murder."

"How did you know she had been strangled?" asked Fulton.

"I didn't know."

"Then why, in your statement, did you describe pressing her throat?"

"I assumed it. I had to explain to the police how the woman was murdered."

"And," said Fulton, "you happened to explain it in just the way in which, according to the doctors, the woman was in fact murdered?"

There was a pause. Finally Field said: "It was a pure supposition."

Fulton sat down without asking any further questions. The jury reached a verdict in thirty minutes, and a few weeks later Field was executed. I have often wondered what strange compulsion made him confess to two murders, for neither of which, in all probability, he could ever otherwise have been convicted.

The following year, I again instructed counsel in a case of murder by a man who had been acquitted of a similar crime on a previous occasion. Once more, the victims had been prostitutes.

The first was a woman named Katherine Peck, alias Rosie,

alias Singing Rose, alias (for some inscrutable reason) "Carbolic Kate." She was found by the police, soon after midnight, lying in the street with her throat cut. One of her known associates was an odd-job man named Frederick George Murphy, with whom she had often been seen in the local pubs. Indeed she had been seen arguing with him outside a public house in Aldgate on the night of the murder.

Murphy had arrived at his lodging house that night about 1 A.M. He left early the following morning and had not returned. An acquaintance of his, named Wood, had met him in the afternoon, and said that Murphy told him he had murdered Mrs. Peck and was on the run. Another man, a vagrant with a criminal record, said Murphy had told him the same thing a few days later.

Although Murphy's photograph was issued to the Press, he wasn't found until six weeks later when he walked into Bethnal Green Police Station, saying he'd heard the police were looking for him. He denied having killed Mrs. Peck and denied having spent the night of the murder in the lodging house. Asked about the clothes he had been wearing that night, he said he had given his overcoat away. He was detained and charged.

But at the trial a vital witness was missing. The second man to whom Murphy was alleged to have confessed had disappeared and was never traced. The only real evidence left was the conversation which Wood claimed to have had with Murphy on the afternoon following the murder: and this Murphy denied. Eustace Fulton, for the Crown, said it would be dangerous to convict Murphy on the evidence now available, so the jury had no choice but to acquit him.

Murphy launched a campaign against Wood, whom he accused of giving perjured testimony and bombarded the police, the Home Secretary, and his MP with angry charges of bribery and dishonesty. He even smashed a window in the Home Office, for which he was sent to prison for fourteen days.

He got a job as a cleaner in a warehouse at Islington Green. He had keys to the premises, which he opened every morning. On May 14, 1937, he wrote to his employers, telling them that there was a dead woman in the cellar of the warehouse, and protesting his own innocence. When the police arrived, he had absconded: but next day he turned up at Poplar Police Station and made a long statement explaining why he couldn't have killed the woman. There were bloodstains on his clothes.

Rose Field, the dead woman, was one of several prostitutes who were known to have spent time with Murphy in the warehouse late at night, and she had last been seen going in that direction with him.

Divisional Detective Inspector Salisbury, like Inspector Halliday in the Clapham case, encouraged Murphy to make as detailed a statement as possible about his movements on the night of the murder. And detail by detail the police were able to prove his statement false. He was convicted and hanged.

The cases of Field and Murphy seemed to me then, and still do seem, relevant to the vexed question of capital punishment. Since neither man was convicted of what was presumably his first murder, no penalty could have prevented the second: but, supposing that, instead of being hanged, they had merely been sent to prison for a few years, does anyone believe that the odds would have been against a third murder when they came out?

The campaign against capital punishment was conducted at a highly emotional level. So clamorous was it, and so ubiquitously pursued through all the media of mass communication, that the surprising thing is not that it should finally have secured the suspension of hanging but that the great majority of people in this country remained unconvinced. Personally I have no doubt that majority was right.

Of course execution by hanging is horrible. Of course there are strong emotional arguments against it. But the only argument which really matters is one, not of emotion, but of reason. Is capital punishment an effective deterrent? Does it help to prevent murders? A multitude of statistics can be produced, many of them contradictory and most of them not really applicable, because they relate to countries or cities too different from our own. But common sense, and the almost universal opinion of policemen (who, after all, have the closest acquaintance with criminal behaviour and whose own lives are most often at stake), suggest firmly that capital punishment is indeed an uniquely effective deterrent.

I am not, I trust, lacking in compassion. I have seen, I suppose, some forty men sentenced to death and I have certainly felt sorry for some of them. I remember, for instance, a simple-minded boxer called Del Fontaine, who had killed his girl friend when he found her double-crossing him. Hanging does not seem to me a necessary or appropriate punishment for *crimes passionelles*.

This is not a question to which sensible people need give an all-or-nothing answer. There are many different kinds of murder and it is silly to lump them all together. Since the reason for capital punishment is that its deterrent effect prevents murders, there can be neither point nor justification in hanging those murderers whom no penalty would deter—murderers who are mentally unbalanced or who kill someone near to them in a sudden fit of rage. This distinction was quite properly drawn in the Homicide Act, 1957. This Act seems to have been widely misunderstood; lawyers found it untidy, and people said that it was inconsistent, if anyone was to be hanged, not to hang, for example, poisoners, who are a particularly unpleasant kind of murderer. Again, they were substituting emotion for thought. The distinction between "capital" and "non-capital" murders was not intended to be a moral or aesthetic one. It was practical. It was meant to apply the strongest deterrent to those crimes which, for everybody's safety, most need to be prevented and which, by their nature, are most capable of prevention by deterrence. It was aimed, in other words, at the professional criminal. The object was to deter him from carrying and using deadly weapons; to prevent just those types of murder which are commonest in other, more violent countries and which threaten, with the growth of professional crime, to increase here.

Few criminals today have any rooted objection to violence, and violent robberies have been one of the fastest growing sorts of crime. Until recently the robbers usually stopped short of killing, and I have no doubt that fear of the gallows was the chief reason for their restraint. Between committing a crime for which the penalty is a few years in prison and committing a crime for which the penalty is being hanged, a manifest gulf exists. Few people are prepared to cross it: but many criminals, as is becoming all too clear, would be prepared to risk an additional prison sentence if, by killing someone who gets in their way, or killing a witness, they can improve their chances of not being caught at all.

If capital punishment is to be abolished completely, we shall have to replace it with some penalty which operates almost as powerfully on the minds of criminals. This means life sentences which really are for life, and there is likely once more to be a strong emotional clamour against them.

Another and perhaps more honest, argument against the death penalty is its irrevocability. Mistakes cannot be rectified. No one, of course, can say that an innocent man has never been, and never could be, hanged. Human affairs admit of no such certainty. But I can say, without any hesitation, that I know of no case—certainly no case which would have been capital murder under the provisions of the Homicide Act— in which an innocent man has in fact been hanged in recent years.

Another argument which the abolitionists advance is that

very few murderers do, or would, kill twice. What they mean, however, is that not many people have been twice convicted of murder; which is hardly surprising since, until 1957, death was the prescribed penalty for convicted murderers, and those convicted on "non-capital" murders since 1957 have mostly not yet come out of prison.

The statistics of murderers who killed twice do not include Field or Murphy, but can anyone doubt that they should? Does anyone seriously believe that Donald Merrett did not kill his mother, even though a Scottish jury found the case Not Proven? Does anyone, except those who are determined to believe that every notorious murderer was innocent, really doubt that Donald Hume killed Stanley Setty?

An even more flagrant and surprising case was that of a fisherman from Hull, by the name of William Burkitt, who was charged in 1915 with strangling a woman with her stocking. The jury at York Assizes found him guilty of manslaughter but not of murder. He was released in 1924. In 1925 he was again standing trial at York Assizes, charged with strangling a woman with her stocking. Again the jury found him guilty of manslaughter but not of murder. He was sentenced to ten years penal servitude and served the full term, coming out in 1935.

Four years later he tied a stocking round the neck of the woman with whom he was living, and was again charged with murder. At Leeds Assizes he was again acquitted of murder and convicted of manslaughter. This time he served fifteen years before being released. He died peacefully, two years later, in his seventy-first year.

If his life had been shorter, the lives of two innocent women would have been longer. In spite of the verdicts brought in by those three Yorkshire juries, I can't help believing that it would have been a just and desirable bargain.

CHAPTER 5

You Can't Offer Pounds to a Judge

If I were asked to specify one crime which was typical of the 1930s, I would instinctively say fraud. I'm not certain why. There are, I'm sure, as many smart operators and confidence tricksters working today as there ever were, and I don't really believe that their victims have become much more sophisticated. As Barnum said, there's a sucker born every minute; the supply is inexhaustibly renewed. Partly, no doubt, my impression is subjective. Because fraud cases tend to be lengthy and complex, they bulked large in the work of the London Side. There have, also, been two real changes. On the one hand, a tightening up of the law and the creation of the Fraud Squad have had a salutory effect in certain quarters: and, on the other, the whole pattern of British crime has become more feverish and violent, making fraud seem nostalgically civilised by comparison.

This is not to say that frauds do no great harm. On the contrary, they can be very cruel indeed. Their victims are not, as a rule, tycoons or millionaires, who are too shrewd and too well advised to be readily taken in, but people to whom small sums of money mean a lot and who are unsophisticated about the wicked devices of this world.

Before World War II sharepushing used to be the commonest City swindle. The sharepusher would set up a nominal business or acquire an already existing one; the only essentials were an impressive name and an impressive address in the City of London. He would then devote himself for a while to building

71

up confidence. He would circularise carefully selected victims—clergymen, widows, and other people whom he knew to be living on small stipends or pensions, eked out by the interest from a little invested capital. They were vulnerable because they were anxious about money; they would welcome any plausible chance of increasing their incomes. They were allowed, at first, to make small profits on one or two transactions, and they were encouraged to submit full details of all their investments.

Once confidence had been established, the sharepusher's high-pressure salesmen moved in, genial, persuasive, well-dressed, and driving expensive cars. They rarely had much difficulty in persuading their victims to buy more shares "of the same sort as had shown a profit already"; the deal might be made in cash or the new shares might be acquired in exchange for securities already owned by the victim.

The new shares were usually genuine but worthless. The sharepusher might have obtained them by buying, at negligible cost, a block of shares in a derelict company: or he might have got control of the company and issued fresh shares. Sometimes, of course, the technique was simpler: the company didn't exist.

Another method was to buy up a moribund company, issue new shares and offer the original shareholders a chance to increase their holdings. Soon afterwards, a smooth-talking gentleman would call on them and offer to buy any shares in the company at a greatly inflated price. The victims, seeing, as they thought, the prospect of an immediate and certain profit, eagerly took up the company's option to increase their holdings. They never saw their impressive visitor again—or any return on their investment.

A variation on sharepushing was the "unit fraud." The sharepusher acquired an orchard or some other piece of productive land (mushroom fields were rather popular), divided it into plots which he called "units," and sold them for, perhaps, £5 each. The unit holder could be shown the land and was guaranteed a proportionate share of the profits. When someone eventually became suspicious and the matter was investigated, many more units were found to have been sold than there were plots. The game could be kept going for a long time by the classic expedient of paying bogus dividends to the earlier victims out of money subscribed by the newer ones.

In one large-scale conspiracy of this kind, the organisers obtained some £900,000 from the public and paid out £500,000. The leader of the group urged his salesmen to "leave them nothing but their eyes to cry with." It was my pleasure to instruct counsel for his prosecution.

He was allowed bail until almost the end of the trial, on condition that he reported to the City police each day. After a harassing session in the witness box, he went to Old Jewry to report, and there bumped into a rival sharepusher, who was also on bail while awaiting trial. "You're a lucky man," said this rival, "they won't give you more than seven days," and then added with a nasty grin, "Seven Christmas Days, that is." The police had to separate them.

Next morning the Judge refused bail, and two days later the sharepusher did in fact get seven years.

Another case which involved me in the mid-thirties was remarkable not for the facts of the crime, which were typical enough of a certain sort of fraud, but for what came afterwards. Between June 1935 and the end of 1936, three firms of "outside brokers," with addresses in Basinghall Street, New Bond Street, and Cannon Street respectively, unloaded worthless shares on to the public for a total of £120,000. An investigation by the City police showed that all three firms had been financed by a company with the vague but resonant title of "Commerce, Industry, and Finance, Ltd." This company had received, and then sold for cash, securities extracted from the victims of the three bucket shops; it had also paid for the printing and distribution of half a million circulars issued by them.

73

The principal figure in the company was Mr. Edward Harold Guylee, an apparently respectable citizen living in Surrey, where he was a churchwarden and highly esteemed by his neighbours. He and two of his associates were brought to trial at the Old Bailey before Mr. Justice Finlay. "Khaki" Roberts led for the prosecution, and Guylee was represented by D. N. Pritt.

His defence was that he had himself been deceived by a financier named Maurice Singer. This gentleman, unfortunately, had disappeared, and there was no evidence of the dealings which Guylee said had taken place between them. "Khaki" conducted the prosecution with his usual skill and thoroughness, and in due course Guylee and his associates were convicted. Few people in Court can have been surprised: but Guylee himself plainly was. He was visibly shaken by the jury's verdict, and still more so when Mr. Justice Finlay, describing the fraud as "gross, cruel, and systematic," sentenced him to five years' penal servitude. His expression was in marked contrast to the cheerful and confident manner he had shown throughout the trial, beaming affably on everyone in Court.

Soon afterwards I slipped on a patch of oil while getting off a bus in Whitehall, and had to spend six months encased in plaster of Paris from thigh to ankle. I hadn't been back at work very long when, in the summer of 1938, I saw Guylee again. The scene was, once more, the Old Bailey, and this time he stood not in the dock but in the witness box, guarded by prison officers. The dock was occupied, I'm sorry to say, by a solicitor's managing clerk and a member of my own profession, F. J. de Verteuil, who had defended one of Guylee's associates in the fraud trial.

Guylee swore that he had paid these two men sums amounting to £11,200 "to grease the wheels of the High Court, to square certain officers of the Director of Public Prosecutions Department, to buy off the Press and to straighten the Judge."

74

He looked grim as he told his story. He had been persuaded to part with £3000, he said—"the money to go three ways"—in order to prevent a warrant being issued. This expenditure proved vain. Then, after his arrest, he had been asked which Judge he would like to try the case.

"And did you express a preference?" asked Mr. Justice Macnaghten.

"I didn't know one Judge from another," replied Guylee morosely. He had been told, he went on, that the Judge would need 2000 guineas because "you can't offer pounds to a Judge." The rest of us apparently would be satisfied with pounds. I say "us" because I learned, to my surprise and, I must admit, annoyance, that I was one of those who were supposed to have received £1000 each. Needless to say, none of the people whom Guylee imagined he had bought had ever been approached with such a suggestion. The defence was that Guylee had made the whole story up: but this time the jury believed him. The two men in the dock were duly convicted and sentenced, just as Guylee had been, to five years' penal servitude.

It's hard to imagine how any intelligent person, living in this country, could have been taken in by such implausible promises. The British legal system is probably the least corrupt in the world. I've known of policemen who took small kickbacks and of shady lawyers, but none holding an official position who could have been bribed in such a way: and I never heard in modern times of a British Judge against whom even a shadow of suspicion lay. Why then did Guylee believe it? One might have thought that, being himself a professional in the fraud game, he would have been quick to smell fraud in others. The reverse appears to have been true. He was so accustomed to dishonesty that he took it for granted everyone else was, or might be, equally dishonest. And so he was hoist, with his own petard.

The "long-firm fraud" was another lucrative manoeuvre, common in the 1930s. In its simplest form, it entails starting a business, ordering goods from the wholesalers and paying for them almost at once. Then, once confidence has been established, the swindler starts giving larger orders and obtaining longer credit. Finally, he sells the goods for cash and absconds with the proceeds. In a more complicated form, requiring several conspirators, three or four businesses are started simultaneously; letterheads are printed, orders are placed and credit is requested. If the wholesalers ask for references, they can be referred to the other firms—from which they will receive a glowing account of the stability and credit-worthiness of the firm about which they were enquiring.

However the thing was done, the result in all "long-firm frauds" was the same. The swindlers, having obtained goods on credit, sold them and absconded with the cash. Occasionally the boldest swindlers didn't even abscond. They salted the proceeds away and, armed with fictitious losses and falsified books, simply went bankrupt. This was considered the most elegant way of rounding off the scheme.

Businessmen are more accustomed nowadays to check credit ratings, and a high proportion of them now work in large firms with security departments which can make discreet enquiries about dubious people and unknown companies. But the essence of all frauds is as old as man: only their details need bringing up to date in each generation. The airline ticket frauds, which have been plaguing the world's airlines and travel agencies during the past few years are only a modern version of the "long-firm" manoeuvre.

Confidence tricksters too are always with us. They are—indeed they have to be—the most engaging of crooks. Perhaps because their victims could more easily afford the loss and were not, as a rule, poor widows or retired parsons, I certainly found them more sympathetic than the other professionals specialising in fraud. They were never violent and they were often ingenious.

Their best target is someone from a distant country who will soon be going back there. Australians used to be favourite victims: and Australians, it's said, also make the best con men. (My Australian friends tell me, not without a touch of pride, that this widely held belief is, in fact, true.) The victims tend to be rich and, in their own estimation, shrewd men of business. It always surprised me to see how easily such men, self-made tycoons very often, fell for such blatant old tricks. Indeed no trick, however blatant, however old, seems unworkable in the right hands. I've no doubt people are still buying Sydney Harbour Bridge and purchasing gold bricks. Where possible, however, the swindlers try to make the purported transaction more or less shady; this, they hope, will increase the victim's natural reluctance to talk about the matter or go to the police.

One of the most successful con men between the wars was Michael Corrigan (if that was really his name—he sometimes called himself Cassidy). He was probably an Irishman, born at Fermoy: but nothing about him was ever certain except his ability as a champion liar. He was quite a small man, square-built and full of hearty charm. The first thing indisputably known about him is that in 1916, at Romford in Essex, he married a girl whom he deserted four years later. He told her he was a Chief Inspector in the Northwest Mounted Police, now called the Royal Canadian Mounted Police.

By 1922 he had become Major Corrigan and rented an office in Kingsway. His business there consisted of borrowing money to exploit oil and silver concessions in Mexico, which, he said, the Mexican Government had given him as a reward for political services. In 1923 he was adjudged bankrupt—in his absence, for Corrigan had disappeared.

In 1924 he replenished his funds. He persuaded a company director to give him £40,000 for investment in Mexican oil shares and, by contracting to buy a coal mine in the Forest of Dean, somehow wheedled nearly £35,000 out of the mineowner. Meanwhile, under his alternative name of Cassidy, he was living very comfortably with a woman who owned a racing stable in Belgium.

The next year was almost as good. Another financier gave him £20,000 to invest in the Mexican concessions. In 1926 he transformed himself from Major to a Flight Commander in the Royal Naval Air Service, resplendent with the D.S.O. and the Belgian Legion of Honour. He also described himself, at various times, as the brother of a well-known millionaire, as a Mexican oil king, and as the personal plenipotentiary in Europe of Mexican President Plutarco Calles. He defrauded a rich Rumanian of £4000 and just failed to get another £5000.

Though his activities were now of keen interest to the police, Corrigan had never been charged with any offence. So plausible was he that several of his victims remained unshakably convinced that their "investments" would still show a profit. One of them even stood surety for him when he was arrested on a tipstaff's warrant. Towards the end of 1926 he was actually convicted—not in Britain but in Belgium, and not for fraud but for entering the country under an assumed name; he was sent to prison for a month.

Next year he acquired a new mistress—and £10,770 from her mother, having told them he was president of the Standard Oil Company. In 1928 he hinted in some quarters that he was a former Secret Service man, and at the same time promoted himself to the rank of General in the Mexican Army. That year he defrauded one man of £4900, still ostensibly for investment in oil shares, and another of £18,320 plus some jewellery. His expenses must have been very high; his way of life was certainly lavish, and he not only backed, but owned racehorses. A few months later he went bankrupt again, with assets of only £30 to set against liabilities of £108,822.

Then in 1930 he suffered his first real reverse. He was convicted of fraud and sentenced to five years' penal servitude. When he was released, he changed from the mythical oil business to an equally mythical armaments business. He was supplying aircraft, he said, to the Australian Government. A businessman who lent him a large sum of money to back this fictitious deal refused to prosecute when the fraud was exposed.

In 1937 Corrigan persuaded the Irish authorities that he was an Irishman who had fought gallantly to liberate the Emerald Isle, and they rewarded him with a passport. He notched up two more petty convictions, neither for fraud: in one case he was fined £50 for helping an alien to land in the United Kingdom without permission, and in the other he was fined £500 for making a false declaration to the Customs.

Not until January 1939 did he appear again at the Old Bailey. I'd heard of him before, but this was the first time I'd actually seen him. I was interested; his virtuosity, I felt, deserved a certain admiration. He was charged with defrauding a French firm which had paid him £7250 for a quantity of arms, and received in return only packing cases loaded with stones and rubbish. He was sent to prison for two years.

He came out in August 1940 and plunged irrepressibly into his old line of work. Claiming that he could sell the rights of a new process for hardening steel to the Armament Corporation of America, he obtained £3685 for alleged expenses. A tough solicitor subsequently forced him to repay £2685, and the other £1000 was recovered from the perfectly respectable, if somewhat naïve, gentleman who had brought Corrigan into the business.

I saw Corrigan next one day when I was having a drink in the Carlton Bar. He strolled in, looking very well and remarkably prosperous. He greeted me most affably, recalling that we last met "at the Old Bailey," as though it had been the Athenaeum. He stood chatting for a few minutes, and hinted that he was currently engaged on secret work of national importance.

When I got back to the office, I telephoned Detective Superintendent Thorp about some other matter, and, before I rang off, asked if he happened to be looking for Michael Corrigan. "We're always looking for Michael Corrigan," Thorp replied. It seemed that the police were indeed investigating a fresh crop of complaints from people with whom Corrigan had lately had dealings. "I'm not surprised that he regards his work as secret," Thorp added.

I saw Corrigan again, many months later, in another bar. I was waiting for Stan Joel to join me for lunch, when Corrigan came in, looking more prosperous than ever and accompanied by a blonde who must have been about thirty-five years younger than him. He waved cheerfully. Stan was, by now, quite a well-known racehorse owner; indeed, he'd just won the St. Leger. Almost as soon as Stan arrived, Corrigan paused at our table, said, "Mr. Jackson, if you and your friend want something good, do so-and-so"—I've forgotten the horse's name—"in the four o'clock," and then followed his blonde into the restaurant.

"Who's that?" Stan asked. I told him at some length. "Good Lor'!" he said; then, after a thoughtful pause, "I wonder if he knows anything. It'll be a decent price."

I thought it most unlikely, I replied, that Michael Corrigan would tell me the correct time, let alone a potential winner. Rather to my relief, the horse was unplaced.

Superintendent Thorp told me later, when I was at Scotland Yard, that Corrigan's activities between 1944 and 1946 were among his most imaginative. He obtained large sums of money in connection with a wide range of fictitious business deals, which included the purchase of land in the United Kingdom on behalf of two South American millionaires; a concession from the Guatemalan Government for cutting and exporting balsa wood; the purchase of Guatemalan bonds; the sale of

No. 145 Piccadilly; payment of demurrage on ships arriving in the Thames and Humber laden with balsa wood; and the bulk purchase of United States Army surplus stores.

Corrigan's story had a sad ending. He was arrested and charged with four offences involving fraud. By then he must have been about fifty-eight, and the prospect of another period in gaol, probably a long one, was more than he could face. On October 16, 1946, he committed suicide in his cell at Brixton by hanging himself with his tie. I was genuinely sorry. It was a dismal end to a colourful life.

The outbreak of the Second World War had checked the big City frauds. Wartime restrictions allowed small scope for them, and many of the operators were away in the Army, perhaps exercising their talents on the Quartermaster's staff. When the war ended, measures were promptly taken to prevent a recurrence.

Sharepushing cases had been more likely to fall within the jurisdiction of the City Police than of Scotland Yard, but many had required investigation by both forces. The two forces worked well enough together, but inevitably the division of responsibility had sometimes meant delay.

In February 1946, after discussions between the Home Office, the D.P.P., the City Police, and the Metropolitan Police, a new bureau was set up, at Scotland Yard called the Metropolitan and City Police Company Fraud Branch, with officers drawn from both forces. Thorp was put in charge, and no one could have done the job better; he was a man of presence, charm, and wide experience. The men under him had no special qualifications except an interest in the work and their ability as policemen. Would it be more sensible to recruit accountants for this kind of work? I doubt it. People point to the remarkably high qualifications of the FBI in America, where every officer has a degree or its technical equivalent. My admiration for Mr. Hoover and his men is unbounded, but they are, I think, educated beyond their need—at least, for routine work. When necessary, an accountant can always be brought in. The difficulty in fraud, as in other cases, is to gather evidence which will secure a conviction: and this is essentially a police problem, not a technical one.

The formation of the Fraud Squad (this more convenient name soon supplanted the ponderous official title) effectually prevented a recurrence of sharepushing on anything like the pre-war scale. Its officers established liaisons with the banks and the Stock Exchange, and with the police of Canada, the United States, and Australia. A useful result of these links was the preventive work which the Fraud Squad had been able to do. When the wrong sort of tourist arrived at a London hotel, he was sometimes unpleasantly surprised to discover that his intentions were known. Two large men would call on him, show their warrant cards and warn him discreetly that his stay was likely to prove unprofitable.

The Fraud Squad was a success from the beginning. Not only does it operate freely within the two London police areas, but its specialist skills are available, on request, to any other police force in the country. It constituted another step along a path which we shall certainly have to pursue much further: the path of very close co-operation between police forces and the integration of their detective departments.

CHAPTER 6

The Bullets Which Wobbled

At the beginning of the war, when there was more fuss and less justification for it than later, a meeting was held to discuss the removal of some government departments from London to other and presumably safer parts of the country. I attended on behalf of the Director's office.

It was a large gathering, and the Chairman began by impressing on us, in the most solemn tones, that we were about to discuss matters of the utmost secrecy. The places to which we might be moving would each be given a code letter, and from that moment on we must refer to them in no other way. The Director's office, I learned from a top secret document which was circulated among us, would be going to Oxford; code name —CB (or something of the sort). As the meeting broke up, I casually referred to Oxford by name and was earnestly rebuked: "Not Oxford, Jackson—CB."

I hurried back to the office to tell my senior colleagues, but found that everybody had gone out to lunch. Everybody, that is, except one of the messengers. He came into my room, and said: "Good morning, sir. I hope we don't have to move. I mean, I don't much fancy Oxford, do you, sir?"

He needn't have worried. After all the fuss, we never did leave London. The office was bombed out a couple of times: we even spent one day temporarily ensconced at Scotland Yard: but we finally acquired a whole floor of Devonshire House in Piccadilly, and there we stayed until the war's end.

These moves made very little difference to the routine of

our lives. Many barristers and solicitors were away in the Army, but most of the Treasury Counsel were still there, none of them being young. I was myself asked to join a government security department but Sir Edward Tindal Atkinson, the Director of Public Prosecutions, refused to let me go. His decision disappointed me at the time but must be seen in retrospect as a piece of good luck, for if I'd gone, I might not have returned to the Director's office in time to be offered the job at Scotland Yard.

As it was I continued to look after the Director's work at the Old Bailey and between sessions to do my share of cases in the Magistrates' Courts.

Sometimes we sat in court outwardly unmoved while the sirens moaned and a flying bomb rumbled along overhead. From my friend Donal Barry, like myself a member of the London Side, I heard of an opponent who ducked under the solicitors' table, continuing his cross examination in muffled tones, and emerging with a smile of satisfaction when the menace had passed over.

The pattern of crime adapted itself to new conditions. A slight diminution in some peacetime offences was compensated by the growth of the black market and the criminal activities associated with it.

In the early part of the war there was a small wave of spy trials, which were my concern because the Director prosecutes in all such cases. Though spies are not criminals in the ordinary sense I had no qualms about prosecuting them in wartime or, when as A.C.C. I was responsible for the Special Branch, about hunting them down during the nominal peace which the Communists regard only as an extension of war by other means.

The German spies who came to Britain, both in the First and in the Second World War, were, for some reason, surprisingly inefficient and ill-prepared, and were, for the most part, quickly rounded up. Why this should have been so is an interesting subject for speculation, whether historical or psychological. It may have been because the genius of the German people is for organisation and administrative rather than for individual initiative, and spies have to operate as individuals. Heinrich Himmler, for example, was essentially a distorted civil servant. The Russians, on the other hand, have Oriental minds and a long tradition of subtle spying both on each other and on their neighbours. At all events, Nazi espionage was never comparable with the vastly more elaborate and successful Communist networks.

In the very early days of the war, four men—Walberg, Meier, Kieboom, and Pons—landed on the coast of Kent from a small boat. They hid for the night, and, at breakfasttime next morning, Meier went into The Rising Sun at Lydd and asked for a glass of beer. His briefing had apparently contained no information about Britain's peculiar licensing hours. He was promptly arrested and his companions were rounded up. At their trial Meier, Kieboom, and Walberg were convicted and sentenced to death. Pons, who was defended by Christmas Humphreys, was acquitted presumably because the jury believed his story that he had come under duress.

Around that same time, just as the uneasy hush of "the phony war" was about to dissolve into the fury of the blitzkrieg, a much more extraordinary crime was committed in London. It was a political assassination, a rare event in British history, and the murderer shot not one, but four distinguished men at close range, three of whom were saved by his ignorance of firearms. Surprisingly few people remember the case today, presumably because the death of a retired proconsul, however eminent, seemed trivial then compared with the death of France and perhaps of all Europe.

On March 13, 1940, in the Tudor Room at Caxton Hall, the East India Association and the Royal Central Asian Society held a joint meeting to hear a lecture on Afghanistan by Sir

Percy Sykes. The Secretary of State for India, the Marquess of Zetland, took the chair; with him on the platform were Sir Louis Dane, Lord Lamington, and Sir Michael O'Dwyer.

The meeting ended at half-past four. The audience was preparing to leave, putting on coats, moving towards the doors, when six shots rang out in rapid succession. A man standing near the platform had fired twice at Zetland, twice at O'Dwyer and once each at Lamington and Dane. Every bullet hit its mark. Lamington was wounded in the hand, Dane in the forearm. Zetland felt a blow above the heart but was apparently unscathed. O'Dwyer was not so lucky; two bullets struck him in the back and he died almost instantly.

The shooting was over in a matter of seconds. It left a blue haze of smoke in the hall and an audience too astounded to move. As so often on such occasions, no one afterwards, even from that assembly of educated and intelligent people, could be certain what had happened. The witnesses disagreed over the number of shots which had been fired. The most common estimate was four—a salutary warning against placing too much reliance on eyewitnesses.

The first person to move was the murderer, and he moved very quickly indeed towards the nearest exit. He would have reached it, too, but for the courage of one of those splendid English ladies of the old school who are nowadays derided. She threw herself in his path, seized him by the shoulders and held him long enough for one of the men in the audience to bring him down, knocking the gun out of his hand. Then the police arrived.

The prisoner turned out to be an Indian, calling himself Mahomed Singh Azad, which is an improbable blend of Moslem and Hindu names. His real name was Udham Singh. The police were soon able to build up a considerable dossier on him. He was a Sikh, born in Patiala State and brought up in an orphanage at Amritsar: and Amritsar had been the scene of the so-called massacre in 1920 when Sir Michael O'Dwyer was Lieutenant-Governor of the Punjab.

After serving for three years in the Indian Army, Udham Singh had travelled, via London and Mexico, to the United States, where he lived for seven years. He had then gone to sea as a Puerto Rican, under the name Frank Brazil, because as an Indian he could not have been employed on an American ship. He deserted in Calcutta, and a month later was arrested at Amritsar for being in possession of illicit weapons and a prohibited newspaper. He admitted that the weapons were for use against the British. He was sentenced to five years' imprisonment.

After his release, he came to London, went to the Soviet Union in 1936 and was back in Britain by 1938. He may have been, in some sense, a Communist, but applied to such men the term seems hardly relevant. What he was, like so many of the terrorists who have plagued our times, was a dedicated revolutionary.

"I didn't mean to kill," he said when he was charged. "I just did it to protest. I didn't mean to kill anybody." He was searched, and in his pocket was found a diary containing the private addresses of Lord Willingdon, a former Viceroy, the Marquess of Zetland, and Sir Michael O'Dwyer. "I did it because I had a grudge against him," Udham Singh burst out. "He deserved it. I do not belong to any society or anything else."

He was reminded that he had been cautioned and was advised to say nothing more.

"I don't care," he said. "I don't mind dying. What's the use of waiting till you get old?"

He was again warned that what he was saying might be used in evidence at his trial. But a little later he asked: "Is Zetland dead? He ought to be. I put two into him right there"—and he indicated his stomach. Later still, when he heard what had happened, he said: "Only one dead? I thought I could get more. There was a lot of womans about, you know."

He was duly committed for trial at the Old Bailey. George McClure, a quiet advocate, known for his fairness rather than for being tough, was chosen to prosecute. The papers were passed to me with an instruction from the Assistant Director that I should prepare a note about the Sikhs, their history, religion, and characteristics. Why this information should have been considered necessary I can't imagine, but I spent an enjoyable time poring over books which had belonged to my father. I produced a learned and lengthy note, of which McClure, needless to say, made no use whatsoever.

The trial began on June 4. Since this was the day on which the Prime Minister announced the hairbreadth rescue of the British Expeditionary Force from Dunkirk, it is hardly surprising that Udham Singh's trial should have received little attention in the exiguous newspapers of the time.

The case against him was plain enough. The only puzzle was why the other men on the platform had escaped so lightly. Dane and Lamington had barely been scratched, and Zetland might almost have been wearing a bulletproof waistcoat; the slug was found in his clothing when he undressed.

The mystery was solved by Robert Churchill, the famous gunmaker and ballistics expert. He was a small man, rather thick-set, with beady black eyes. He made a fine witness, not only because his knowledge was unrivalled, but because he was really interested, with all the enthusiasm of a skilled amateur, in forensic problems. The police had the highest regard for him; he used to coach the Special Branch in pistol shooting. But he was as ready to testify for the defence as for the prosecution. Since he retired, there has been no independent ballistics expert of anything like his stature available; which is a serious lack.

Udham Singh, he told the Court, had used .40 ammunition

in a .455 Smith and Wesson revolver. The bullets had fitted the barrel of the gun so loosely that, when they were fired, they wobbled out without engaging the rifling. It was rank bad luck, Churchill remarked to me, that O'Dwyer "caught the two that flew straight and hard."

Udham Singh's defence was that the killing had been an unfortunate accident. He never meant to shoot anybody, only to fire into the air as a protest: but somebody—some unidentified person—saw him draw the gun and knocked it down just as he pressed the trigger. He was defended by St. John Hutchinson, K.C., Reggie Seaton, now Chairman of London Sessions, and no lesser champion of Indian independence than Krishna Menon in person. They did their best, but inevitably the jury found him guilty. He was asked, in the traditional formula, whether he had anything to say why sentence of death should not be passed upon him.

He had a great deal to say. Fishing a piece of paper from his pocket, he began a lengthy and impassioned diatribe. From time to time, he consulted his script, and he stumbled over some of the longer words.

"I say down with British imperialism!" he shouted. "If you have any human decency, you should die with shame . . . The so-called intellectuals who call themselves rulers of the world are of bastard blood . . ." (Much of it was incoherent and, to me at least, incomprehensible.) "Bloodthirsty . . . brutality . . ."

He went on and on. As I watched him, I thought he wasn't finding it easy to read from the document in his hand. The speech had been drafted, I was inclined to suspect, by someone who knew more English than Udham Singh, and it had been drafted for this occasion.

After a while, Mr. Justice Atkinson interrupted him. "I am not going to listen to a political speech," he said quietly. "If you have anything relevant to say, say it. But you are only to say why sentence should not be passed according to law."

"I do not care about sentence of death," Udham Singh shouted in reply. "It means nothing at all. I do not care about dying or anything . . ."

And he resumed his harangue. At last the Judge stopped him. Udham Singh put away his spectacles and shouted: "Down with British imperialism! Down with British dirty dogs!" Sentence of death was passed. Before leaving the dock, he spat at the Judge. Eight weeks later he was executed.

Even in wartime ordinary police work has to continue; international crimes against humanity may overshadow, but do not preclude, ordinary crimes against human beings. There were slight changes in the frequency and complexion of crime: otherwise, the job of the C.I.D. continued, between 1939 and 1945, much as usual. Some policemen were allowed to join the armed forces and some were needed for special duties, but their loss was compensated by the help available from the military police and the tighter control which wartime regulations imposed on everybody's activities. During the blitz burglars were no more enthusiastic than the rest of us about venturing into London's dangerous streets. Only when the tide had turned and victory came, however dimly, into sight did the characteristic wartime rackets, the black market, and the exploitation of shortages really become a major cause of crime.

Though many crimes continued as before, many criminals were now in uniform; a fact which presented both extra facilities and extra difficulties to the detectives who were hunting them.

A typical case, in which the Metropolitan Police were asked to help, began with the disappearance of two little girls in Buckinghamshire. They were last seen, by several other children, asking for a lift in an Army truck. One girl, an evacuee from London, tentatively identified a driver called Hill, who wore Army issue spectacles with steel frames. A twelve-year-old boy by the name of Norman Page confirmed that the man had worn spectacles and was able to describe the lorry in considerable detail.

An identification parade was arranged, but, before anyone could stop him, Hill went up to the children and said: "I'm not the soldier you saw driving those girls away, am I?"

"No," replied the children in chorus.

Eighty drivers were then lined up. The only one of the five children to pick anybody out was Norman Page. He picked Hill.

A discrepancy of twenty miles was found on the speedometer of Hill's truck, but he insisted that he must have covered the extra distance in camp. When the police asked for another identification parade, they were told that the regiment was under orders to move. The best that could be done was to arrange that the children should stand at the crossroads and watch the lorries go by.

Again Norman Page picked out Hill.

The following day, a pair of Boy Scouts found the bodies of the missing girls. They had been stabbed and strangled. The Chief Constable of Buckinghamshire telephoned the Yard, and next morning Chief Inspector Hatherill arrived, accompanied by Sir Bernard Spilsbury. After examining the wounds, Spilsbury described the blade which must have caused them: and this, Hatherill soon learned, matched the width of an Army clasp knife. A khaki handkerchief with a laundry mark—RA 1019—had also been found near the bodies.

Hatherill and his sergeant went to Suffolk, where Hill was being detained. In Hill's kit, Hatherill found a pair of steel-rimmed spectacles, an out-of-date clasp knife with a broken blade, and signs that a pair of trousers and a denim blouse had recently been washed. The rest of his clothing was dry, but several items bore the mark RA 1019. Hatherill then ex-

91

amined the truck which Hill had been driving. It tallied with Norman Page's description.

In the long interrogation which followed, Hill proved quick-witted and clever, not at all easy to catch out. His clasp knife, he said, was kept in his kit; he hadn't seen it for several months, and it was in good working order then. The handkerchief, he suggested, must have been returned in someone else's kit.

Hatherill asked him to take off his battledress blouse and cardigan. He did so—and was revealed wearing a khaki shirt with the sleeves torn off. His explanation was quite ingenious. He said that his shirt had come back from the laundry torn, and he had therefore ripped the sleeves right off, thinking it would do for the summer.

Hatherill took all the clothes back to London and gave them to Dr. Roche Lynch, the government analyst. A few hours later, Dr. Lynch reported that stains on the shirt and trousers were human blood.

When Hill had been charged, Hatherill set to work, tying up the loose ends. He talked to more than a hundred soldiers, took statements from the officer who had read Hill's speedometer, from the Medical Officer, who said that Hill had never re-ported any kind of haemorrhage, from the Quartermaster Ser-geant, who said that Hill's kit had been stored in a dry place; from the men who had shared a hut with Hill and from the mess orderlies, who couldn't remember having seen him at tea on the day of the crime. Meanwhile, two further items of sci-entific evidence emerged: Dr. Lynch found a smear of human blood in Hill's truck, and on a gas mask container which one of the dead girls had been carrying a faint fingerprint was dis-cerned—faint but recognisable, the print of Hill's left middle finger.

The most interesting feature of the trial was the evidence of Norman Page. He was one of the most impressive witnesses I've ever seen. The examination and cross-examination of children, so as neither to confuse them nor to alienate the jury, is a difficult art: but a good child witness can be most convincing, perhaps because his mind is fresh and takes impressions like a photographic plate. Norman Page had been right all along, and certainly nothing was going to shake him now. Hill was convicted and sentenced to death.

Hatherill told me afterwards that he went up to Norman as they were coming out of court, and said: "You're a clever boy, when you grow up you ought to be a detective."

"What, me?" replied Norman. "Sit on my arse doing nothing all day? Not bloody likely."

Not many days later, Charles Wallace told me that he thought after so many years at the Old Bailey I ought now to hand over to another member of the Department and devote myself to the heavier cases on the London Side. These were, for the most part, the kind of prolonged fraud cases from which I had been largely precluded by the necessity of spending a fortnight in every month at the Old Bailey. Because the change meant that I should see less of my friends in the Bar Mess and among the Court officials, I was sorry: but as far as the work itself was concerned, I had no strong feelings one way or the other. I have found that almost any case is absorbing while one does it, though it may seem boring in retrospect.

During my last session at the Old Bailey, there was another case which, in ordinary times, would certainly have become a national sensation. The protagonist belonged worthily to the horrific line of mass murderers which includes Jack the Ripper and, more recently, the Hammersmith killer.

The case began with the discovery of a woman's body in an air-raid shelter at Marylebone. She had been strangled and her handbag taken. Next morning another woman, a prostitute, was found with her throat cut; her handbag had been ransacked. Three days later, another woman was found dead; there was a stocking round her neck and her body had been mutilated with a razor. Chief Inspector Greeno was still busy at this woman's flat when he heard that yet another woman had been found, strangled and mutilated, in a flat at Paddington; her handbag and wardrobe had been rifled.

Since at least two of the murdered women were prostitutes, Greeno began the delicate task of cajoling information from other members of that profession. It might be supposed that prostitutes would be the keenest people in London to help catch this kind of murderer, but in fact, as the Hammersmith case has shown again, they are always extremely reluctant to talk. Presumably, like many people in more respected walks of life, they feel "it can't happen to them." The dangers of allowing a killer to remain at large therefore seem remote, compared with the immediate disadvantages of talking to the police. Not only do they regard the police as natural enemies, but they are frightened that, if they were too frequently seen conversing with a detective, they would be blamed by the criminal fraternity when some thief whom they knew was arrested: and, since most prostitutes live among, or at least in contact with, criminals, such a risk is not to be taken lightly.*

However, after hours of patient work, Greeno found a woman, called Mrs. Kathleen Mulcahy, who had been assaulted by a strangler on the same night as the last of the known victims had been killed. The attack had taken place in her flat at Paddington. Mrs. Mulcahy had screamed and fought so violently that the man ran away. She described him, and said he had been wearing an Air Force uniform.

No sooner had he begun to follow up this information than Greeno learned that an airman had just been remanded in custody for having assaulted a woman in the West End. The man's name was Gordon Frederick Cummins, and the assault

* Between February 2, 1964 and February 16, 1965, the bodies of six prostitutes were found in the Hammersmith area. All had been strangled and all were nude. The killer has not, at the time of writing, been detected.

had occurred shortly before the attack on Mrs. Mulcahy. He had been interrupted while throttling a woman whom he had tried unsuccessfully to pick up, and the police traced him through the service number on a gas mask he left behind.

He said he was drunk and didn't remember what had happened. Prima facie, there was nothing to connect him with the murders, but Greeno instituted a full-scale search of his quarters. The result was spectacular and conclusive. A bizarre collection of trivia which had belonged to the dead women came to light—a cigarette case, a pencil, a fountain pen, a handkerchief, a comb, a wristwatch.

He was committed for trial, charged that within a space of five days he had murdered four women and attempted to murder two more. Each murder was, of course, the subject of a separate indictment and, at the Old Bailey, Cummins was only tried for the murder of Evelyn Oatley. For that offence, however, he had two trials, or, to be accurate, one and a half. At the first hearing an album of photographs relating to one of the other murders was put in by mistake, thus revealing to the Jury that Cummins was accused of more than one murder. This Jury had to be discharged, and Cummins was tried and convicted by another and in due course hanged. His wife, who stood by him to the end, said he was so gentle he wouldn't hurt a fly.

The war continued and crime continued and my work continued. And in my personal life there were two eminently satisfactory events. Mary and I moved from the flat where we had lived ever since we were married to a house in Virginia Water. We found ourselves in a most agreeable community, for commercial affluence and the depredations of the Welfare State had not yet changed the character of such places. I joined the Home Guard. We were to stay in Virginia Water until 1953, when we moved to Ewell—partly because my brother-in-law lived at Ewell, partly because it had pleasant associations with the far-off days when I was at my private school, and not least because it lies just within the border of the Metropolitan Police District.

The other event was more personal still. In 1944 our daughter, Virginia, was born.

CHAPTER 7
Secretary Among the Bandits

The Secretary of the Commissioner's Office is not a glamorous figure. His duties provide little scope for drama, either in fiction or in real life. But he ranks as an Assistant Commissioner, and, since he deals with all official correspondence, he is on the inside of most things which go on at the Yard.

The Civil Staff, of which he is the head, has been an integral part of the organisation since the Metropolitan Police were first created. In 1878 a Home Office committee suggested that "some gentleman placed in the position of Secretary, through whom all papers should pass from the various departments at the headquarters to the Acting Commissioner would be of considerable value to the Commissioner and Assistant Commissioners in the management of what may be called the office staff."

Bureaucracy acted with characteristic speed. Almost fifty years later the title of Chief Clerk was changed to "Secretary." Eleven more years passed before the Secretariat became a department of the Commissioner's Office. Finally, in 1931, Howgrave-Graham was given the status of an Assistant Commissioner. Like many jobs, its scope depends largely on the calibre of the man occupying it, and Howgrave-Graham, though he shunned the limelight, was a tough man who liked to be considered an *eminence grise*. The position he handed over to me was, I suspect, a good deal wider and more influential than the one he himself had inherited.

When I arrived at Scotland Yard in January 1946, I knew

hardly anyone there except Ronald Howe and a number of C.I.D. officers whom I'd met during my years in the Director's office. The first thing I wanted to do, therefore, was to put faces to the names I had so often seen on the Metropolitan Police List. Admirable organisation though it is, Scotland Yard has not escaped the trammels of bureaucracy. A newcomer needs to learn the administrative structure.

The Commissioner's Office, as I already knew from that familiar list, was divided into six departments. Four of them were police departments, each controlled by an Assistant Commissioner—"A," "B," "C," and "D."

The Assistant-Commissioner (A) was John Nott-Bower, a most distinguished policeman, who had won the Queen's Police Medal for Gallantry during a gunfight in Delhi. At the time of my arrival, he had been temporarily seconded as Inspector-General to the Allied Commission in Austria. "A" department was being run by Major J. F. Ferguson. The AC(A)'s duties are described as "administration," but they include such diverse subjects as the strength and establishment of the Force, its discipline, promotions, and ceremonials; licensing; keeping a watchful eye on betting and gaming, and on disorderly houses; the Mounted Branch; the Women Police; and control of the "Back Hall." The Back Hall was a most important part of Scotland Yard. When the main entrance is closed at night, a small lobby at the side of the building, with a duty Inspector in charge, became not only the physical means of access but an Orderly Room for the whole place.

"B" Department deals with traffic problems and is responsible for police motor transport. Its head was Sir Alker Tripp, who had been a member of the Civil Staff.

The Assistant-Commissioner (C) was my friend Ronald Howe. Like me, he was a barrister. He had come to the Yard at Lord Trenchard's invitation from the London Side of the D.P.P.'s office. Indeed, I had first met him playing poker with

Charles Wallace, the Assistant Director. He was keenly interested in Continental police methods: after the war he played a leading part in the revival of Interpol: he was, and is, a strong advocate of a national, and separately recruited, C.I.D. That he was a man of considerable capacities has always been obvious: and, since his retirement, he has underlined the fact by proving himself a very shrewd and successful businessman.

The AC(D) was Sir George Abbiss, a handsome man with a huge white moustache, whose long years of service had made him a walking encyclopaedia of police lore. He had joined the Metropolitan Police when I was three years old and had been an Assistant Commissioner since 1935. His responsibilities included recruiting, training, maintenance of buildings and fixtures, communications and the Information Room, clothing, and the medical, dental, and nursing services.

The other two departments were "L" (for legal) under Macdonald Baker, Solicitor to the Commissioner, and "S," which was mine. There was also the Assistant Commissioner without a department, Sir Maurice Drummond, a charming old man who was the Commissioner's Deputy. I remember listening to the Derby with him in June of that year when a horse called Airborne, owned by my old friend Ian Ferguson, cantered in at 50 to 1. Since I had put a pound each way on Airborne at even better odds—66 to 1—simply on the grounds, as my wife said, that "we should look so silly if it won and we hadn't backed it," the occasion has remained vividly in my memory. Drummond retired soon afterwards, to be succeeded by Nott-Bower. Indeed, I'd hardly learned to recognise the Assistant-Commissioners, when all the faces changed again. Ferguson went off to be Chief Constable of Kent, and was succeeded by Philip Margetson: Alker Tripp was succeeded by Henry Dalton: and "D" Department was taken over by Arthur Young, who had been Chief Constable of Hertfordshire, and later found his métier as Commissioner of Police for the City of London.

The Civil Staff at Scotland Yard, for whom as Secretary I was responsible, are not part of the Civil Service of the Crown but are organised on unmistakably civil service lines. As well as the executive and clerical officers, the Civil Staff included scientists in the forensic laboratory, solicitors in "L" Department, dentists in the Metropolitan Police Dental Clinic and nursing staff in the Metropolitan Police Nursing Home.

When I took over from Howgrave-Graham, they numbered about 575. When Gilbert Carmichael succeeded me in 1953, they had increased to 820. By the time I left the Yard in 1963, there were no fewer than 4845, though this grand total admittedly included 1500 school crossing patrols and 500 traffic wardens. Parkinson's Law, which is of universal application, was perhaps responsible for some of this growth; but much of the increase—the addition, for example, of 94 civilian fingerprint officers—was justified by the recommendations of a committee set up in 1949 to consider the proper employment and distribution of manpower in the Metropolitan Police.

The Chairman was Sir Arthur Dixon who had been head of the Home Office police division; there were six other members, including me. It was fashionable then to describe such committees as "working parties." We were known, therefore, as the Dixon Working Party, a name which particularly amused a local councillor at Salford, where we had gone to observe a scheme in which policemen were moved round in cars, dropped and picked up again. After looking us over one by one, the councillor observed, "Workin' Party? I've never seen such a fine lot of callused 'ands," and resumed his lunch.

One of the main questions to be considered was whether, and to what extent, the detective officers manning the Correspondence Branch of "C" Department, the Fingerprint Branch, and the Criminal Records Office could be replaced by civilians. All sorts of arguments were advanced in opposition to such a change. It was said that, while civilians might be able to perform certain routine tasks, there were many occasions which needed the experience of a trained police officer; that service in these Branches was valuable to officers who might afterwards go back to ordinary C.I.D. duties; that members of these Branches often had to visit the scenes of crimes and therefore ought to be police officers; and that civilians would not provide the uninterrupted day and night service which was essential in the Fingerprint Branch and the Criminal Record Office.

We were not convinced. We recommended a cumulative degree of civilianisation in all three Branches. This policy has, I think, worked well, and went some way to relieve London's chronic shortage of policemen. The shortage continues, however, and has become even more serious in relation to the soaring crime rate. Further civilianisation is often proposed, and the same arguments are advanced by the Police Federation against it.

These arguments are not wholly without validity. Civilians never are quite as good as members of a disciplined force; they dislike working round the clock, and are more likely than a policeman to find the job duller than they expected. It is also true that, when provincial policemen make use of the Yard's facilities, they feel happier talking to other policemen.

In theory, of course, the distinction is invalid, since the police are a civilian service, merely citizens in uniform. In practice, however, it is real.

There is what one might call an intermediate class between civilians and police—retired policemen. They are already quite widely used at the Yard—for example, as messengers—and more could probably be employed. There are undoubtedly clerical jobs still being done by policemen which could just as well be done by civilians. But it would be wrong to suppose that such reforms could solve, or even begin to solve, the manpower shortage.

The Dixon Working Party had barely ceased its labours when I was invited by Sir Harold Scott to join a very different committee of enquiry, a Mission no less. The Mission was to visit Malaya and advise the Government of the Federation on certain police problems which had arisen; the Federation Police apparently were not only struggling with the Emergency but had domestic difficulties as well.

I discussed it with Mary, not because I had any real doubts that I wanted to go, but simply because I have always discussed everything with her. It meant being away for three months. I had every hope that they would be extremely interesting months.

The head of the Mission was Sir Alexander Maxwell, who had been Permanent Under-Secretary of State at the Home Office and was a great civil servant. I had only met him once or twice before, but during those three months I came to know him extremely well. I can see him now, sitting on a verandah in the Malayan dusk, reading Horace. His wisdom and humanity were equalled by his modesty and simplicity. Though he was much older than I and Jock Ferguson, who was the other member of the Mission, we could never persuade him to take things easy. When eventually he became ill with some digestive upset, we had, almost literally, to force him on to an aeroplane which would take him back to Kuala Lumpur, while we made a long journey down the east coast by road.

A tour of Malaya at that time—we were there from November 1949 to February 1950—was not without hazards. We visited every state save one, and called at all manner of establishments from rubber plantations to the jungle training school. We travelled by plane, boat, and car. What we didn't travel in were armoured cars, because the police didn't have any; a weakness we subsequently criticised. We usually had an armed escort, often a Bren Carrier, but Ferguson and I were inclined to think it might have been better to go flat out in a fast car unescorted as the planters did when travelling through the countryside. On almost our first day out of Kuala Lumpur, we arrived at Seremban to discover that a party of Malay police, moving through a pass parallel to the one we had traversed, had been ambushed and many of them killed. The Chief Police Officer of the State had just heard the news. We could hardly blame him for not giving his full attention to welcoming us.

The Emergency was then at its height, and there was no real sign of when or how, or indeed if, the battle was going to be won.

I believe unrepentantly that the British Empire was a good thing and that its dissolution has been a tragedy for the world. Malaya was, by any standards, one of the countries where we did best. We created Singapore from a swamp. An English sea captain brought a rubber plant illegally from Brazil (which had a monopoly) to Kew, and from that precarious beginning we gave Malaya her chief industry. Colonial rule was a matter of business arrangements with the Sultans, who remained important and respected. It was a happy country and a beautiful one, green and glossy.

But the seeds of trouble were there from the beginning. In every Malayan village you will find one house not on stilts: the Chinese shop. Infiltration across the frontier is so easy, and the balance of prosperity so tempting, that the Chinese population has risen steadily until the whole country is now divided fifty-fifty. And the Malays and the Chinese are temperamentally incompatible. Some British civil servants tended to approve of the Chinese, who are clever and hard-working; others loved the Malays, who are polite and lovable but less industrious. Welding the two races into a single nation was to prove no easy task.

In Malaya, as in so many other parts of the world, the growth of the Communist conspiracy after the war was blandly ignored until it erupted into bloodshed. It is a country of high hills and thick jungle; extreme range was often no more than thirty yards. The tide was only turned eventually by General Templar, who deprived the bandits (how curiously old-fashioned the term now seems!) of their commissariat, and patiently undertook a long-drawn-out process of cleaning and securing one area after another.

The Americans in Vietnam have learned some of the lessons of Malaya and failed to learn others: but their problems are infinitely greater. The Communists have also learned lessons. The techniques of guerrilla warfare are far more sophisticated in Vietnam than they ever were in Malaya. Another advantage which the Americans lack but which was an essential element in the defence of Malaya is the presence of a robust European community with no intention of being driven from its plantations.

We had luncheon with one of these planters, who was known locally for some reason as the Baron. I remember a yellow tent, made of parachute silk, which he had pitched on his lawn. (Typically he proved to be the son of a man I'd once met at Frinton.) He had organised his own defence force of special constables and kept the peace in that district very well. I heard too of a former Lieutenant-Colonel in the Gurkhas who had, rather unusually, persuaded a number of Gurkha ex-servicemen to work on his plantation. When the bandits started to harass them, they sallied forth and brought back a few heads. Now, we were told, the bandits make long detours to avoid that plantation.

I enjoyed our travels in Malaya, and we emerged unscathed except for the extremely painful wounds incurred when Maxwell and I stepped on a nest of kringgas or fire ants. They are, I understand, the only creatures from which driver ants will turn aside. The driver ants are wise.

We settled down finally to write our report in a place called Frazer's Hill. It was fresh and misty, very like an English village, except that in English villages there are no gibbons swinging through the trees and no hornbills flying over the gardens. Its idyllic quality was rather spoiled in retrospect by the knowledge that shortly after we left Malaya Sir Henry Gurney, the High Commissioner, was ambushed and killed while on his way there.

Many of the problems with which our report dealt have long been forgotten. The Malayan Police, which before the war had been one of the best in any colonial country, had to be built up again after the years of Japanese occupation. The Communists launched their campaign of terrorism while the returned European officers were still struggling to restore morale, root out corruption, renew obsolete equipment and cope with a nonpolitical crime wave which included piracy on the West Coast as well as more orthodox forms of murder and robbery. Our report discussed questions of police organisation and training; tried to soothe tensions, both personal and racial, within the force; and made a number of recommendations. These recommendations were particular to the circumstances of the time and are probably of no great interest now. But, reading our report through again, I noticed one passage which may be worth recalling because of its application to problems nearer home.

"If the higher posts in a Police Force are always filled by promotions from within," we wrote, "there is a danger that the Force may stagnate from lack of fresh ideas and from ignorance of methods which have proved successful elsewhere. A junior officer who has useful new ideas is seldom capable of getting them adopted; his suggestions are liable to be rejected either because he has not the experience and wisdom to present them in an acceptable form, or because senior officers have become too set in their outlook to recognise their value. To enable the Force to keep up to date, to profit from the experience of other Forces, and to be continuously on the lookout for ways of improving its methods, it is desirable that from time to time there should be appointed to senior posts one or more men who have acquired experience in other fields."

This is an unfashionable view. But I believe it was true of Malaya then, and I fail to see why it should not be true of Britain now.

The Mission returned to England in the middle of February, and, with my mind still full of what we had seen, I went back to my desk at Scotland Yard. The streets of London seemed very safe after Malaya. Nobody was likely to shoot at me in Whitehall in 1950.

The chances of being shot by a criminal in London have, nevertheless, increased and are increasing. Most British policemen dislike the idea of carrying guns, but their view will inevitably change if too many criminals start to use firearms. "Good" crooks keep away from guns because they bring heavy extra trouble. The organiser of the London Airport raid in 1949 is said to have searched his men, before they set out, to make sure that none of them was carrying a pistol. But a new generation shows ominous signs of being less scrupulous or less prudent.

Guns can be obtained readily enough in the underworld market for perhaps £10 or £20 each. To obtain them legally is almost impossible. The granting of firearms certificates was one of the matters dealt with by "A" Department. The policy was strict. Pistol and rifle clubs could get licences, but very few private individuals were able to satisfy the police that they needed a gun.

A seventy-five-year-old cripple in a lonely house was not allowed to keep a small pistol for his own defence: but anybody could go into a shop and buy a 12-bore shotgun, which will blow a man's head off. Not only is a shotgun more deadly than a pistol, but it is easier to explain away if a criminal is caught with one in his possession. Not surprisingly, .410 shotguns have been the chosen weapon in quite a number of recent crimes.

Other branches of "S" Department are responsible for the Map Room and for crime statistics, both extremely important functions.

The Map Room, situated in a basement underneath Scotland Yard, is partitioned by huge sliding wall maps dotted with different coloured pins. Its staff are civilians, but it is a very useful, as well as an interesting, place for policemen to visit. Only there can one get a bird's-eye view of what's happening in London. The Map Room reaches a more sophisticated approach to crime, showing how patterns form and spread, and indicating that the old days of the local criminal, though not quite gone, are fast disappearing.

Statistics also provide a kind of retrospective bird's-eye view. It is important to get them right, but equally important not to rely on them too much or draw elaborate inferences from them. All statistics are liable to distortion and criminal statistics are more liable than most because they contain so many variable and unknown elements: and they cannot include the large number of crimes which are never reported to the police at all.

The Metropolitan Police crime statistics are now, I think, about as accurate as one can get. Even so, any superficial conclusions need treating with caution; and this applied to our own internal analysis no less than to the conclusions drawn by outside experts.

It is necessary to ensure that the crimes which are reported are correctly classified. When I was A.C.C. I found that robberies "with violence" were being classified not according to the definitions in the Larceny Act 1916, but according to the classifiers notion of what constituted violence serious enough to bring it within the category. I changed that. How the practice started I don't know; possibly from some idea of preventing public alarm. I could see no merit in this argument. I thought and still think that rather than being fed pap about these matters the public should know exactly how bad the situation is.

One of the most important functions of "S" Department, arising from the simple fact that the Secretary writes the letters, is that he must act as a channel of communication between, in one direction, the Commissioner and the Home Office, and, in another, between the Commissioner and the Press. He has to collect any information necessary for answering Parliamentary questions. Since the Metropolitan Police is the only police force in the country for which the Home Secretary is directly responsible, such questions were by no means infrequent in my day: and, as the wave of anti-police propaganda increased, so did the number of questions.

Press relations are certainly no less, and nowadays, whatever civil servants and politicians may suppose, perhaps more, important for the satisfactory working of a public service. Summing up a case at the Old Bailey in 1933, Mr. Justice Rigby Swift said: "There has been some mention of a so-called Press Bureau at Scotland Yard. I do not know what this purports to do, but I have not heard of it before and I do not wish to hear of it again. It sounds to me a most improper thing." The Press Bureau had, in fact, already been in existence for about ten years. Just before I became Secretary, Sir Harold Scott persuaded the Home Office to authorise a Public Information Officer as well. More recently still, on the recommendation of a Home Office committee, one civilian officer in each police district of London has been given the job of dealing with the Press. And at the beginning of 1967 a senior Public Relations Officer was superimposed on the structure.

It would be idle to pretend that public relations were well handled by the police. The Press officers, who are civilians, admittedly have a very difficult job; the police complain that they want to tell too much, the newspapers that they tell too little. There is, or appears to be, a genuine conflict of interests.

The Press believes that all news should be freely given unless publication would clearly be harmful. Many policemen tend to share the view of Mr. Justice Swift, and believe that nothing should be published about a criminal investigation unless it would clearly be helpful to the police. Tension and bad feeling often result.

This conflict ought to be reconcilable. To talk about "the Press" is, in any event, a misleading generalisation. The Press consists of a number of newspapers and a number of journalists: they are of different kinds, and different degrees of responsibility, and should be treated accordingly. In my experience, however, most newspapers and most senior crime reporters (particularly those from the mass-circulation papers which some people affect to despise) are firmly on the side of the police and anxious to behave responsibly. They repay trust.

What constitutes behaving responsibly may raise legitimate ethical questions. The Press rightly resents any attempt to muzzle them. What the police want concealed—as in the Sheffield scandal—ought sometimes to be revealed. A difficult problem arose in the case of Neville Heath. Heath was wanted for the murder of a woman, and it was known that he might kill again. The newspapers already possessed a photograph of him. If they published it, a potential victim might recognise him and be saved: but publication would prejudice the evidence of identification without which Heath could not be convicted. The newspapers were asked not to publish his picture: they complied: and another girl was killed. Since Heath had walked into a police station at Bournemouth and not been recognised although the officers had his photograph in front of them, I doubt whether publication would have saved the girl. If I had been Assistant Commissioner, I too would have advised against it; the situation might be different today, with the much greater coverage which television offers. But the problem was a real one, and the Press approached it responsibly.

To tell the Press nothing seems to me almost always wrong, if only because it will not necessarily result in nothing being published. The police are not the only source of information about a crime. Neighbours, bystanders, relations, underworld contacts, are usually eager enough to talk. What they say may or may not be accurate. In either event its publication may be harmful; it may colour the evidence of witnesses; it may even affect the mind of the investigating officers; and it may alert the criminal. But the police, having refused to co-operate, have deprived themselves of any influence with the Press.

This is foolish and unnecessary. Newspapermen can be very useful allies. They too are investigators, they too receive information: criminals sometimes give themselves up to a newspaper rather than to the police, not always with the happiest results. In the long run, however, working journalists need the help of the police more than the police need the help of journalists. A relationship of mutual confidence can therefore be turned to good advantage. Such relationships are in fact established between sensible senior officers and trustworthy journalists. The fact remains that, in conveying any information to the Press, at all, the officers are committing a disciplinary offence.

As Assistant Commissioner I made a point of being accessible to editors and to the crime reporters I knew I could trust. Some when they had acquired doubtful information, used to ring up and ask me about it. I gave them, as frankly as I could, one of three answers: "This is true and no harm will come if it is published," "This is true but ought not to be published because it will hinder our investigation," or "This is untrue." I was very rarely let down, and I'm sure the benefit, in terms of public relations, was considerable.

My views on this, as on a good many other matters, were clarified by my experience as Secretary. I had known for some while that I might be offered the job of A.C.C. and the time came in 1953, when Sir Harold Scott retired. Sir John Nott-Bower moved up to be Commissioner and Ronald Howe became Deputy Commissioner, a uniformed job which personally I wouldn't much have liked but which he valued partly because it was arranged that he should retain his connection with Interpol. My appointment was announced on August 12. Technically it was a sideways move rather than a promotion, but it brought a higher salary and a better pension: and, much more important, it restored me to a milieu where I had always felt at home. I was not, by nature, an administrative civil servant. I was a criminal lawyer. Now I was to deal once more, and in the most direct way, with crime.

CHAPTER 8

You Are Surrounded by Thieves

How John Harriott, the fighting man, and Patrick Colquhoun, the Scots lawyer, joined forces to create the first real police force in England, patrolling the Thames in small boats, armed with cutlasses; how they withstood a full-scale siege at Wapping New Stairs Police Station; and how they broke up the gang of river pirates which, rather than admit defeat, threatened to burn all the shipping in the Pool of London—these earliest police adventures make a marvellously romantic tale, and they were the historical prelude to the Metropolitan Police.

The River Officers were strictly enjoined that their cutlasses were never to be used or shown except in self-defence, and that they must conduct themselves "with all possible civility to all persons." This tradition was inherited by the Force which Sir Robert Peel created in 1829. The General Instructions compiled by the first Commissioners laid down the duties of London's policemen very clearly:

"It should be understood, at the outset, that the principal object to be attained is *the prevention of crime*. To this great end every effort of the police is to be directed. The security of persons and property, the preservation of public tranquillity and all the other objects of a Police Establishment will thus be better effected than by the detection and punishment of the offender after he has succeeded in committing the crime."

Harriott and Colquhoun, and Peel, and the Commissioners, were all acutely aware that the very idea of a police force was regarded with profound suspicion by all classes of British society. Nothing much could be achieved until those public fears had been soothed. There must be no resemblance to the secret police forces of the Continent. Largely for this reason, no provision was made at first for a detective branch.

Such detection of crime as occurred had been, for seventy years, the prerogative of the Bow Street runners. These were originally a group of thief-takers specially recruited about 1750 by Henry Fielding, the novelist who wrote *Tom Jones*, to tackle a notorious gang of street robbers. Fielding's blind half-brother, Sir John, succeeded him as the Bow Street magistrate, and took personal command of the runners or "Robin Redbreasts," who wore scarlet waistcoats beneath blue coats and were armed with a small baton, a pistol, and handcuffs. Their basic pay was a guinea a week, but anyone could hire them for a guinea a day plus 14 shillings expenses.

They were by no means ineffective. They made it their business to frequent the taverns and "flash houses" where thieves, pickpockets, and robbers could be found; they consorted with criminals and reaped a harvest of information. Some of them, particularly after Fielding's death, were not above making private deals for the return of stolen property.

The most famous was called Townsend, "a man," as the contemporary joke said, "that's known from town's end to town's end." The arch-gossip, Captain Gronow, in his *Reminiscences and Recollections,* described the Coronation of George IV in 1820 with "little Townsend, the Chief Police officer of Bow Street, with his flaxen wig and broad hat, hurrying about assuming immense importance" and "hullooing with all his might 'Gentlemen and ladies, take care of your pockets for you are surrounded by thieves'"; in spite of which excellent advice, an unprecedented number of watches and purses were snatched.

Townsend made a practice of attending the Old Bailey, in

order to memorise the faces of criminals and their methods of work. In 1816 he gave evidence before a committee which the government had set up to examine the causes of crime and the conduct of police and magistrates. Townsend, like every generation of his successors, blamed low rates of pay, and also the bad effect of giving rewards which the officers shared. In the same year, a runner by the name of Vaughan was convicted of inciting young boys to commit crimes, and then arresting them for the blood money.

After a prolonged flurry of committees, Robert Peel, the Home Secretary, finally acted. He established the new Metropolitan Police Force under two Commissioners, Colonel Rowan, a soldier, and Richard Mayne, a lawyer. They would be Justices of the Peace with executive but no judicial functions, while the other Justices (except for the Bow Street Magistrate, who kept his runners) would from then on have only judicial ones. Two thousand men were recruited. Most of the Superintendents and Inspectors were ex-Army, but, to avoid any taint of militarism, they were dressed in plain blue coats and reinforced top hats. Only on very special occasions were they allowed to work in plain clothes, and they were strictly forbidden to enter public houses on duty; which placed them at a severe disadvantage in the investigation of crime.

The result was that they had the worst of both worlds. The public continued to regard them as spies and they caught too few criminals.

In 1839 the last of the Bow Street runners retired, and for two years, London had no detectives at all. Then, in 1842, a man by the name of Daniel Good murdered the woman with whom he had been living at Roehampton. He escaped from a policeman who found him with the mutilated corpse. His footprints were lost in a muddy field at Putney, and for ten days he was at large. There was an unprecedented hue-and-cry, and a great deal of public alarm, before he was finally captured at

Tonbridge. People had been thoroughly frightened, and it concentrated their minds wonderfully. The Commissioners seized the opportunity. They persuaded a not very enthusiastic Home Secretary to allow the formation of a small detective branch.

This consisted of two Inspectors and six Sergeants, wearing plain clothes and with an office at Scotland Yard. Inevitably there were unfavourable comparisons with Bow Street, but at least the nucleus had been formed and experience was being gained. Training in observation soon proved its worth. An article in *Household Words* described how a detective found a button at the scene of the crime and scrutinised all the suspects until he found one with a button missing.

A corruption scandal in 1878, resulting in the deplorable case known as the Trial of the Detectives, produced yet another Home Office committee, specially charged with examining the conduct of the detective branch.

A briefless young barrister named Howard Vincent saw his opportunity and, with commendable energy, took it. He hurried over to Paris, introduced himself to the Prefect of Police and to the senior detective officers, and, after a short but intensive study of their methods, wrote a detailed report for the Home Office committee. They found it useful: and, more important, they now knew his name. When the question arose of appointing a new head of the detective branch, Vincent applied, enclosing a commendation from the Attorney-General.

Howard Vincent's admirable grasp of how to get on in the world was very properly rewarded. He was appointed the first Director of Criminal Investigation at Scotland Yard—a title clearly borrowed from the French Directeur des Recherches Criminelles—at a salary of £1100 a year.

He increased the strength of his department, now called the C.I.D., to 800 men; warned them that any pecuniary transactions with the public, unless personally authorised by himself, would bring immediate dismissal; and instituted new systems of exchanging information, centralising the criminal records and consolidating the work of the various branches and divisions.

Vincent's appointment began the tradition, of which I was perhaps the last exemplar, of appointing barristers from outside the police force to head the C.I.D. It was, I believe, a sensible tradition, but few, if any, of Vincent's successors can have done as much for the department as he did. *The Police Code and Manual of Criminal Law*, which he compiled in 1882, is still, having been continually revised, an essential part of every detective's equipment. One of his last reforms, before he resigned to stand for Parliament, was to improve the *Police Gazette*, which had originally and rather charmingly, been called the *Hue and Cry*; he introduced descriptions and drawings of wanted men, and wood engravings of stolen articles.

There was still one more innovation before "C" Department became recognisably the organisation which I commanded. On the evening of March 1, 1883, Vincent was sitting in the library of his house in Grosvenor Square when the room was shaken by an explosion. A constable in the street outside told him it had come from the direction of Parliament. When he got there, he found a big crowd of Cabinet Ministers, MPs, and journalists. A bomb had exploded in some government offices, killing nobody but breaking nearly every window in Parliament Street. The Fenians had begun their dynamite campaign.

The battle against these Irish-American terrorists was dramatic and often perilous. A new branch of the C.I.D. was formed to wage it—the Special Irish Branch. The Fenians struck back with an attempt to blow up Scotland Yard; dynamite was placed in a public lavatory at the rear of the building, causing a good deal of damage and the loss of some records.

The Special Irish Branch did excellent undercover work. Information was garnered, arrests were made, and finally the explosions stopped. But scarcely had the Fenian terror ended when the anarchist terror began. The French President was assassinated and Russian nihilists were said to be active all over Europe. A comic song of 1894 had the resounding chorus:

> "It's a B.O.M.B. bomb!
> It's a B.O.M.B. bomb!
> They say it's very hard
> On Scotland Yard.
> It's a B.O.M.B. bomb!"

Anarchists were neither a joke nor a myth, though the Special Branch found itself investigating the usual plague of hoaxes and false alarms. The word "Irish" had been dropped from its title. The Special Branch was clearly going to be needed indefinitely, and its field of action would include all threats to the security of the state or to the lives of the Royal Family, Cabinet Ministers, and visiting dignitaries.

Organisations have an inherent tendency to grow and to spawn new departments like an amoeba. When I became Assistant Commissioner, "C" Department consisted of eight separate branches, besides the Special Branch. When I left, there were eleven. This growth was necessary, and I make no apology for having myself created three new branches: but Parkinson's disease is so endemic in Whitehall, and so serious, that nothing which looks like spontaneous bureaucratic growth ought to pass unscrutinised.

The nucleus of "C" Department is C1, Central Office; which was originally just what the name implies—the central office of London's detective force. The correspondence branch, C2, also dates back to the beginning of the detective force; it deals with all the paperwork relating to crime, with case papers, with prisoners' petitions referred by the Home Office for comment, with applications for evidence in civil proceedings, and with enquiries from insurance companies. All this adds up to a formidable flood of paper; in 1964 the number of insurance queries alone came to 48,500.

The Fingerprint Branch, C3, has a statutory duty to provide a service, not only to the Metropolitan Police, but to police forces throughout the country. The usefulness of any fingerprint collection depends entirely on its system of classification and filing. C3 is responsible for maintaining and searching the Main Collection, for filing the sets of prints which are constantly being received from the police and from prisons, for attending scenes of crime, photographing prints *in situ*, and examining articles submitted.

The Criminal Record Office, C4, has similar national responsibilities, laid down as long ago as 1871 by the Prevention of Crimes Act. It maintains a number of separate indexes: a register of all convicted criminals; an index of crimes reported but not solved, and of wanted men; a Method Index, in which criminals are grouped by modus operandi, a Property Index, recording stolen property; and a Motor Vehicle Index, recording stolen cars. C4 also has a Publications Office, which produces the *Police Gazette* and the *Metropolitan Police Informations*, useful broadsheets circulated regularly to all police stations.

C5 is the Assistant Commissioner's private office. A small staff, mixed police and civilians, make special enquiries for him and handle the internal administration of the department—promotions, transfers, personal records, complaints, discipline, and general instructions to the C.I.D.

C6 is the Fraud Squad. Its work is not only more complex, but has become more widespread, than that of any other branch of the department. One result of its success was that we were constantly being asked for the loan of a Fraud Squad officer to advise, or help with some problem, in the provinces.

Such requests are never refused; and Commonwealth coun-

tries have a specific right to ask for help. During my time at
the Yard, quite a number of officers from Central Office went
on missions abroad; to solve murder cases in Malta, Bermuda,
and the Bahamas, to investigate a shipboard explosion in the
Persian Gulf, to check—at the special request of the Ceylon
Government—the police work which followed the murder of
Mr. Bandaranaike.

C7 is the Detective Training School, with students drawn
not only from the Metropolitan Police but also from provincial, Commonwealth, and foreign police forces.

C8 is the Flying Squad. This name, like most interesting
names, was invented by the Press. In the 1920s, a number of
detective officers from C1, who were known to have particularly good informants, were given a roving assignment. The
whole of London was to be their hunting ground, and they
were equipped with motorcars. The newspapers and the public
found them romantic: criminals found them tough and effective: and if there were (as indeed there still are) occasional
touches of jealousy between the Flying Squad and the Divisions, the results have more than justified the experiment.
The Squad soon became a separate branch.

C9, C10, and C11 were all created while I was Assistant Commissioner. C9, the Metropolitan and Provincial Crime Branch,
originated in a discussion between the Home Office, certain
County Chief Constables, and myself, soon after my appointment.

The Home Counties were suffering from a plague of big
country-house breakings, and two Chief Constables in particular—John Ferguson of Kent and Joe Simpson of Surrey—
were convinced that London crooks were largely responsible.
I invited these two and the Chief Constables of Buckinghamshire, Hertfordshire, Essex, and Berkshire to a conference in
my room at the Yard. The fruit of our meeting was a small new
branch of C Department, in which officers of these county
forces worked together with London detectives. They pooled

information and shared their resources but C9 officers never made arrests. There were two reasons for this rule: first, that we didn't want to tread on local toes, and, second, that we didn't want the faces of the provincial officers to become familiar to London crooks. Other County forces soon asked to join in the scheme, and C9 was officially named the Metropolitan and Provincial Serious Crime Squad. Unofficially it was called the Home and Colonial.

C10 deals with stolen cars, a variety of crime which has hugely increased since the war. And C11 is the Criminal Intelligence Section, a pet project of mine, which can perhaps more conveniently be discussed in the next chapter, since the need for it sprang directly from the new pattern of crime which we found ourselves facing.

An ancillary service, for which I was also responsible, was the Forensic Science Laboratory. This laboratory serves the whole of South-Eastern England, and its staff were, and I imagine still are, grossly overworked; which means that they have less time than they should for original research. Forensic science has made great advances in recent years, notably in the grouping of dried blood and in the identification of minute particles. One of the difficulties is to make working policemen aware of what has become possible. The laboratory is staffed by civilian scientists but there are a number of police liaison officers attached to it: and, if we are not perhaps quite as science-minded as, for example, the Germans, the facilities provided at Scotland Yard, and the use which is increasingly made of them, certainly stand comparison with the work of the Home Office laboratories in other parts of England.

Quite separate from the C.I.D. but also coming under the A.C.C., is still the Special Branch. Spy mania grew so acute during the First World War that, at one stage, the Assistant Commissioner left the direction of the C.I.D. to his second-in-command and devoted his whole time to Special Branch business. When peace came, the Superintendent of the Special

121

Branch, a man named Patrick Quinn, was knighted on retirement. To the best of my knowledge, this is the only knighthood which has ever been given to a Superintendent of the Metropolitan, or indeed of any other Police force.

When I became A.C.C., my deputy in charge of the Special Branch was an old friend Commander Leonard Burt. He was well-suited for the job. Although his entire pre-war police career had been in the C.I.D., he had served with distinction in M.I.5. during the war and on his return to the force was put in charge of the Special Branch. He reported to me almost daily, and sometimes, when we had dealt with the matters which brought him there, would spend a few minutes talking of the old days. He retired in 1958 and was succeeded by E. W. Jones. Even Jones's whole service was in the Special Branch. I had known him too in my Old Bailey days and had a high opinion of his ability, fully justified in the years which followed. There was no lack of work for the Special Branch. It was a period of big espionage cases—Blake, Lonsdale, Vassal. The menace of spies, if not the fear of them, was more serious than anything which Superintendent Quinn had to tackle. Blake, Lonsdale, and Vassal were all entirely different from each other and actuated by entirely different motives; but they were part of the same relentless underground war which has been, and still is being, waged against the West.

In Patrick Quinn's day helping the enemies of one's country was generally regarded not merely as criminal but as dishonourable. Now patriotism is considered outmoded. Britain's Security Services are efficient enough but they can only gather information. They cannot alter the climate of opinion or force a government to take action. Neither the fight against spies nor the fight against crime can ever be completely won: but both can be lost, and the blame for losing them rests more often with the public and the politicians than with the Security Services or the police.

CHAPTER 9

The "Coolest" Thing to Be

The growth of crime during the past decade has been so continuous and inexorable that people tend to think of it as though it were a phenomenon of nature, certainly as something which has been going on steadily ever since the war. Surprisingly, this isn't true. Crime always tends to increase in wartime, and the number of indictable offences recorded by the Metropolitan Police duly rose from less than 96,000 in 1938 to nearly 129,000 in 1945: but then the figure started to drop again. Year by year it fell: 127,796 in 1946, 127,458 in 1947, 126,597 in 1948, 106,077 in 1949. By 1954 it was down to 93,937, lower than before the war.

That was the position when I became Assistant Commissioner. My predecessor, Ronald Howe, and I were surely justified in thinking that the battle against crime was going well, that I was taking command of a victorious army, and therefore that the job of A.C.C. would become, if anything, progressively easier. In the event, however, we were quite wrong.

In 1955 the crime figure edged up again, and the following year it zoomed. By 1958 it had broken all previous records: 151,796 indictable offences in the London area. The rise has continued, unchecked, ever since. In 1963, the year I retired, the total reached 229,107, and there is no sign yet that this mushroom growth is even slowing down.

The causes have been endlessly discussed and remain anybody's guess. Every commentator trots out his own *bête noir*; some blame the Welfare State, others the capitalist system;

some talk about the decline of religion, others about the weakening of parental authority. But one thing at least has become quite obvious. The chief cause of crime is not, as the liberals of previous generations believed, poverty. Poverty can cause crime; few people would really prefer to starve rather than steal. But the relief of poverty and a drastic reduction of economic inequality have brought no comparable lessening of crime. On the contrary, booming crime rates seem to be characteristic of an affluent society. This is not a new discovery. In 1751, when he was Magistrate at Bow Street, Henry Fielding wrote a treatise, called *An Enquiry into the Cause of the Late Increase in Robbers,* in which he concluded that the growth of crime was a by-product of growing public wealth. In his experience, he said, most thieves stole luxuries rather than necessities. The policemen and magistrates of today would confirm his observation.

The causes of crime are multiple and complex; a combination of greed and boredom, of resentment, arrogance, disrespect for property, of vanity and a lack of imagination or compassion. There is no single or simple explanation or simple cure.

The official crime statistics present only a rough and incomplete picture; rough because they lump disparate incidents together under the same headings, and incomplete because they cannot take account of "the Dark Figure," the crimes which are never even reported to the police. Dr. Leonard Radzinowicz, Professor of Criminology at Cambridge, described in a lecture how this Dark Figure comes about:

"It is an agglomerate of many elements. Often people are not conscious that a crime has been committed at all. Sometimes they think it to be something else: accident or just loss. Frequently, very frequently indeed, they are fully conscious but nevertheless unwilling to report for a variety of reasons that may act singly or in combination. Such are the wear and tear inherent in bringing a case forward; reluctance to appear vin-

124

dictive or pity; considerations of loyalty or protectiveness; fear that further damage to the victim may ensue; even lack of confidence in the system of criminal justice."

Professor Radzinowicz is a most sober and sensible criminologist. No one would accuse him of making wild guesses or of exaggeration. His conclusions must therefore be taken seriously and they are extremely alarming. He calculates that the crimes which are brought into the open and punished constitute no more than 15 percent of the crimes which have been committed.

Any policeman knows that the Dark Figure is a reality. Bits of it, like the tops of icebergs, are occasionally illumined. A convicted criminal, for example, may ask for other offences to be taken into consideration. He only confesses, of course, to crimes which he thinks may be brought home to him anyway, but, very often, some of them are in fact new to the police. Sometimes, too, the police, while investigating one crime, stumble on evidence of another. This happened after the Great Train Robbery, when all the coverts were being flushed. A team of Flying Squad officers, acting on a tip that he had been involved in the robbery, descended on a metal dealer's yard at Harlesdon. The dealer proved to have no connection whatever with the train robbery: but in a locked room behind his office, the police found a printing press and excellently designed plates for forging £5 notes.

A more curious case, which revealed quite a number of previously unreported crimes, occurred in London a few years earlier. A diamond merchant had complained of losses from a strong box which he rented in the Hatton Garden Safe Deposit. The circumstances were intriguing, and I instructed Detective Inspector Millen of the Fraud Squad to investigate.

The safe deposit was believed—always a rash belief—to be impregnable. It was built like an underground fortress. Nothing short of dynamite could have blasted a way in, and no force seemed to have been used at all. The main door was made of heavy steel, controlled by two combination locks. One combination was known only to the managing director and to the manager, the other only to the custodians of the vault. Behind this door lay a metal grille, which was locked with two different keys. The strong boxes themselves also had two locks each; one which could be opened only by the company's key, the other by the individual renter's. There were three custodians, two of whom were always on duty during the hours of business. One stayed outside the grille unlocking it for each renter who called: the other was stationed inside and used his key to undo the first lock on the strong boxes. Each renter had to sign an entry book, showing the times of his arrival and departure. All the custodians had been with the company for a number of years and knew every renter by sight and by name.

When the diamond merchant opened his strong box one Monday morning, he found that two small parcels of gems were missing. They had been there when he locked it the previous Friday. He was sure they had—and yet he couldn't believe it. How could they have been stolen from such a place? People who deal every day with valuable goods or large quantities of money become extraordinarily casual about them. Like a housewife who feels sure she put her purse in a drawer and then wonders if she really did, the diamond merchant evidently had doubts. Though the loss was more than £1000, he didn't report it.

Three weeks later, however, on another Monday, he opened the strong box and found that a tin containing diamonds worth almost £5000 had disappeared. This time he told the police.

The managing director admitted that several losses had been reported to him in recent months, and Inspector Millen soon discovered others which had not been reported. At least twenty-four larcenies had occurred; in some instances, the same strong box seemed to have been pillaged two or three times. The true total was almost certainly greater. Not everyone who rents a strong box is anxious to discuss its contents with the police. But the twelve renters who did talk to Millen about their loses were honest enough. Why hadn't they told the police earlier? The answer seems to be that, like the diamond merchant, they doubted the evidence of their own senses and their memories. Since the safe deposit was impregnable, they thought it must be they who had been careless or forgetful: and what was missing was never more than a small proportion of the contents of any one box.

Millen sat down to work out how the job could have been done. It was clear that no renter could have opened somebody else's strong box, even if he had the key, without the collusion of the custodian inside the grille. And, since keys were issued direct to the renters in sealed packets, the custodians could have had no opportunity to copy them in advance. But if a renter was careless while inside the safe deposit, a dishonest custodian might well have been able then to take an impression of the key. Armed with this duplicate, another renter could come in later, and between them they could open the victim's strong box without attracting any attention.

Millen put his deductions to the test by having the three custodians watched. One of them was found to be spending money lavishly and to be in the habit of coming to work from his home in Bethnal Green by taxi. His wages were £7 a week. Among his cronies were two Hatton Garden jewellers. A discreet check showed these jewellers both had strong boxes and were among the few renters who frequently visited the safe deposit on Saturday morning.

We held a conference at the Yard, and decided to mount simultaneous raids on the houses and business premises of the three suspects. Millen's men, reinforced by the Flying Squad, swooped—and found quite enough to support the arrest of all three. In a classic understatement, the taxi-riding custodian protested, "I'm not the brains behind this." They got thirty months each.

The most frightening aspect of the criminal statistics is not so much the total rise in the number of offences but the disproportionate rise in certain types of offence—crimes by young people, crimes accompanied by violence, organised professional crimes.

Robbery, which by legal definition entails violence or the threat of it, was rare enough before the war to be unimportant; in 1938 there were only 162 cases in the Metropolitan area. In 1955 there were 237. From then on, the increase in robbery was twice as fast as the general increase in crime. In 1964 there were 1266 cases. The profits of robbery have also been soaring. Between 1962 and 1963 the amount taken rose from £799,117 to £1,032,205: and the latter figure, of course, includes none of the £2,500,000 stolen in the Great Train Robbery, which took place just outside the Metropolitan area. Twenty percent was recovered in 1964, but this was an unusually high proportion; the average amount recovered has been less than 10 percent.

Two opposite delusions are perhaps worth mentioning. It is often said that there was no increase in robbery with violence following the abolition of corporal punishment in 1948. For the first few years this is true: but, since 1958, the sort of robberies which used to render a criminal liable to corporal punishment have multiplied rapidly every year. It may well be that the abolition of flogging encouraged their increase, but it does not follow, in my view, that corporal punishment for adults ought to be re-introduced. The birch has some value for juveniles, not because it hurts, which is forgotten in half an hour, but because it teaches them that the United Kingdom doesn't tip up whenever they set foot on the Isle of Wight. But the flogging of adult criminals is too apt to make martyrs, and too uncertain because some of the most vicious offenders are medically unfit to receive their punishment. Long prison sentences are more appropriate and more effective.

The crimes which matter most, and which are most ominous for the future, and which should therefore be most rigorously prosecuted and most severely punished, are those committed by professionals. Such crimes are a minority, perhaps quite a small minority, of the total number of recorded offences. It is unlikely, for instance, that professional criminals were responsible for most of the 71,747 "miscellaneous simple larcenies" which appear in the statistics for 1963.

The category of "professional criminal" needs a sub-division. Some of those "simple larcenies" will have been committed by congenital lay-abouts, hopelessly weak and ill-disciplined characters, who steal, without much thought for the future, whenever the opportunity presents itself. They are, I suppose, professionals of a sort. They are the little fish, a nuisance to the community but not dangerous, on whom the net or preventive detention used to close, while the big fish swam free. The big fish, the true professionals, regard them with contempt.

The true professional treats crime as a business. He plans: he takes no unnecessary risks: he calculates the profitability of each new enterprise before embarking on it, and he adapts his activities to suit any change in the market. Every city in the world has a hard core of such men. They are not reformable. They have no intention of giving up a life which provides them with excitement and prestige as well as a great deal of money. If they are successful, they become aristocrats in their own milieu; a milieu in which, even more than elsewhere, money and ruthlessness are the criteria of success.

Organised crime has been such a flourishing industry in recent years that recruits are plentiful. Profits have been big, risks low.

Affluence and over-full employment meant that more money

than ever before was being kept in office safes (often out of date); accumulated for pay day and conveyed from place to place in small vans, in scantily guarded trains and even on foot. Valuable and easily sold commodities, such as tobacco, were constantly being moved, from factory to wholesaler, from wholesaler to retailer, in more or less unprotected vehicles. To hit these modern targets, the criminals used modern methods and modern equipment. How to organise an assault, commando techniques, a knowledge of explosives—such useful lessons may have been learned originally from serving in the Army, but they were not forgotten when conscription ended; they had become part of the underworld's conventional wisdom.

Criminal gangs nowadays are less likely to be permanent entities than teams selected for a particular operation, like the group which did the Train Robbery. Drivers and strong-arm men are readily available, but crime has become so much more mobile, so much less local, that it would not be thought unusual now, for example, to bring to London a miner accustomed to working with explosives. Any skill and any equipment can be bought if the money is available. Much of the equipment is not, in fact, at all difficult to obtain. Every scrap yard has a thermic lance, which is the most up-to-date and effective instrument for safe-cutting: most quarries have a stock of explosives: stored, for safety, in isolated sheds: and, when 250,000 cars are parked each night in the streets of London, no gang of robbers need go short of a Jaguar or Dormobile to be used in a quick raid and then discarded. Manpower is more expensive, because the team may have to be paid regular wages while waiting, and rehearsing, to do a job. And some specialists, in the criminal world as in Harley Street, expect high fees. Obtaining their services can be costly for several reasons. I know of at least one safe cracking for which an expert had to be specially got out of Wandsworth gaol. But underworld financiers are usually prepared to advance the money for a likely enterprise.

Looking back, I can see, much more clearly than we could at the time, several indicators of what was happening, milestones in the development of the new pattern.

The first, perhaps, was the abortive London Airport raid of 1949. The police had been tipped off about a plan to raid a warehouse at Heath Row; the contents were worth about £380,000. The Flying Squad laid an ambush, and, when the gang appeared, there was a ferocious fight. Nine men were arrested, and subsequently sent to prison for long terms. If their plan had succeeded, the fashion for large-scale robberies might have been established then. As it was, the growth of the crime industry was checked.

Checked but not stopped. If I were asked to give a single date for the opening of the new era, I would suggest May 21, 1952.

It was a Wednesday. At 4:20 A.M., in Eastcastle Street in the West End of London, a post office van was suddenly blocked by a private car. The van stopped, and was immediately attacked by a number of armed men. The automatic alarm siren failed to work; it had been sabotaged in advance. The van's crew were hauled out of the cab, and the van itself was driven off. It was discovered some hours later in an enclosed yard about a mile away. The mail bags had presumably been transferred to another vehicle. At all events, they were gone; except that, for some reason, perhaps because they were disturbed, the thieves had left behind thirteen bags containing £156,000. However, since the van had been carrying more than £400,000 in untraceable notes, it wasn't a bad haul. The raiders had evidently known what the bags contained, which van would be used and what its route would be. The post office men could offer no clue as to the identity of their assailants. There were no other witnesses and, of course, no fingerprints.

The police had little doubt who was behind the raid; proving it was another matter. Which is often the case. They pursued every scrap of information, every angle of approach, but never found evidence which would stand up in court. The organiser of the mail van robbery had an unbreakable personal alibi; he planned the crime, gave the orders and took a large share of the profits, but smaller fry put on the masks and did the job. No one was ever charged. The organiser, like any other successful businessman, went on from strength to strength, enlarging his interests and launching new enterprises. Today he is said virtually to have retired.

His success, and the success of that first mail van robbery in particular, had a strong effect on the development of crime in Britain. As a result of that night's work, the organiser was seen to have become a rich man and to have acquired immense prestige. He was admired by other criminals, and admiration leads to emulation. Even more important was the realisation that, with profits on this scale, crime had become big business. For such a haul it was worth taking trouble, worth laying careful plans, buying information, corrupting employees. If anything went wrong, there would be plenty of money to pay for the defence of any member of the gang unlucky enough to be arrested: and, if the worst came to the worst, his wife and family could be properly looked after while he was away.

Once the new pattern was established, its development was cumulative. Each successful operation provided capital for the next. This is where the raw crime statistics were deceptive. Because the total number of indictable offences was still falling, we didn't realise the subterranean change which was taking place.

Overt robbery was not the only type of crime in which the new generation of gangsters indulged, but it was the fastest growing for the simple reason that it produces the largest reward for the minimum number of incidents.

Lorry hijacking is a good example. The normal pre-war method was the "jump-up"; thieves would follow the lorry until the driver stopped for a cup of tea, then jump into the back and throw parcels down to their confederates. Lorries containing valuable cargo are much less vulnerable nowadays, but the crooks too are much more sophisticated. In 1964 over 5000 lorries were stolen and the value of the goods taken exceeded £915,000 of which less than a tenth was recovered. The first suspect in a lorry hijacking is always the driver, but many innocent drivers have been tricked into stopping and opening their doors by some highly imaginative methods. The gang which drove past the target lorry, waving a number plate which was a duplicate of the lorry's own as though to suggest that it had fallen off the back, surely displayed a resourcefulness worthy of a better cause. The loot, especially if it consists of perishable goods, is generally sold to a receiver in advance.

The old-fashioned fence was often a pawnbroker: but in the affluent society pawnbrokers are few and far between. The modern fence usually runs a genuine business through which he can conveniently dispose of stolen goods. Cigarettes and whisky can be sold through a hundred channels, but jewels need a jeweller and sides of beef need a large refrigerator. Businesslike crooks make sure of their market, and obtain a quoted price, before doing the job. Some fences, alert to the danger of informants, negotiate through a "placer," a go-between or broker whose function it is to know what goods are available, who can dispose of them and at what price. Stolen money is a specialised commodity and there are dealers who buy it, at a discount of perhaps five shillings in the pound.

Fencing, the disposal of stolen property, is an essential substructure of almost any criminal pattern, and it is not uncommon for the fence himself to be the organiser of crimes. There is one sort of crime, however, which needs no fence, and it has been increasing in London lately: the protection racket. This again is an essentially professional activity, flourishing best in shady surroundings. It has been greatly encouraged by the legalisation of betting shops and gambling clubs. Such establishments not only provide a tempting target but constitute an atmosphere in which criminals, most of whom are natural gamblers, feel at home.

A very small dose of violence can put a club or restaurant out of business. Almost always the violence is committed by the hired help, very seldom by the big fish. Increasingly, large-scale crime is planned by experienced men with bad records but carried out by younger and more reckless men with little "form" to embarrass them in court. The result, many police officers believe, is greater viciousness.

As the '50s wore on, the new pattern of professional crime became unmistakable. I discussed it with my deputy, Commander Hatherill, and with the two Deputy Commanders, Rawlings and Spooner. We all agreed that a campaign against criminals of this calibre ought to be backed, like a military campaign against jungle terrorists, by an efficient intelligence service. It was a pity, Spooner said, that policemen who retired should take valuable knowledge about criminals with them into oblivion. From this remark sprang the Intelligence Section at Scotland Yard, though Spooner never got the credit he deserved. He was gravely ill when the branch came into existence.

My recommendation to the Commissioner was that we should form a small unit, which initially would be part of C5, my own private office, to obtain, collate, and disseminate information exclusively about hard-core professional criminals and their associates. The Commissioner agreed, and this new Section began its work in March 1960 with a carefully chosen and high-powered staff.

There was an obvious danger of demarcation disputes. The Intelligence Section must not seem to be usurping the function of the Criminal Record Office or of the specialised indexes or of the huge and somewhat unwieldy Central Register, which catalogues not only crimes and criminals but complaints and correspondence and almost everything else which ever comes to the notice of Scotland Yard. It was to avert this danger that I made the new Section part of my private office, with accommodation just two doors down from my own. One of its objects would be to ensure that the Assistant Commissioner was kept up to date about which criminals constituted a serious menace.

Demarcation disputes would, in any event, have been unjustified. The Intelligence Section had quite distinctive functions. The Criminal Records Office lists only the names of people who have actually been convicted: the Intelligence Section covered people who have never been caught but about whom the police need to know. The Central Registry contains too much for anybody to grasp: the Intelligence Section had only a handful of files and a card index. The other indexes provide categorised facts: the Intelligence Section offered information about a criminal's associates and background, which might seem, to a bureaucratic eye, tangential but which could be extremely useful to detectives in the field.

It constitutes—or at least I hoped it would constitute—a new way of thinking about London's crime. The pattern, as we had been made painfully to realise, was not static; as circumstances changed, the pieces shifted like a kaleidoscope, but they were still the same pieces, with a few being added and a few subtracted. The Intelligence Section was designed to present a complete current picture of what the major professional criminals were doing, where they were and with whom they were associating. The official records could contribute to this picture but were not enough in themselves. Other sources had to be constantly tapped. In accordance with Spooner's original suggestion, a Detective Inspector from the Intelligence Section was assigned to each of the four Metropolitan Police districts. His job was not only to make himself available to any policeman with facts to contribute but deliberately to seek out those officers whose long experience ought to be drawn on before it was lost.

The Intelligence Section rapidly proved its value. The dozen or so officers who manned it found their work snowballing as more and more information came in; information which they didn't merely analyse and file but from which they frequently derived suggestions and warnings worth passing on at once to investigating officers or to the Flying Squad. Before long, the new Section had clearly outgrown the protective wing of the A.C.C.'s private office. It acquired the dignity of its own number: C11.

This change in the quantity and quality of crime was one of the two unexpected developments which faced me soon after I became Assistant Commissioner. The other development was parallel, equally unexpected, and, in some ways, even more sad and frightening. At this most inappropriate juncture, there was a substantial increase in public woolliness and sentimentality about criminals, and in propaganda directed against the police, the courts and all forms of established order.

Earnest liberals wrote books about the Challenor case, about Timothy Evans, about Hanratty. I accept that they were well-meaning and sincere, though their conclusions were, in my view, quite simply wrong: but they were also unmistakably contributing to an anti-police mood. They at least intended to do good, though what good they expected to achieve was often —to me at least—obscure. Others had less excuse.

For glossy magazines to print glamourised pictures of criminals; for journalists and sociologists to write articles making heroes out of petty crooks and brutal thugs; for radio and television producers to put out programmes which deride and attack the police while deliberately working up sympathy for thieves and murderers—such behaviour seems to me either irresponsible or malicious. The attack developed on many different fronts; it was sometimes crude, sometimes subtle. It appeared in a lot of new-wave television plays and it was a recurring element in the so-called satire programmes, which tended to assume as axiomatic that policemen were brutal and corrupt.

Richard Burton and Elizabeth Taylor seriously contemplated making a laudatory film about the Great Train Robbery. A note in *Radio Times* said, without apparent disapproval, that a train robber was the "coolest" thing to be. Several fashionable writers suggested that crimes against property were not really immoral, and a clergyman in a parish magazine went so far as to describe burglary as merely a way of redistributing property.

The whole campaign was part of a general revolt against authority. It went with protesters who sat down in the road and agitators who threw ball bearings under the hooves of police horses.

In the old days children were taught to trust the police and go to the nearest Bobby if they were in difficulty. Now an entire generation has been taught—not perhaps by their parents but by pressures of publicity all around them—to dislike and distrust the police and to despise what the police stand for. How vicious the propaganda can be was vividly exemplified in a nuclear disarmanent magazine which has extended its interests to all the other leftist agitations which excite young people. It contained a parody of a police recruiting poster. Beneath a picture of a smiling constable, the text read:

Fred and I were out on patrol last night. Suddenly we saw this old drunk reeling along the pavement. Funny, how your training comes in useful all the time. I kicked him in the crutch, while Fred knocked his teeth in and broke his arm in two places.
Then we arrested him for being drunk and disorderly, obstruct-

137

ing an officer in the course of his duty, and, when we'd got his trousers off, indecent exposure.

Back at the station we drank our cocoa. Another routine beat over.

And then in large letters:

IT'S A REAL THUG'S LIFE
IN THE NEW POLICE FORCE!

Such blatant rubbish may in fact do less harm than the steady drip-drip of more sophisticated cynicism. But the cumulative effect over the course of a generation is incalculable and extremely disturbing. Bringing young people up in this way, alienating them from the law and encouraging them to admire or condone crime, is surely as wicked and mad as anything Sergeant Challenor did, and in the long run, more far-reachingly dangerous to us all.

This shift in public opinion gave a great boost to the criminals' morale. They were gratified to find themselves widely depicted as clever, amusing and even rather endearing people.

Less irresponsible but hardly more helpful or sensible is the view advanced by so many progressive, and therefore fashionable, sociologists that almost every crime is due to mental sickness. That a large number of psychiatrists agree fails to convince me of its truth. Psychiatrists, like other enthusiastic experts, are apt to interpret everything in the light of their own speciality. I would sooner accept the opinion of a friend of mine, a judge with a vast experience of crime, that perhaps seven percent of convicted criminals need psychiatric help.

I don't want to appear a harsh penologist. Indeed I don't profess to have any *a priori* views about the proper way to treat or punish lawbreakers. The starting-point of my argument is very simple. Punishment has one main purpose: to diminish crime. If there was any evidence that psychiatry helped to achieve this purpose, I would welcome it into the courtroom.

138

There seems unfortunately to be no such evidence. Since the psychiatrists and liberal theoreticians began to make their influence felt, crime, far from diminishing, has increased. They are, I fully recognise (indeed I recognise it rather more clearly than some of them), still exploring. If they find an effective answer, I shall be delighted: until they do, I prefer to abide by the old-fashioned theories of common sense.

Policemen usually take a tougher view of professional criminals, not because policemen are brutal, or even because criminals are their enemies, but because they see at first hand the misery which crime can cause. It is the police officer, not the progressive thinker, who finds the body of a raped and murdered child half-hidden in a ditch, and who has to inform her parents and ask them to identify their daughter. It is the policeman, not the left-wing clergyman talking blandly about "redistribution of property," who sees the senseless filth and destruction which burglars leave behind. It is the policeman who meets the victims, often elderly people selected for their innocence, whom a sharepusher has robbed of their savings, leaving them "only their eyes to cry with." It would be a brutal and heartless policeman indeed who, having seen these things, could still accept the attitude of those television pundits who seem to think a crime becomes admirable if only it has been planned with sufficient ingenuity and carried out with enough ruthless efficiency.

As the new mood spread, both the criminals and the police soon realised that any complaint against a policeman was certain to find a ready and credulous audience, and would be so publicised and magnified by the media of modern mass communications that, even if the complaint could be ultimately disproved, the truth would never really catch up the lie. For several years now there has been a growing feeling in the police, and particularly among C.I.D. officers, that the odds are stacked against them; that the barriers protecting criminals are being reinforced; and that the public is indifferent or hostile.

The continual increase of crime is an intractable and frightening development, but at least there are positive ways in which it can be fought. The Criminal Intelligence Section helped; stiffer sentences would probably help: a reorganisation of Britain's detective forces might help: and an improvement in police recruiting, especially in London, would help a great deal. But this other development, this corruption of public opinion, is much harder to fight. Its roots are deep and complex, its branches wide and tangled: and it casts a most unhealthy shadow.

CHAPTER 10

Father Brown and the Podola Case

The anti-police campaign—and to describe it in that way is really not an exaggeration—reached its height in 1959, when two murder cases, both singularly unpleasant, served for propaganda and as rallying points.

There was a third murder case that spring, which has stuck in my mind, partly no doubt because of the murderer's remarkably appropriate name, and partly because the public reaction, or lack of reaction, to it made an interesting contrast with the others; a contrast which did not go unnoticed by the police.

The man was called Joseph Chrimes. On the last day of the previous year he had broken into a bungalow, battered an elderly woman to death with a tyre lever and stolen a clock, a cigarette lighter, and a number of other small items. In March 1959 he was tried at the Old Bailey, convicted and sentenced to death. The case aroused no public interest. There was no agitation for a reprieve, even from the confirmed opponents of capital punishment.

But, at the same session of the Central Criminal Court, Ronald Henry Marwood also stood trial for capital murder and was also sentenced to death. A well-organised and highly publicised campaign for his reprieve was immediately put in train. Much emphasis was laid on the fact that "poor Ron Marwood" was only twenty-five: no one mentioned that his victim had been two years younger. There was another difference, besides the ages of the people involved, between the Chrimes and Marwood cases; a difference which may or may not have weighed with the campaigners but which certainly concerned the police. The man Marwood killed was a policeman.

Police Constable Summers, a young officer with less than two years service, had been stationed at Holloway. He seems to have been well enough liked, not only by his colleagues and by the law-abiding people on his beat, but also by the young toughs who proliferate round there.

Just before 10:45 on the evening of December 14, he had been on patrol in the Seven Sisters Road when he saw a small crowd milling about in front of Grey's Dance Academy. He saw the flash of knives. Most of the crowd belonged to one or other of two local gangs of youths, known as the Angel Mob and the Finsbury Park Lot. These gangs had clashed a few evenings before in another dance hall. Somebody had flicked a pellet of silver paper at the other gang's leader; a piece of lese majesty which was now to be punished in blood.

Summers came on the scene just as the two leaders were squaring up for a duel, one armed with a carving knife, the other with an axe. Summers strode into the crowd and some of the youths ran off. Others stood their ground. Summers seized the biggest of them by the arm, and began marching him along the pavement towards the Police Station. He brushed aside some of the gang who tried to rescue their comrade, and had gone about forty yards when Marwood drew a knife and stabbed him in the back.

He staggered a little way and then collapsed. The youths scattered and ran. The bystanders merely stared. Only three of them, young girls aged sixteen, fourteen, and twelve, made any attempt to help Summers as he lay on the pavement. Then a passing motorist saw what had happened, stopped and telephoned for an ambulance and for the police. Before the ambulance arrived, another driver took Summers to hospital in his car; but the policeman was dead when they arrived.

The Information Room at Scotland Yard had sent police

hurrying to the scene. Two officers in a police van stopped Marwood and another man about half a mile away. There was blood on Marwood's hands and three of his fingers were cut.

Both Marwood and his companion said they had been nowhere near the Seven Sisters Road that evening. The cuts on his hand had been caused, he said, during a fight at a Finsbury Park hotel. When Marwood was questioned by Superintendent Fenwick at Holloway Police Station, he elaborated: someone had swung at his head, he put up a hand to protect himself and felt a sharp pain. Next morning, he and his companion were taken to the hotel. They separately indicated the positions where they claimed to have been standing and correctly described the musical entertainment provided in the saloon bar. They were then released.

Later that day Marwood left home and didn't return. About the same time, the knife which had killed Summers was found on a compost heap in a private garden. It bore no fingerprints.

The murder had been committed in a well-lighted street in front of a large crowd of witnesses. Both Marwood and Summers were well known to many of them, and must, anyway, have towered above the scuffle, since they were both about six foot three in height. But no one came forward to identify the killer, and though statements were taken from more than a hundred people, not one proved both able and willing to help the police. A few said they wanted to help and admitted to having seen the incident, but their descriptions of the murderer were so varied as to seem deliberately misleading.

On one point only did they all vehemently agree. They couldn't remember seeing Ron Marwood.

Meanwhile, Marwood's disappearance increased the suspicion against him. I received regular reports of such progress as the police were making. They had broken down the Finsbury Park hotel alibi, and discovered that Marwood's hand had been cut accidentally by a member of his own gang who had been brandishing a chopper outside the dance hall. But neither this youth nor any of the others would say that it was Marwood who attacked Summers. Even the one whom Summers had arrested, "Big Mick," though he finally admitted everything else, persisted in saying that he didn't know who had rescued him.

Some arrests were made. Eleven youths, including both gang leaders, "Big Mick" and the one who had been picked up with Marwood after the murder, were convicted of making an affray and given sentences ranging from a £20 fine to fifteen months' imprisonment.

Then one evening, six weeks after the murder, Marwood walked into the Caledonian Road Police Station. He was twice punctiliously cautioned, but said "You can write it all down. I did stab the copper that night. I'll never know why I did it. I've been puzzling over in my mind during the last few weeks why I did it but there seems no answer."

So they wrote his statement down, read it to him, invited him to read it over himself and make any changes he wanted. He read it through and signed it.

In this statement he said that someone had swung a chopper at him. He had deflected it but had been knocked down. He got up, feeling dizzy and sick, and saw Mick a couple of yards away being pushed along by a copper. Marwood walked up behind the policeman, who "sort of half turned," said "Clear off," and struck Marwood on the shoulder. "I remember I had my hands in my overcoat pockets. I pulled out my hand, intending to push him away. I must have had my hand on the knife." He aimed a blow at the policeman's arm. The policeman fell down, and Marwood ran away. As for the knife, he maintained that "some bloke" had given it him earlier in the evening. "When he gave it to me, he said 'Here you are. You might need this.' At the time I thought it was a bit silly and I put it in my overcoat pocket. I had forgotten all about it and

I never realised I had it until I struck the policeman with it."

In fact, as we knew, the knife had been in Marwood's possession for several months. He was charged with murder next day.

At his trial a few weeks later he said he hadn't stabbed Summers and hadn't confessed; his statement was a forgery by the police. After deliberating for three hours, the jury found him guilty and he was sentenced to death.

Immediately, the campaign for his reprieve was put in motion. The usual people began whipping up feeling. A local vicar organised a petition, which 150 Members of Parliament signed. Hostile crowds gathered outside Pentonville Prison on the evening before and the morning of his execution, and when these scenes were shown afterwards on newsreels, angry audiences shouted cat-calls against the police. Joseph Chrimes had enjoyed no such sympathy and support: but then he hadn't murdered a policeman.

Only two months later, another policeman lost his life in a still more sensational case. His name, which was quickly forgotten, was Raymond Purdy. The name which has been remembered, as in the Marwood case, was the name of the murderer: Guenther Podola.

Deputy Commander Spooner came into my room and said: "You'll be sorry to hear, sir, that one of our sergeants has been shot. He's dead." The story, as I soon learned, had actually begun five days earlier. Detective Sergeant Purdy was on duty at Chelsea Police Station when a message came in from an American lady, named Mrs. Schieffman, saying that she had a blackmailer on the phone.

The call had been expected. Mrs. Schieffman's flat in South Kensington had been broken into, about ten days before, while she was away. As well as a mink stole and some jewellery, the burglar had taken her passport. Two days later, she received an express letter signed *R. M. Lavine, Detective, U.S.A.* The writer said he had been hired to check on her activities, had amassed photographs and tape recordings, and was now prepared to sell them to her for five hundred dollars; in consideration of this sum he would also send a favourable report to his employer. He gave her a few days to think it over. Like a sensible woman, and having done nothing to be blackmailed about anyway, she immediately showed the letter to the police.

On July 12 the blackmailer rang, asking for her decision. Following a plan which had been agreed with the police, she said she would pay. The blackmailer promised to ring back later with instructions about the method of payment. Mrs. Schieffman told the police, who arranged for any further calls to be traced.

Next morning the man phoned again. He instructed Mrs. Schieffman to draw five hundred dollars from the bank and then wait for another call. It came in the afternoon. She kept him talking while a neighbour notified Chelsea Police Station. Quickly the Post Office engineers traced the call. It came from Knightsbridge 2355, a public phone box at South Kensington Underground Station. Sergeant Purdy and Sergeant Sandford raced to the scene in a police car. They saw a man in the call box, speaking into the telephone and holding a small black notebook. They burst in, seized the man and took the notebook. Purdy identified himself to Mrs. Schieffman over the phone, and then told the man he was being arrested for demanding money with menaces. They started marching him towards the police car, but before they reached it he broke away.

Purdy stumbled. Sandford commandeered a taxi cab. They piled in, and swung after their quarry into Onslow Square. They saw him dart into the entrance of a block of flats. They raced in pursuit, and caught him hiding behind a pillar in the hall.

Purdy made the man sit on a windowsill and told him to behave himself, while Sandford crossed the hall and rang for the porter. There was no reply. "The porter must be out," he called to Purdy. For a moment Purdy turned his head towards him. Sandford saw the man begin to slide off the windowsill and his hand going inside his jacket. He shouted a warning, but, before Purdy could react, the man had pulled out a gun and fired point-blank at Purdy's chest.

Purdy fell, gasping. The man ran out of the door. Sandford started after him and then, realising he couldn't catch him, returned to see what he could do for Purdy. A couple who had heard the shot came and helped, while Sandford phoned Scotland Yard and Chelsea Police Station. The two senior detective officers from Chelsea, Superintendent Hislop and Chief Inspector Acott, arrived just in time to see Purdy die.

Then began the grimmest and most serious of all manhunts: the hunt for an armed and ruthless criminal, who had already murdered a policeman and had now vanished into the great maze of London. He had left us with only two clues, his palm-prints on the windowsill and his thumb prints on the little black notebook. The contents of the notebook, which might have provided further clues, were so cryptic that they defied our powers of detection. Pages were headed with single words, such as HORSES, TRAINS, LAUGHS, WATER, CRASHES. Under CRASHES came these four entries:

CAR: Paul Temple etc and suitable other crashes 1903
TRAIN: Good with steam 20B49
WOOD-SPLINTERING: 3B23/25
COW: 1B68

Sherlock Holmes or Lord Peter Wimsey would no doubt have solved the puzzle very quickly, but it mystified my officers, who consoled themselves with the thought that, even if they could decode it, they weren't likely to be helped much in their search for Purdy's murderer. The mystery wasn't, in fact, solved until much later, when the ownership of the notebook was traced to a studio manager at Broadcasting House, who had lost it in

147

a burglary. The notes were references to items in the BBC's library of sound effects.

Meanwhile, we did at least know what the murderer looked like: aged about thirty; height, five foot nine or ten; clean-shaven; thin build; brown hair, crewcut; American-style green-blue tinted sunglasses; soft-spoken, American or Canadian accent; light sports coat, light grey trousers, light brown suede shoes. Sergeant Sandford supplied all these details, and, for once, we could be quite sure that the description was accurate. It went out immediately on the teleprinter to all stations in the Metropolitan Police District, and then to all other police forces throughout the United Kingdom. Just two hours after the murder, it was also put out on radio and television news bulletins.

At that stage, the public was very much on our side. Everyone wanted to help. Messages of sympathy and encouragement —as well as the usual crop of well-intentioned but false sightings—poured into Scotland Yard.

Naturally both the Commissioner and I were very concerned about the progress of the hunt. Both of us visited Chelsea Police Station, but we followed the cardinal principle of never interfering with the men on the job. I returned to my office to await further news.

The police worked late into the night. Hundreds of reports from the public were investigated, and at the same time a great comb-out was taking place through all the coverts of the underworld. Whispers began to come in; whispers about a man calling himself Mike Galento or Colato, who had recently appeared in Soho. He had come to England, the rumours said, for the first time in his life, but had quickly bought a gun and scraped acquaintance with some well-known rogues. His description fitted.

Superintendent Hislop and Chief Inspector Acott were piecing these hints together in the early hours of the following day, when they received another item of information. Hislop went to a hotel near West London Air Terminal and took possession of the register. What interested him was an entry dated May 21. The signature, in a Continental script, appeared to be *G. Podola*: the address was *Montreal*. The description given by the hotel staff matched "Galento" and matched the man who killed Purdy.

An enquiry was radioed to the Royal Canadian Mounted Police. A few hours later, the reply came from Ottawa:

OUR RECORDS DISCLOSE PERSON NAMED GUENTHER FRITZ ERWIN PODOLA WE ARE FORWARDING AIRMAIL TODAY FINGERPRINTS CRIMINAL RECORD AND PHOTOGRAPH.

Podola, we learned, was a German citizen, who had been deported from Canada a year before. We, therefore, radioed to Interpol at Wiesbaden, asking for Podola's fingerprints and photograph from their files.

Now we knew whom we were looking for. He was born in Berlin in 1929, had emigrated to Canada in 1952 and had been deported in 1958 after serving a prison term for housebreaking and theft. He had gone back to Germany, then come here. We picked up his trail at London Airport. He had been directed to the nearby hotel: after ten days he had moved to a guest house in the Cromwell Road, from which he had been ejected on June 23 for not paying his rent. And there the trail ended— until Sergeant Purdy saw him in the phone box.

Before releasing Podola's photograph to the Press, Hislop showed it to Sergeant Sandford, together with photographs of eleven other men, and asked him which, if any, of these twelve had shot Purdy. Without a moment's hesitation, Sandford pointed at Podola.

Around noon on the same day, Acott heard that a man answering to Podola's description was staying at a hotel in Queensgate. A raiding party was assembled and given pistols.

Acott and another senior officer from Chelsea, Inspector Vibart, entered the hotel first. They examined the register and found that a Canadian from Montreal had signed himself in as *Paul Camay*. The writing was unmistakably Podola's. Acott showed Podola's picture to the manager's wife and she identified him as "Camay." He was in Room 15, she said.

While Vibart stood guard in the hotel, Acott went to fetch the others, who were waiting nearby. They followed him back into the hotel at discreet intervals; Hislop first, unarmed, because, like many British policemen of the old school, he preferred, even then, not to carry a gun; Detective Sergeant Chambers and two others, all with pistols; and finally a dog handler with a police dog called Flame.

At Hislop's request, the hotel manager went upstairs to check that "Camay" was still in Room 15—and reported that he was. The officers took up their positions round the door. Vibart handed his gun to one of the others and charged the door. It didn't give. He stepped back and shouted: "Open. Police. Open this door."

For about fifteen seconds there was silence. Then they heard a slight metallic click inside the room. It sounded like a gun being cocked. Sergeant Chambers hurled his 230 pounds against the door.

This time the door flew open. It hit Podola in the face and sent him staggering back across the room. Chambers hurtled in after him. Podola cannoned into a chair and finished up on the floor, face uppermost, with his head in the fireplace. Chambers fell on top of him.

The dog Flame was brought into the room but kept under control near the window. Podola was struggling violently, while Chambers held his arm down to stop him getting at a gun. The others crowded in, seized Podola's arms and furiously kicking legs, and he suddenly went limp. They searched him where he lay. He had no gun. The click they heard had been Podola unlocking the Yale lock on the door.

They put Podola on the bed. He seemed to have been knocked out; he had a cut eye and blood was flowing down his face. They washed his wound and staunched the bleeding. A few minutes later, he sat up, watching them with his right eye; his left eye was now completely closed. He drank several cups of water. In case he was shamming, they handcuffed his hands behind his back, and then let him stand up and walk round the room. From time to time he broke into violent shaking. When he seemed fit to be taken to the police station, they helped him down the three flights of stairs to the ground floor.

Summoned by some mysterious jungle telegraph, reporters, photographers, and sightseers had gathered outside. Since the only witness to the murder had already identified a photograph of Podola, the routine precaution was not strictly necessary: but routine is routine, and not lightly to be departed from: so Acott ordered Podola's head to be covered. Then he was put in a car and driven straight to Chelsea Police Station.

The Divisional police surgeon, Dr. Shanahan, was summoned at once. He examined Podola carefully and found no injuries apart from an abrasion over the left eye, which he cleaned and dressed. Podola refused to talk and appeared to be in a state of collapse; he was suffering from a withdrawal syndrome, the doctor thought, and possibly recovering from concussion. Dr. Shanahan ruled that Podola was not yet fit to be charged but was fit to be detained at the police station.

After the doctor had left at about 5:30 P.M., Podola was kept under continuous observation. He slept, or seemed to sleep, most of the time, but, at one point, he managed to smoke a cigarette and drink a cup of tea. His condition was still far from normal, however, and at 11:30 P.M. Dr. Shanahan was summoned again. He made another examination, found that

Podola was not recovering as he had expected, and recommended admission to hospital.

Podola was taken on a stretcher to St. Stephen's, where he was examined by the consultant physician, Dr. Philip Harvey, who suspected there might be a brain injury. Podola's skull was X-rayed, but showed no fracture. A lumbar puncture was performed. Dr. Harvey decided that Podola had suffered concussion and some mild contusion of the brain; nothing worse. Three days later, Podola was pronounced fit, taken back to Chelsea Police Station and charged, in the presence of his solicitor, with the murder of Sergeant Purdy. He was then taken to West London Magistrate's Court, remanded in custody for a week and driven to Brixton Prison.

These are the simple facts of the arrest and detention of Guenther Fritz Podola. I am quite certain that they are as I have given them. All the officers concerned acted properly and with considerable courage. But, within a very short time, public anger against Purdy's murderer had been converted into an extraordinary storm against the police. This change was precipitated by accounts of the affair which appeared in certain newspapers. One, for example, told how "police dog Flame was slipped into Room 15 and, snarling, went like an arrow for the man on the bed. The powerful brindle Alsatian caught him on the cheek." Another described the dog as going for Podola's arm. Both versions were wholly fictitious; the dog never went near Podola. Such inaccuracies were harmless enough, however, compared with the other tales which began to spread. These tales would not have been believed if a lot of people hadn't wanted to believe them, nor would they have spread if some people hadn't wanted to propagate them.

On July 20 Mr. R. T. Paget, Q.C., Labour Member of Parliament for Northampton, asked a question of the Home Secretary, Mr. R. A. Butler: "What happened to Guenther Podola during the six hours at Chelsea Police Station which necessitated his removal to hospital on a stretcher?" Mr. Butler replied that Podola had been allowed to leave hospital and that as he was being charged with murder it wouldn't be proper to say more.

"I am not concerned about the charge against Guenther Podola," said Mr. Paget. "I am concerned about the people who beat him unconscious. Have charges been preferred against them?"

Later in this exchange, Mr. Paget said: "I gather from the Home Secretary that no charge has been brought as to an attack on Mr. Podola, in which, according to some accounts, he received injuries to his skull and jaw. Surely the attack on him when in police custody cannot possibly have any bearing on whether or not he committed a murder previously." He added that people should be safe in British police stations and the idea that either vengeance or beatings up should occur there was utterly unacceptable.

Hard pressed, Mr. Butler finally said: "I am absolutely satisfied that this man was not beaten up in the police station." This ambiguous reply failed to allay the anger and suspicion which had been aroused by the Home Secretary's earlier answers.

Inevitably, the rumours about what the police had done to Podola proliferated; one version said that every police officer in the Station had been invited to hit Podola once. The messages of sympathy we had received after the murder were replaced by a torrent of angry letters. A thick file of them was brought to me each morning, but in the end I simply gave up reading them. Voluble members of the lunatic fringe write to the police about every sensational crime: the letters about Podola were all the more sad and irritating because quite a lot of them came from ordinary citizens, who were filled with righteous anger about what they thought had happened. Some people, of course, took a different view. They said that the police were fully justified in beating Podola up; he deserved it. The police forces of other countries with which I was in touch couldn't understand what the fuss was about. They thought Podola was lucky not to have been shot. All in vain did I insist that Podola had not only not been shot, he hadn't been beaten up either; nothing had happened in Chelsea Police Station. Everyone was quite sure it had.

Podola's trial took place in September, about five months after Marwood's. Interest really centred on the preliminary issue of whether he was fit to plead. His Counsel, F. H. Lawton, Q.C. (now Mr. Justice Lawton) maintained that Podola had no memory of anything which occurred before July 17, the day after his arrest. "In all fairness," Lawton added, "I should state specifically that there is no evidence of any kind that any violence was done to Podola at Chelsea Police Station. Indeed, such evidence as exists points the other way. His shock is the shock of his arrest and the circumstances of it."

The Prosecution replied that Podola's amnesia was a fake. Nine doctors were called to give evidence on one side or the other. Dr. Shanahan said that Podola had shown "a withdrawal reaction," and agreed that there had been no physical injury except the cut above his eye and the swelling round it— and no additional marks in the evening which hadn't been there in the afternoon. Dr. Harvey recalled his diagnosis of concussion and mild contusion of the brain. Dr. Colin Edwards, a neurologist who had examined Podola while he was on remand in Brixton, disagreed about the concussion and said he thought Podola's amnesia was hysterical and of purely psychological origin. Another neurologist, Dr. Michael Ashby, took much the same view, and at the same time revealed a rather curious opinion about the proper duty of the police.

Podola claimed that, shortly after his arrival at St. Stephen's Hospital, he heard the voice of Superintendent Hislop whispering in his ear: "I am your friend. Say it went off accidentally." Maxwell Turner for the Prosecution asked Dr. Ashby if he believed this story about Hislop.

"I tried to catch Podola out," replied Dr. Ashby. "I don't see that it's improper for anyone else to. I feel it's the duty of the police to try to trap criminals."

"Come, come, come, come, Doctor!" exclaimed Mr. Justice Davies.

Dr. Ashby said he was sorry if he was wrong, but he didn't exclude the possibility. The Judge then pressed him: "You tell the jury you thought it was entirely a proper thing for a police officer to try and trap a man on a murder charge by saying words of that kind. That was your view, was it, as to the propriety of someone doing that?"

"I hadn't thought out very carefully," Ashby replied, "about propriety and the rules."

"Don't bother about the rules. Does it strike you as being the sort of thing which a man with the faintest ideas of rectitude could bring himself to do?"

"If he thought or assumed that this act had been done, I would have thought he was merely trying to establish what he thought was a fact. If he was in any way trying to establish and create a false fact, it would be a most shocking thing to do."

"It is trickery, is it not?" asked the Judge.

"A trick to establish the truth is a point I find it difficult to necessarily assume is improper," Ashby answered.

"Then," said the Judge, "taking that view of the propriety of a police officer using a device of that kind, the approach was this, was it: since it was not an improper thing to do, it was a quite feasible thing for this senior police officer to have done?"

"I am afraid, my Lord," said Dr. Ashby, "I view this as a scientist accepting or rejecting evidence, and I tried to view it quite objectively without any reference to what was proper or improper."

The Defence then called Dr. Edward Larkin, a psychiatrist,

who agreed with Edwards and Ashby that there were no signs of physical damage to the brain; any concussion there might have been was trivial and could not have caused loss of memory. He was inclined to think that the story of Superintendent Hislop's whisper was a morbid hallucination, and he believed that this had started Podola's hysterical amnesia. Later, when he was being cross-examined, Dr. Larkin said he thought the amnesia had begun in the hotel room at the time of Podola's arrest. Maxwell Turner pointed out that this wasn't what he had said before. "No," Dr. Larkin agreed blandly, "you've made my mind clear. Thank you."

The Prosecution then called Francis Brisby, the principal medical officer at Brixton Prison, who said that, in his opinion, Podola was malingering: and, after him, Dr. Denis Leigh, a consultant psychiatrist, who had been invited to examine Podola because of a recommendation by the Royal Commission on Capital Punishment that the defendants in all murder cases should be examined by an independent psychiatrist. Dr. Leigh had seen Podola on ten occasions. He thought Dr. Harvey's diagnosis of contusion of the brain couldn't be correct, said that Superintendent Hislop's alleged whisper was either a lie or a hallucination, and expressed the view that Podola's amnesia was definitely feigned.

The Defence called one supplementary medical witness, rather a celebrated one because he frequently appears on television, Dr. Stafford Clark. Dr. Clark had not examined Podola and admitted that he had not followed the details of the case closely, but he gave his views on hysterical amnesia with illustrations from cases he had seen.

The jury decided that Podola was not suffering from genuine loss of memory and was fit to stand trial.

The trial itself was much shorter than the hearing of this preliminary issue. On September 24, Podola was found guilty and sentenced to death. After the rejection of his appeal, three weeks later, he suddenly recovered his memory and tried to establish an alibi. He now said that, at the time of the murder, he had been breaking into a flat in Sloane Avenue. The police duly investigated and found that the flat had indeed been broken into on the day of the murder and that the thief had not been caught. The address of the flat, written in Podola's hand, appeared in the black notebook, so Podola probably was the housebreaker: but, as he could have entered at any time between 8:30 A.M. and 2:30 P.M., this hardly constituted an alibi.

Podola now remembered something else. He had a double named Bob Lavine, he said, whom he'd known both in Canada and in Germany. They were alike as two peas. He and Bob had arranged to meet at 105, Onslow Square, the place where Sergeant Purdy was killed. Podola hadn't kept the rendezvous, but his prints were there because they had previously cased the joint together. Dutifully we asked the Canadian and German police if they could find any record or trace of Bob Lavine. They found none. Podola was hanged.

In spite of the evidence at the trial, especially that of medical witnesses for the Defence, the police never received a word of apology for the wild accusations which had been levelled at them by people who should have known better. A leading article in the *Police Review* suggested that Mr. Paget might now withdraw his remarks, which had received very wide publicity and were highly damaging to the officers concerned. Paget replied, criticising the *Police Review* for failure to grasp the difference between a question and an assertion; he had merely asked the Home Secretary a question based on "the information available." His letter ended: "I would like to say now that I am entirely satisfied that Podola was not assaulted at Chelsea Police Station and I have no criticism at all to direct against the police conduct. I have, however, no apology to make either for asking the question or for pressing for an answer."

The *Police Review* published this reply, but the editor added a note defending his ability to distinguish between questions and assertions. "Mr. Paget," he wrote, "asked the Home Secretary whether charges had been preferred against *the people who beat Podola unconscious*. In our opinion the words in italics contain an assertion, not a question." The editor's logic seems to me unanswerable. Certainly it was never answered.

Of course policemen do sometimes behave with less than perfect propriety. Dealing with violent men, they are sometimes rough. The party which went to arrest Podola was no doubt nervous, as indeed they had every reason to be, and might well not have been gentle in taking him. But the story about his being beaten up in the police station was intrinsically implausible. They wanted Podola hanged, not beaten up. Their instinct would have been to behave towards him with scrupulous correctness, careful to give the Defence no excuse for distracting attention from Podola's crime by attacking them.

There is a story by G. K. Chesterton called *The Scandal of Father Brown* in which the priest's motives are grossly misinterpreted. The false report is corrected half an hour later, but it never quite catches up—"and so the two Father Browns chase each other round the world for ever." Most people, I'm sure, still think of Podola as the man who was beaten up at Chelsea Police Station, and will continue to do so as long as his name is remembered at all. The truth of the matter can only run limping and panting behind.

CHAPTER 11

Murder Bag in Hand

It is extraordinary how many quite important officials there are in Britain about whom the public knows practically nothing. I don't mean of course the mushroom crop of petty civil servants who have come into being since the war and whose diminution would be both more remarkable and more admirable than their continued existence but senior officials doing necessary and rather interesting jobs. There is, for instance, the Receiver for the Metropolitan Police District, of whom few people outside Whitehall seem to have heard. But to the Metropolitan Police he is business manager, financial watchdog and Minister of Works all rolled into one. He is independent of the Commissioner, has a staff of over a thousand and spends about £60 million on maintaining and equipping the force and the Metropolitan Magistrate's Courts. The job was created by Peel as part of his police plan and is therefore as old as the force itself.

During my years at Scotland Yard I knew three Receivers, Sir Frederick Johnson, Sir Joseph Baker, and Mr. W. H. Cornish, who still holds the post.

All three had been officials of high rank in the Home Office with wide knowledge of police matters, and all contributed to my education from the time I entered the Yard until I left it. I was reminded of them by reading again some remarks by Sir John Moylan written in 1929 when he was Receiver.

"Scotland Yard," he said, "unlike most Continental and American police forces, has no specialist departments, no Homicide Bureau, for instance, and no branch devoted solely to the investigation of fraud." With the setting up of the Fraud Squad eighteen years later this ceased to be true, but we still have no Homicide Bureau. What the Press sometimes calls the "Murder Squad" is simply the group of senior officers in C1 or Central Office.

Central Office, which in Moylan's day coped with all the detective work now undertaken by the specialist branches, is now split into ten sections, each headed by a Superintendent and each specialising in a particular type of crime. The crimes concerned are those which can be better dealt with centrally than by divisional officers such as counterfeiting and coining, drug-peddling, passport offences, international crimes and those which may require extradition proceedings; crimes, in other words, which are not local and which may entail Government action. These Superintendents have another duty too. They form a stand-by rota to assist any provincial Chief Constables who ask for help.

Murder is not the only crime for which Scotland Yard's help may be asked. The Chief Constable of Buckinghamshire immediately called us in over the Great Train Robbery, and the Fraud Squad is frequently consulted. But murder, because it is both so important and relatively so rare, is the crime for which provincial police forces most often feel—or used to feel —the need of experienced help.

The Superintendents of C1 are not specialists in murder. They are specialists in investigation and particularly in the questioning of witnesses and suspects. The provincial forces used to be considerably less sophisticated and less well equipped than Scotland Yard, but that situation is changing. Many of them have now set up specialist departments of their own, and the smaller forces can consult the larger ones: a process which will be taken a step further by the current policy of amalgamating forces into larger units. Nevertheless, Scotland

Yard, by the mere fact of its being the Metropolitan Force, inevitably has experience and techniques which other forces have had less need to develop: and it is only sensible to draw on them.

In the horrible case of Stephanie Baird, for example, the girl who was murdered and her body mutilated at the YWCA hostel in Birmingham, some senior officers from Birmingham visited the Yard to consult our files. Commander Hatherill summoned an unofficial conference of Detective Superintendents with experience of large-scale murder investigations. They discussed the case and put forward certain suggestions about the drawing up of a questionnaire from which to collate information in a mass enquiry. This system was applied and proved effective. When the killer, Patrick Byrne, was arrested, the Chief Constable of Birmingham sent a telegram to the Commissioner thanking the Metropolitan Police for their help.

The normal procedure for calling us in was that the Chief Constable telephoned me—or sometimes Commander Hatherill—personally and told me briefly what had happened. I then ordered the Chief Superintendent of C1 to send the next Superintendent and Sergeant on call. They telephoned their wives, informed the provincial force when they would be arriving, picked up the "murder bag" (which contains everything needful for the investigation of a homicide) and were on their way within the hour. Their task when they got to the scene of the crime involved a certain amount of diplomacy. They had to establish friendly relations with the local officers, and they were responsible to the Chief Constable for all matters affecting the case: but once a week they came back and reported to me. And when the case was over, solved or not, I always sent the Chief Constable a copy of their report.

As soon as they had left the Yard, their names were replaced on the call list by the next Superintendent and Sergeant due to go. With the usual cussedness of human affairs, a lull in provincial cases was generally followed by an overwhelming spate of requests. At one point in 1963 I had eight Superintendents and Sergeants away on provincial enquiries at the same time. The extra three were Divisional Superintendents. I didn't like denuding the Divisions, but I had no option. I was obliged to comply with every request for assistance. I raised the matter with the Chief Constables who were members of a Home Office subcommittee on the organisation of Criminal Investigation Departments, of which I was Chairman. We decided to recommend that assistance should equally be made available by any neighbouring county or city force: and this has taken some of the load from Scotland Yard.

One of the members of C1 in my day was the late Superintendent Wilfred Daws, known as "Flaps" because his ears were somewhat large. In the autumn of 1956 he was summoned to Huntingdonshire to help with the Fens Murder. This case intrigued me at the time because it seemed to come straight from the last century. The setting was bleak and remote. I could picture Superintendent Daws, clad in an ulster, his ears projecting beneath a flat-crowned bowler, driving in a hansom cab across that sinister countryside. Only the intrusion of frogmen spoiled the scene.

A farmer called Arthur Johnson had disappeared from his home during the night of October 15. Bloodstains were found in the farmyard, and there was another patch of blood half a mile away in a stubble field beside a dyke. Then Johnson's van was found. It had been abandoned at Two Pole Drove, a rough track some two and a half miles from the farm; there was a lot of blood in it and there were some bloodstained sacks.

Arriving at Crowtree Farm, Superintendent Daws and Sergent Humphries learned that Johnson had been a bachelor, living alone. He was last seen at about ten o'clock on the night he disappeared, driving in his van towards the farm. The whole

162

area round about consisted of fields bounded by ditches and dykes, which in turn flowed into larger dykes that the local people called drains or rivers. Narrow tracks led from the farm to the fields, crossing the dykes with wooden bridges. These tracks were difficult enough by daylight. Anyone who tried to drive along them by night would almost certainly have got bogged down in a sugar-beet field or fallen into a dyke, unless he had known the route. So it seemed a fair deduction that the van had been driven to where it was found by a local man.

While frogmen searched the deep fen canals for Johnson's body, Daws and Humphries explored Crowtree Farm. They found Johnson's jacket and spectacles, laid aside as though he had been preparing for bed, and more than £80 cached in various places, usually only two or three pound notes together. Johnson, Daws had learned, was reputed to be rich, but he was also a reticent, even a secretive, man—a characteristic which scarcely distinguished him from everybody else in those parts.

When Daws entered the sitting room, he was struck by the damp, musty smell. At first he thought it just the smell of a room which was seldom opened. Then he realised it was dry rot.

This room contained a safe and a roll-top desk. Inside a drawer which was slightly open Daws found two bands, which had been used as wrappers for bundles of bank notes: another similar wrapper lay on the floor nearby. There was no money in the desk. A cloth over the safe had been turned back, but the safe itself was locked and the keys nowhere in the house. When it was finally opened, with the aid of the local bank manager, the only money Daws found was £16 14s. 5½d. in an old handbag.

The police, meanwhile, had acquired a suspect—Morris Arthur Clarke, a twenty-seven-year-old lorry driver. He lived in Peterborough, about seven miles from the farm: but, what was more important, he used to live in the farm itself, when his wife had been Johnson's housekeeper. He had left in January 1954. Johnson had lent him £100 so that he could start in business as a haulage contractor. The venture had not been a success; by September 1956 he had no lorry, no capital, and debts of more than £1000. On October 1, two weeks before Johnson's disappearance, Clarke took a job as a shunter-driver, working a night shift from 6 P.M. to 6 A.M. His creditors were pressing him for payment and threatening legal action. On October 5 he gave one of them a cheque for £200. It bounced. At 5:25 P.M. on October 15 Clarke had assured his angry creditor that the cheque would be met if it was presented again in the morning. And met it was, because at 10 A.M. on October 16 Clarke paid into the bank £200 in notes. He had never paid cash in before. An hour later he settled his account with another creditor, this time for about £33.

Clarke's sudden affluence coincided with the night on which Johnson disappeared.

Daws and Humphries went to Clarke's house very early, at 7:50 A.M., to avoid reporters. He said he hadn't seen Johnson lately, that he had never driven his van, and that he had been at work, lorry-driving, throughout the night of October 15–16. The £200 was money he had saved; and he had saved it secretly without the knowledge of his wife. He added that there was still £20 in his bureau, the remainder of his savings. He raised no objection to being fingerprinted and to having samples of his blood and hair taken and scrapings from his fingernails.

Daws also took possession of his working clothes, his boots, and bicycle. In a bureau drawer were twenty ten-shilling notes. Daws sniffed them, and asked Humphries to smell them too. They bore the unmistakable odour of dry rot: and so did some more notes, found in a pocket of Clarke's blazer.

The notes were sent to the Fingerprints Branch at Scotland Yard and the other specimens to the Forensic Science Laboratory at Nottingham. Investigating Clarke's account of his

164

movements on the night of October 15–16, Daws found that he had no alibi between 9:55 P.M. and 1:30 A.M.

Although the police had been searching the fens for more than a week, there was still no trace of a body. Daws returned to Scotland Yard for a discussion with me and Commander Hatherill. "I should think the body will turn up about Thursday," said Hatherill with gloomy confidence. "The gases will blow it up till it floats to the top."

And he was absolutely right. On Thursday, October 25, Johnson's body, bloated with the gases of decomposition, came to the surface. A horrified fisherman found it. Half covered in a sack, it was floating in a dyke some three miles from the farm. An autopsy showed that Johnson hadn't been drowned. He had been bludgeoned to death with a blunt instrument. His right leg was broken, too; the blows to his head, according to the pathologist, had probably been administered while he was lying on the ground.

Even now there wasn't enough to connect Clarke with the murder. There was blood on his overalls, but his group was the same as Johnson's and the bloodstains might have got there when he had had some teeth extracted shortly before.

Clarke was interviewed by Duncan Webb, the crime reporter of *The People*, and protested his innocence, saying that on the night of the murder he had spoken to three police officers and a blonde woman around midnight. Daws checked this story and found it was perfectly true—except that it had happened not on the 15th, but on the 17th of October.

A bloodstained stick, which, the pathologist said, could have inflicted Johnson's head injuries, was found in a barn at Crowtree Farm. Daws questioned Clarke again, and was given the same story which Duncan Webb had been told. When Clarke had finished his statement, Daws told him that he had a warrant to search the house.

In the bathroom Daws started to climb a ladder leading to a

trap door into the loft. Sergeant Humphries saw Clarke go white and begin to shake as though he were about to collapse. Inside the loft Daws found a Dundee cake tin and a canvas bag. The cake tin contained £641 in notes: in the bag was an old purse filled with sovereigns and half-sovereigns.

"Come and smell this," Daws said to Humphries and the two local policemen who were with them.

They all sniffed the paper money, and again there was the same unmistakable smell of dry rot which had pervaded Johnson's sitting room.

"What's this?" Daws asked Clarke, pointing to his find.

"It's Johnson's money," Clarke said in a low voice.

"Johnson the dead farmer?"

"Yes. I killed him."

Daws left the money in the cake tin, which he carefully wrapped up in an endeavour to preserve the telltale smell. "I am sanguine enough," he wrote in his report, "to hope that the smell will still be present at the trial."

I can't remember if it was. At all events, Clarke was convicted and sentenced to death, though the sentence was afterwards commuted to life imprisonment. So ended this hauntingly old-fashioned story of the tight-fisted tight-lipped farmer killed among the fens, with the mist wreathing up outside and the foul smell in a little-used parlour waiting to betray the murderer. "Talk about foreign countries," Daws said to me afterwards. "Down there, half of them don't even speak English."

CHAPTER 12
The 4604th Palmprint

Detective fiction, as everyone knows—detective story writers not least—diverges from real life detection in many ways: but one of the biggest differences is among the least noted. Police detectives in fiction are almost invariably attached to Scotland Yard. In real life the great majority of London's detectives, dealing with all sorts of crime, are not at Scotland Yard at all but in the divisions; to be precise, the total strength of the C.I.D. at the last count was 1820, of whom five hundred were attached to the Yard.

London was divided, when I became Assistant Commissioner, into four districts and twenty-three divisions—an extra division has been added since. Each district was headed by a uniformed Commander, and at his headquarters there was a Chief Superintendent in charge of the detectives. The C.I.D. officers in each division were commanded by a Superintendent, with an Inspector heading each sub-division.

The Dixon Working Party recommended a maximum case-load for any one officer of 150 complaints of crime a year. With the flood tide of crime rising steadily higher, and the shortage of policemen becoming more rather than less acute, this figure has never been more than a pious hope. The case-load actually being worked varies from division to division, but it rarely drops below 250 complaints a year and sometimes rises above 350. Sherlock Holmes could reject cases which failed to interest him: police detectives cannot. But no detective, however brilliant or conscientious, can properly investigate 350 crimes a year. The result is frustration; frustration for the detective who knows that he can do little or nothing for most of the people who have suffered thefts or burglaries, and frustration for the victims who, after years of being chivvied about minor traffic offences, now look for help to the police and cannot get it.

Brilliant detection is, in any event, extremely rare. I can scarcely think of a case which was solved by one man's acumen, as opposed to thoroughness and teamwork. The crime on which fictional detectives most frequently exercise their genius, murder, is in real life the least likely to be solved by individual cleverness. The very fact that a mysterious murder is so sensational and so urgent means that a large number of men are likely to be working on it; all the resources of the machine are brought to bear. Whereas a complicated fraud case may be investigated by an Inspector and a Sergeant working patiently for six months, a murder case is more likely to occupy three hundred men for three weeks.

A good example of a case which stretched the machine to its uttermost, while remaining a divisional responsibility, was a murder on the golf course at Potters Bar.

Oddly enough, it was the second murder which had taken place there. Parts of a man's body had been dredged up from a pond on the course in 1954. They were identified as the remains of a railway fitter called Albert Welch, who had lived nearby and disappeared a year before. And that was all the police ever did discover. There were times during the investigation of the second murder when I feared that history was going to repeat itself.

This case began at 11 P.M. on April 29, 1955, when a man telephoned South Mimms Police Station to say that his wife had not returned from her evening walk with the dog. She had gone out, as usual, at about 8:15, leaving him watching television. When she wasn't back by half-past nine, he grew anxious and went to look for her. His anxiety increased when he found the dog in the garden but no sign of his wife. He followed her invariable route to the end of the road, through a tunnel under the railway and on to a path across the golf course. It was growing dark, and he knew she was frightened of the dark. But she was nowhere to be seen.

The police organised a search which continued until 1:30 in the morning, and, after a brief rest, was resumed at dawn. It was still hardly light when a uniformed constable found the body, lying about fifteen yards from the path, in rough grass between a hedgerow and the seventeenth tee.

Half an hour later, the body was being examined by the local police surgeon. He was joined by Detective Superintendent Crawford and Detective Inspector Hawkins of S Division, and by two Scotland Yard experts, Detective Superintendent Law of the Photographic Section and Detective Superintendent Salter, the police liaison officer at the laboratory. The dead woman was lying on her back with her legs spread apart and her own red coat covering her head. Her clothes had been pulled up round her waist, there was blood on her thighs, and the grass between her legs had been flattened as though someone had knelt there. When the coat was removed, her face was seen to have been savagely battered. Her head was lying in a pool of blood, and one of her stockings was round her neck. It wasn't a pleasant sight.

The weapon which the murderer had used was obvious. It lay only a few feet away: an iron marker for the seventeenth tee, painted green and weighing about three pounds. It was stained with blood, and some of the dead woman's hairs were sticking to it. And, more important, there was a smear which at first seemed just a smudged bloodstain, but on closer examination proved to be a small section of a palmprint.

Dr. Francis Camps performed an autopsy that same morning. He found fractures caused by at least four blows from a heavy sharp linear object, presumably the tee-marker, and bruising on the woman's neck from an attempt at strangulation: but he found no evidence of sexual interference.

I knew, as soon as I heard about it, that this would be a difficult case. The motive, in spite of the medical evidence, was obviously sexual, and the great trouble with sex murders is that, unlike most crimes, they are rarely committed by professionals; a fact which renders useless the two most valuable instruments of detection, the informer and the Criminal Record Office. The police are looking for an ordinary man doing an ordinary job: and they know that, unless they find him, the first murder may well be followed by a whole series of similar killings. Motive, which is a clear pointer in most crimes, is unlikely to show them their man. There is a motive, of course, but, instead of being something simple like the desire for money, it remains hidden in the murderer's mind, often quite unsuspected by his family and friends. The challenge and the terrible implication of such cases make an ominous scarlet thread through the history of London's crime.

So the detectives at Potters Bar knew what they might be up against. Even sex murderers do sometimes turn out to have committed other crimes—Neville Heath, for example, had a record—so the first step was to compare the impression on the tee-marker with Scotland Yard's collection of palmprints, about 6000 at that time. A check was also made on men with records of sexual violence; they were interviewed by the police in six counties and asked where they had been on the night of April 29, and their palmprints were taken. A similar check was made on anyone known to have escaped from a mental institution. But they were all eliminated.

So there were no short cuts. We had to look for a man who had no criminal record and wasn't ostensibly deranged. We started with men who had been in Potters Bar on April 29 but had since left the district. We wrote asking for inquiries to be made and palmprints taken in thirty-one counties and twelve cities of the United Kingdom and in an extraordinarily far-flung variety of places to which residents of Potters Bar had chosen to travel in this short time. The Garda Siochana in Dublin, the Provost Marshal's Department in Germany, and police forces in California, Canada, Australia, Eritrea, and the Gold Coast, all co-operated in the attempt to trace the owner of that one small patch of skin. But the only result was to eliminate another group of people.

The local enquiries being made by Inspector Hawkins and his men were no more fruitful, although they quickly found two people who had been on the golf course, only about 250 yards from the scene of the murder, at the very time when it was being committed. A young man and his fiancée had been walking there, when they heard a noise which he thought was dogs yapping but which she described as "muffled screams." Dimly in the dusk the young man had also seen two shapes moving which he thought at first were dogs but afterwards decided were human. The noises stopped, and the couple walked on.

The dead woman's husband was a lorry driver: the woman herself had been working part-time in a shop. They had been married eighteen years, had few friends and led a very quiet life. The woman had taken the dog for a walk—the same walk—every fine evening for the last four years.

On May 4 the police began a house-to-house check on all men and youths living in Potters Bar or the surrounding neighbourhoods. This was a huge job, entailing visits to more than seven thousand houses. I supplemented Hawkins' team with another twenty-seven detectives. Beside the house calls, they visited all the local factories, offices and shops, taking palmprints from two thousand employees who worked in Potters Bar but lived elsewhere. Twelve officers from the Fingerprint Branch devoted their whole time to the laborious task of com-

171

paring these prints with the fragmentary impression on the tee-marker. A palmprint can be as good as a fingerprint, but the detail is harder to identify, particularly when you don't know what part of the palm you are looking at—or even, for certain, whether it is a palmprint at all.

Still there were no results. Superintendent Crawford and Chief Superintendent Mahon, the senior C.I.D. officer in No. 2 District, came to my office to discuss the case. There was nothing for it, we realised, but to extend the search still further. I authorised them to take the palmprints of the entire male population of Potters Bar—or, at least, to try to do so.

The British police can no more compel innocent people to be fingerprinted or palmprinted than they can compel them to answer questions. They have to rely on persuasion, and they usually succeed. A few people object out of mere bloody-mindedness: some refuse for the best, or worst, of reasons—that they have something to hide. Experienced policemen can generally distinguish between the two, and the fact of refusal is itself sometimes a useful pointer. The suggestion has now been made, without apparently provoking any great public indignation, that the entire population should have their fingerprints on record. I don't myself think this would constitute a serious diminution of our liberties, but whether it would be helpful enough to justify so huge, and unpopular, an effort is perhaps less certain.

At all events, we had no such powers in 1954. As they worked their way from house to house through Potters Bar, the police received a few rebuffs and the occasional insult, but most people co-operated readily enough. The officers taking the palmprints had become extremely dextrous by now; indeed, they'd worked out a new roller technique which has since been adopted by most European police forces.

The flow of prints into Scotland Yard became a deluge. In the Fingerprint Department, Chief Superintendent John Livings, always a dedicated enthusiast, organised the men on the Potters Bar job into groups of three, working in shifts round the clock. It must have been stiflingly tedious, and it was much more difficult than a straightforward fingerprint comparison, because nobody knew which hand, or what part of the hand, had made the impression on the tee-marker.

On August 19 the collecting of the prints was almost complete. I was in conference with some Special Branch officers, when Livings peered round the door; a thin face, bald, with piercing blue eyes. Seeing that I was busy, he at once apologised and withdrew. But he had looked excited and pleased. I broke up the conference and sent for him. "We've got it, sir," he said as he came into the room. "The Potters Bar chap."

"Thank goodness for that," I said. "I suppose someone's told S Division the good news?"

"Mr. Crawford and Mr. Hawkins are on their way to see him now, sir."

Nearly nine thousand prints had been taken, and 4604 of them had been examined before the right one came up. It belonged to a young man called Michael Queripel, employed as a junior clerk by the Potters Bar Urban District Council. Crawford and Hawkins interviewed him at the Council Offices.

"Do you know why we want to see you?" asked Crawford.

"Yes, I know what it's all about."

"What is it all about?"

There was a pause. Then he said: "I found her. She was dead."

"Your palmprint was on the tee-plate. If you found her, why didn't you tell the police?"

"You wouldn't have believed me." Crawford allowed another long pause to stretch out. Finally Queripel said: "I hit her, then I tried to strangle her."

"Say no more now," Superintendent Crawford warned, and they took Queripel off to Barnet Police Station. Once there,

173

he was cautioned and asked if he wanted to make a statement. He did, writing it in his own hand:

"I had a migraine attack when I got home from work. I always go for a walk when I get them, and I walked up and down the line path for a bit. I then walked under the tunnel on to the Golf Course. I wandered around and I went into the pillbox under the pipe. I saw her walking towards me with her dog. She walked along the path and I waited until she was out of sight behind the trees. I walked over to the green and waited behind the trees. She came back. I walked through the hedge and ran up behind her and tried to knock her out. She turned just as I was going to hit her. She struggled until I managed to hit her on the jaw. Then I tried to strangle her. I thought she was dead and dragged her over to the hedge where I tried to interfere with her. She was still alive and I had to hit her with the tee-iron to kill her. I hit her several times until we were both covered with blood. Then I ran across the railway line and home through the wood to the Hatfield Bypass and through Bridgfoot Lane.

"I remember that while we were struggling she screamed and talked to her dog which ran away. She told me not to be silly as I would only get into trouble. She said, 'You silly boy, you'll only get into trouble.' It was then I hit her, she fell against a flag post and hurt her back. I put my hands round her throat and tried to strangle her. Then I dragged her over to the hedge where I undressed her. Her coat and blouse were torn in the struggle. I ripped off most of her underclothes. She started to come round and I pulled off one of her stockings and tied it round her neck. It broke straight away and then I hit her with a piece of wood which I found under the hedge. The wood broke as well and so I hit her with the tee-iron. I had to hit her several times before I was sure she was dead. I was growing more and more frightened, but I had to make sure she was dead before I ran away.

174

"I remember she was wearing a red coat and red shoes. I put the coat over her face as she was bringing up blood.

"I wiped my hands on her coat, blouse and knickers. I threw the knickers to one side.

"After I left the golf course I washed most of the blood off my clothes and in the stream at the end of Bridgfoot Lane.

"I then went home and my parents were in bed. I told them the next morning that I had cut my arm round the garage. I told my mother, a few days later, that I had found her and just picked her up to see if she was still alive, to explain the blood on my clothes. My mother told this to my father some days later, when we burnt my clothes.

"I had cut my arm with a razor blade after I got home and I showed the cut to my parents to explain the blood on my clothes because they asked me how it came to be there. I have read this statement and do not wish to add to it or make any further alteration."

This last sentence was added at Superintendent Crawford's request. All the rest were Queripel's own words. It was the only explanation he ever gave for what he had done. The great majority of murder victims are in some way predisposed to their fate. They may be nightwatchmen guarding valuable property, or prostitutes exposed to the obscure passions of their clients, or policemen for whom violence is an occupational risk, or criminals for whom violence is a way of life, or simply husbands and wives so exasperating that they seem to invite murder. All these types are murder-prone. What strikes me as so chilling in Queripel's statement is its reminder that perfectly ordinary people, going on their lawful occasions, taking the dog for an evening walk, may be only a hedge's thickness away from murder. Any of us may have been in that position, without knowing it, and been lucky. The woman on Potters Bar Golf Course was unlucky. She was the one the lightning struck.

Checking back, we found that the police visited Queripel's

home very early in their house-to-house enquiries. Michael was out, but his mother told them that, on the evening of the murder, he had been with a friend at a garage in Barnet. They called again a month later.

When asked if he was willing to have his palmprints taken, Queripel had replied: "No. I've been told in my office that it isn't compulsory."

"It's quite voluntary," said Superintendent Crawford, "but we're hoping everyone will co-operate."

Queripel hesitated, and then said: "Well, all right. If you want mine, you can have them." As it turned out, this was a fatal decision: But I suppose he calculated that the chance of his palmprint not in fact being identifiable was a better risk than calling attention to himself by continued refusal.

On October 12, at the Old Bailey, he pleaded guilty to murder, and was ordered, in the formal words of the statute, to be "detained during Her Majesty's pleasure." He was seventeen and a half years old.

We still possessed the palmprints of nearly nine thousand innocent citizens. I arranged that they should be available for collection at Potters Bar Police Station between 10 A.M. and 9 P.M. every day for two weeks. We put a notice to this effect in the papers, but only 847 prints were claimed. This is much the proportion I would have expected. Most people do not, and indeed have no reason to, share the alarm expressed by those *soi-disant* champions of "civil liberties" who are congenitally suspicious of everything the police do. Chile, I believe, has the most comprehensive form of identity card, including fingerprints as well as all personal details: and foreign visitors, instead of feeling grateful to be spared such tyranny, frequently ask for an identity card, fingerprints and all, because it helps them to cash cheques and get credit.

CHAPTER 13

"W.G." *Stands for . . . ?*

I remember another killer who left his fingerprints behind. It was a very different sort of case, but again it involved both Scotland Yard and Divisional detectives, and presented a challenge not only to our resources but also to our deductive imagination. The man we were after had committed homicide, attempted murder, a serious wounding and several burglaries. Unusually in these days when most criminals know better, he had virtually signed his work with his fingerprints. But the fingerprints weren't in our files.

All save one of these crimes were committed in October and November 1959. The exception was a killing which had occurred nearly a year before. A prostitute, named Veronica Murray, had been found battered to death with a dumbbell which she kept as an ornament on the mantelshelf in her Kilburn flat. We had a detailed description of a man who was presumed to be the murderer—about thirty years old, five foot six or seven in height, stockily built, ruddy complexion, round face, tightly curled sandy-red hair with long sideburns, long pointed nose, wearing a blue-grey belted overcoat, looking like a seaman or labourer, unkempt: and we had his fingerprints. But he had never been found, and it looked as though he never would be—until one day, ten months later, the same fingerprints were found in a room on the seventh floor of the Westbury Hotel.

The suite happened to be occupied by a very old friend of mine, George Sanders, the actor, whom I'd known when we were both boys, living near Worthing. The thief had taken a white raincoat, some jewellery, a bottle of whisky, a grip bag, a pair of size seven men's shoes and a quantity of Parliament cigarettes. George, of course, couldn't resist the opportunity to ring me up and tell me that crime in London was getting out of hand. The unkindest cut, he said, was the loss of his Parliament filter-tips, which at that time were hard to come by in England. It so happened that a visiting FBI man had recently given me a packet, so I promptly sent them round to the Westbury. That small gesture was about all we succeeded in doing for George.

Not that there was any lack of clues. The thief had apparently entered the hotel through a door at the back, walked up a staircase to the roof and then dropped on to the balcony of George's suite. Besides collecting about four hundred pounds' worth of property, he had, for no apparent reason, ripped away two chandeliers and a pair of dummy bookends from the walls. He then walked out of the suite, wearing the raincoat and the shoes and carrying the rest of his loot in the grip bag. He coolly rang for the lift. The night porter who took him down described the man as about nineteen years old, five foot five in height, with fuzzy hair and thick lips, well spoken. And he had left one very promising clue: the Clue of the Discarded Shoes.

Like the ones he had stolen, they were size seven: but, unlike George Sanders' immaculate footwear, they were very old and worn and had obviously been repaired by an amateur. The left shoe bore an identifying mark which nobody could remember ever having seen or heard of before. A number of brads had been driven through the sole from the outside, and bent over inside the shoe to form, crudely but unmistakably, the initials W.G. They must have made walking extremely uncomfortable, if not painful; which may have been why the thief had decided to change shoes when he came across a pair which fitted him. The trouble was that we had no idea what the initials meant.

The thief had told the night porter he wanted a taxi because he had a train to catch from Waterloo at 4 A.M. Taxis proved as elusive as they always are when you really need them, and eventually the man had walked away. Twenty-four hours later, he nearly killed a second woman.

At 12:30 A.M. the following night, he struck up a conversation with a woman on an Underground station, and she let him go back with her to her home in Fulham, where she invited him in and made some coffee. She was thirty-one years old, divorced, with three children. He asked if he could go to bed with her. She refused: whereupon he knocked her unconscious, tore her clothing, tried first to rape her and then to strangle her with one of her own stockings. He left her for dead, and went away taking with him some money and a miniature bottle of whisky. She was found by her children, several hours later, still unconscious on the floor. She had to spend more than two months in hospital.

Her assailant had again left his fingerprints and again we had a detailed description, including a few extra touches. She said he was about twenty-seven years old, five foot nine or ten, leanly built, tanned complexion, light brown hair with a gingery tint, dark eyes, small nose with a broad base, and with a distinctive one-inch scar running horizontally below his right eye. He was wearing a short white overcoat. His name was "Mick" and he had spoken of having recently been discharged from a Guards regiment. He lived near Chelsea Barracks, he told her, and was employed as a drummer or flautist in a night club.

We now had three descriptions. They didn't match perfectly —the killer of Veronica Murray, for instance, was said to have had "an English accent," whereas this man was described as speaking with an Irish accent: but these discrepancies were not unduly worrying. Descriptions of the same man or the same

179

event, given by different witnesses, always do vary. But, with the fingerprints as confirmation, they seemed close enough.

Just over a week later, another woman was nearly killed in her home at night. She was a widow of seventy-one, living alone in a small cottage near Sloane Square. At about 1:30 A.M. she had been asleep in bed on the first floor when she was suddenly attacked by a man hitting her over the head with a poker. She screamed, and he escaped through the front door. The woman was taken to hospital, suffering from severe head injuries. She couldn't describe her attacker, but his fingerprints were the now familiar ones of "Mick." He had entered the house through a small open window on the stairs. The front ground-floor room had been ransacked, but nothing seemed to have been taken except a blue corduroy jacket and an umbrella.

The fingerprints appeared again the following week in the offices of a shipping line in Pall Mall. The building had been entered by way of a neighbouring roof and a lavatory window. Desks and cupboards had been ransacked, but no property was missing. Mick did an extraordinary amount of breaking and entering for very little profit.

A few days later, on Sunday, November 1, he burgled three houses in Chelsea within the space of fifty minutes. The first was in Beaufort Street. He entered it, at 2:30 in the morning, through a ground-floor window, went into a bedroom—and the occupier promptly woke up. Mick escaped without taking anything. Half an hour later, he was climbing on to the roof of a public house in the Fulham Road. He went in through an open first-floor window. A seventy-year-old woman awoke to find him lying on the floor beside her bed with his hands underneath the bedclothes. She screamed. Mick ran downstairs, broke a window with a chair and escaped. All he took that time was a key, which he left at the scene of his third burglary. This occurred at 3:20 in Melbourne Grove. Again he entered through a window, again he tiptoed into a bedroom. Again a woman woke up and shouted. Again he ran downstairs and escaped, taking with him some loose change, a purse, and a fountain pen, his total haul for the night.

On November 4 we held a conference at Scotland Yard. Mick was obviously a very dangerous man to have at large. Because his trail cut across several police Divisions, the case was being handled by Central Office. But, since all his recent exploits had occurred in either "B" or "C" Division, and he had told the woman in Fulham that he lived near Chelsea Barracks, I decided to transfer the headquarters of the investigation to Chelsea Police Station, which was roughly the centre of the area. Unless we caught him, he would certainly commit more crimes and very possibly another murder. Catching him was therefore a high priority job. We agreed on a plan to blanket "B" and "C" Divisions every night with a small army of plain-clothes officers, who between the hours of 9 P.M. and 5 A.M. would stop and check any man resembling Mick. The Fulham woman's description seemed the best to use, since she had spent two hours with him before he tried to kill her.

Chief Inspector Acott formed a special squad, consisting of two Detective Inspectors, nine Detective Sergeants, one Detective Constable, seventy-two Aids to C.I.D., thirty-six uniformed branch constables in plain-clothes, and five dog-handlers. They divided the area into patrol sectors and fixed points, the latter including five bridges over the Thames and all the Underground stations in the area. Each suspect would be taken at once to Chelsea Police Station, where an experienced fingerprint sergeant would be on duty. This rapid procedure would, we hoped, minimise complaints: and in the event, though a large number of people were checked, we received no complaints at all.

Meanwhile, by day, Acott's men followed up every slender clue we had. They made enquiries at Chelsea and Wellington

Barracks, took fingerprints from every guardsman in the London district who seemed to answer the description, and obtained a list of all the men who had recently been discharged, or deserted, from Guards regiments.

Mick had also told the Fulham woman that he was a drummer or flautist, so they dredged through all the night clubs in London, checking not only drummers and flautists but the buying, selling and pawning of flutes and drums. They covered all military bands and the Royal College of Military Police.

Everyone associated with the Fulham woman, including her ex-husband, was eliminated by fingerprints. She had described a scar on Mick's face, so enquiries were made at the Casualty Departments of all the London hospitals. Hostels and lodging-houses were kept under surveillance. Hotels and restaurants were visited. Pawnbrokers were asked to look out for Mick's exiguous loot, and Left Luggage offices were checked for the hold-all which he had taken from George Sanders' room. Every public house, club, cafe, dance hall, and men's hairdresser in "B" and "C" Divisions was visited by some member of Acott's squad.

The dilapidated shoes found in the Westbury were submitted to the Footwear Research Association at Kettering, besides being examined at the Metropolitan Police Laboratory: and a description and photographs of them were published in the *Police Gazette*. Special enquiries were also made at Winton Green Hospital, Birmingham, and Wharf's Grange Hospital at Wetherby in Yorkshire, these being the only mental hospitals in the country with the initials W.G. It was an ingenious idea, but fruitless.

Mental institutions were an obvious place to look because of Mick's apparently unbalanced state of mind. We thought, too, that if he had been a voluntary patient somewhere, this might explain the curious gap in his activities between the murder of Veronica Murray in December 1958 and the hotel robbery in

October 1959. He couldn't have been in prison or we should have had a record of his conviction. But none of the mental hospitals knew him. He might perhaps have been at sea, so a detective sergeant went to Cardiff and waded through the records of more than 300,000 merchant seamen in the files of the Registrar-General of Shipping.

A daily check was made of the fingerprints of all prisoners arrested anywhere in the British Isles. Another huge task was undertaken by the Criminal Record Office: to turn up the files on all men with the initials W.G. and on everyone, including deserters and absconding lunatics, whose description tallied even remotely with Mick's. The Flying Squad mounted extra patrols in the West End and kept watch at Waterloo Station each morning to see who was on the trains leaving at about 4 A.M. The Special Branch went through the Main Index and their Irish photo albums, and made enquiries in all the places where Irishmen customarily meet. The Royal Ulster Constabulary in Belfast and the Garda Siochana in Dublin did their best to check every Irishman who had come back from England since November 1.

This vast trawl caught nothing. We were no further forward than we had been in the beginning. Meanwhile, Mick seemed to have given up crime and our resources were stretched to the limit. Acott's special squad had made several arrests for other crimes and caused a good deal of annoyance to the local criminals, but we couldn't continue indefinitely to employ more than a hundred men a night on this single job. We would have to try something else, and the obvious course was to seek the assistance of the Press.

We hadn't done so before, because our best chance of finding Mick was to catch him on the job and we didn't want to scare him off. But now he seemed to have stopped anyway. The newspapers were straining at the leash already. They knew about the nightly check in "B" and "C" Divisions, and some of them had copies of the photographs which had appeared in the *Police Gazette*. So I decided to issue a full statement, together with a description of Mick and of the W.G. shoe.

Mick, we learned afterwards, read the story and reacted in a way quite opposite to what we had expected. He promptly came to London, on Friday, November 20, spent all evening drinking, then burgled four Chelsea houses in rapid succession, beginning at 1:40 A.M. Our special squad was still fully at work, and Mick's operations took place in the heart of the area we were supposed to be blanketing; a remarkable feat.

Three of the houses were in Jubilee Place, off the King's Road. Mick was heard and challenged in each of them. After his third rebuff, he climbed over the garden wall at the back into the garden of a house in Markham Street. He entered this house by the back door, and, after switching off the power and pulling away the telephone wires, he watched lights flashing outside and policemen searching for him. He mixed a stiff drink, helped himself to cigarettes from a box and sat in an armchair for several hours. Eventually, he pocketed a couple of cigarette lighters and a pair of gloves, and went upstairs. He took a packet of cigarettes off a bedside table and was just picking up a pair of bootees, when the woman in the bed woke up. He ran downstairs and out into Markham Street, and walked calmly to the King's Road. The time was about 6:15 A.M. He took a taxi to Waterloo Station, and caught a train.

That he should have slipped so blatantly through our net was most frustrating, but we did have a possible new lead. One of the lighters stolen from Markham Street had been of an unusual design, and we were able to get a photograph of a similar model. This picture appeared in the London evening papers on November 23 and in the nationals next day.

That same morning, a soldier in the Welsh Guards, stationed at Pirbright Camp in Surrey, told a policeman that he had seen another Guardsman, named Dowdall, with a cigarette lighter just like the one in the papers.

Detective Sergeant Simmons of the Surrey Constabulary went at once to the camp, where he learned that Guardsman Michael Dowdall was confined to the Medical Quarters suffering from scabies. Simmons saw him and asked him about the lighter. Dowdall said he'd never had one like it. Simmons then telephoned Chief Inspector Acott, and told him that Dowdall closely resembled the description of Mick.

At Acott's request, Simmons continued to question Dowdall, who finally admitted having had such a cigarette lighter. He bought it, he said, from an unknown man on Waterloo Station just before catching his train back to Pirbright on the 21st: but, when he saw the photograph in the paper, he threw it into some long grass at the camp, for fear of being charged with receiving stolen property.

Simmons found the lighter in the grass just where Dowdall said he had thrown it. Meanwhile, Acott was checking the trains from Waterloo and found that someone leaving Markham Street at 6:15 would have had no difficulty in getting back to Pirbright for a nine o'clock parade. He told Simmons to keep Dowdall well guarded, collected a fingerprint man and hurried down to Pirbright. Dowdall's fingerprints were taken. And we had Mick at last.

A search of the camp produced several of the stolen items. Confronted with them, Dowdall made a statement admitting everything, including the killing of Veronica Murray and the attempted murder of the woman in Fulham. In due course, he was tried for murder: but he was found to be suffering from diminished responsibility, convicted of manslaughter and sentenced to life imprisonment.

The Fulham woman's description had proved accurate enough, except that he was shorter and younger—eighteen years old, not twenty-seven: and his accent wasn't Irish. With the advantage of hindsight, our failure to interpret the principal clue seems absurd. Dowdall himself explained it. His shoes, he said, had been repaired by a drummer in his regiment. He didn't know why this amateur cobbler had hammered nails so uncomfortably into the soles. Presumably it was just a whim. What they stood for, of course, was *Welsh Guards*.

CHAPTER 14
In Full Possession of His Senses

The case of Michael Dowdall is remembered, I suppose, only by the people he robbed or attacked and by the police who were involved in the hunt for him. There is another divisional murder case, however, which may be worth recalling both for its curious features and because its outline is so well known—to criminologists at least. The investigating officer was "Flaps" Daws, whom I'd just put in charge of the C.I.D. in "T" Division. This case was stranger than anything he'd seen in those East Anglian fens, and, before it was over, it took him farther afield.

The story began, as far as Daws was concerned (though its real beginning, one might say, was almost thirty years earlier), on February 14, 1954. An elderly woman by the name of Lady Menzies and her married daughter, Vera Chesney, ran an old people's home in a big house at Ealing. Their eighteen-year-old housemaid, Eileen Thorpe, was usually woken by Lady Menzies at 6:30 in the morning, but that day she slept on until 7:45. She then got up, and found Lady Menzies' bedroom which was on the ground floor, empty except for the two Chow dogs who always slept there. A couch looked as if it had been slept on and the electric fire was burning, so Eileen assumed that Lady Menzies was attending to the residents upstairs. Shortly afterwards, she found that Mrs. Chesney's room was empty too, though again the bedclothes were rumpled.

Eileen made breakfast for the nineteen residents. None of them, apparently, had seen Lady Menzies or Mrs. Chesney.

When she had finished washing up, she looked in again at Lady Menzies' room, and this time noticed a key lying on the tea-tray. Meanwhile, two ambulance men arrived with a new resident for the home. They joined Eileen in a search for the missing women, and, when they could find no trace of them, agreed to inform the police. An hour or so later, two plain-clothes officers came, made a note in their books and left.

Vera Chesney's adopted daughter, Mrs. Trull, who lived nearby, was told what had happened and came round to help. After luncheon, she and Eileen Thorpe made another inspection of Lady Menzies' room. Mrs. Trull was struck by the fact that it was the couch which had apparently been slept on, not the larger sofa near the window which Lady Menzies normally used as a bed. They went up to Mrs. Chesney's room. The bed, Mrs. Trull thought, though certainly disturbed had been disturbed too neatly: and she noticed that Mrs. Chesney's clothes and handbag were all still in the room.

Another nearby relation, Miss McNeish, was summoned, and the three of them made a more thorough inspection of the whole house. They found that the first-floor bathroom was locked, and there was no key in the lock.

At this juncture, Superintendent Daws arrived. He glanced round and went into the garden, while Eileen and Mrs. Trull began the washing up. It suddenly occurred to Mrs. Trull that the key in Lady Menzies' room might belong to the locked bathroom. They took it, and tried it, and it fitted. They opened the door.

Eileen let out a piercing scream, which brought Daws running from the garden.

Mrs. Chesney was lying dead in the bath, wearing a black nightdress and a pink woollen cardigan. The lower part of her clothing was damp, and her hair wet and soapy, but there was no water in the bath itself, though the plug was in. There was no towel in the bathroom.

188

While he was still absorbing these details, Daws was told that Miss McNeish had found another corpse downstairs. He locked the bathroom, and went down to inspect the body of Lady Menzies. She lay on the floor in a back sitting room, concealed under a pile of chair covers and cushions. On her right leg she wore a stocking, but her left leg was bare. Another stocking and a blue belt were tied tightly round her neck. A tartan scarf was wrapped about her head. There were splashes of blood on the wall and furniture.

Daws followed a trail of blood marks through the hall and into the room where Lady Menzies usually slept. He found evidence there of a fierce struggle. He also discovered a broken and bloody metal coffeepot.

The murder of Lady Menzies wasn't difficult to reconstruct. She had been attacked first in the hall and then in her room, bludgeoned with the coffeepot and finally strangled to death. For a woman of seventy-three, she had put up a tremendous fight. There were blood splashes all over the place—on the floor, but the carpet covering them was free of blood; on the wall behind a bookcase, but there was no blood on the books of the case. The murderer had tidied up the room very carefully, with the object, presumably, of postponing discovery. He had taken the body into the back sitting room where it was less likely to be found later than if he had left it in the bedroom, and he had concealed it from anyone just glancing in; successfully concealed it, for Miss McNeish hadn't been the first person to look into the room that morning. Daws would have been surprised to find any fingerprints on the coffeepot. Nor were there any; it had been wiped clean. The murderer, he decided, must be a man of some cunning and resource.

Eileen had found the back door into the garden unlocked and unbolted, so the murderer had presumably gone out that way: but he couldn't have come in through that door, unless he had been let in or was already inside before it was bolted at 10 P.M. While Daws was considering this problem, he found a small screw on the floor of the back sitting room beside the french windows. These windows, which opened onto the garden, seemed to be locked on the inside, but the screw had evidently fallen from the latch. Daws tried the handle and found that the latch was useless; the windows were kept shut only by a large stone outside. He replaced the screw, went into the garden, removed the stone and pulled the french windows. They opened at a touch—and the screw from the latch lay once more on the carpet inside.

The murderer, Daws thought, had probably known about the latch in advance; a theory which was supported, in true Sherlock Holmes fashion, by the behaviour of Lady Menzies' dogs in the nighttime. They growled and barked and tried to bite Daws. Eileen said they always behaved towards strangers in this way, and that she was a light sleeper and would certainly have heard if there had been any barking in the night.

Mrs. Chesney's death was less easy to reconstruct. She had been a heavy secret drinker and might conceivably have been trying to wash her hair in the bath when she fell over and was drowned; a defective plug accounted for the lack of water. But there was no getting round the fact that the bathroom door had been locked and the key taken downstairs.

Daws quickly decided that the man he most wanted to see was Mrs. Chesney's husband, Ronald, who had called at the house a couple of weeks earlier and been greeted by the dogs, so several witnesses said, as a friend. Mrs. Chesney had also been heard to say that her husband was asking for a divorce, so he could marry a German girl, but she had told him she would never agree to it, both because she was a Catholic and because she was determined that no German woman should be helped to obtain a passport by any action of hers. Indeed, Mrs. Chesney had apparently said that she was frightened her husband might kill her. Daws learned that Chesney would benefit from his wife's death to the tune of £10,000.

And there was more. Chesney proved to be well known to the police. His real name was John Donald Merrett—which rang a very loud bell with any student of famous crimes. He had been convicted in 1927 of uttering forged cheques on his mother's account, but a Scottish verdict of "Not Proven" was given to the simultaneous charge that he had murdered his mother.

Proven the charge may not have been, but few people today can have any serious doubt that he was guilty: that he shot his mother through the head with an automatic pistol. The police work seems to have been notable for its inefficiency. The pistol was never even tested for fingerprints. Mrs. Merrett had been in the middle of writing a letter when she died, an ordinary chatty letter complaining about a servant—which seems improbable behaviour for someone on the point of suicide: but the letter was never even produced in evidence. The main reason for Merrett's acquittal, however, seems to have been the evidence for the Defence given by Bernard Spilsbury and Robert Churchill. This formidable combination of expert witnesses simply bulldozed aside any other considerations, though the scientific evidence was, in fact, dubious at the very least. Which is a useful warning against deferring too readily to experts, however distinguished.

Since then, Merrett's career had been checkered. He was only seventeen-and-a-half when he killed his mother. During his eight months imprisonment for forgery, an old friend of his mother, Mrs. Mary Bonnar, visited him several times. When he came out, he lived at her home in Hastings for a short while, and then eloped with her daughter Vera. Within a month, Vera was back with her mother and Merrett was back in prison, convicted of obtaining goods by false pretences.

At the age of twenty-one, he inherited £50,000 from his

grandfather. He was persuaded to settle £8400 on his wife—
but the capital was to revert to him if she died. Merrett soon
spent the rest of his legacy and returned to crime; he lived by
stealing, blackmail, fraud, and smuggling. Like many other
criminals, he had quite a respectable war. He served with the
Navy in the Mediterranean and became a Lieutenant Commander, RNVR though by all accounts he was ready, even
then, to make a little illegal money on the side.

Afterwards, he went back to crime again and back to prison.
Released from a British gaol, he devoted himself to the black
market in Germany, while his wife and her mother ran the
old people's home in Ealing. For some reason, Mrs. Bonnar
now called herself Lady Menzies: and no one, including the
coroner who presided at her inquest, was so impolite as to question the title.

Chesney's description was now issued to the Press and circulated to all police stations. He was a huge man with a beard
and a bulbous drooping nose: his resemblance to a strip-cartoon
pirate was increased by his habit of wearing a single gold earring. A port warning was sent out, with a note that he had
sailed from Harwich to the Hook of Holland on February 4,
less than a week before the murders, but was believed to have
returned later. We knew about this departure because he had
gone out of his way to attract attention. Flamboyant with his
beard and gold earring, he had bumped into a policeman at
the barrier and made jokes to the Immigration Officer about it.

A man looking very much like him, but without the earring,
had been seen in Ealing, carrying a briefcase, shortly after 6
P.M. on February 10. A motorist who thought he recognised
Chesney had slowed down to give him a lift, but the pedestrian
turned his head away and walked quickly on. Later that same
day, a man answering Chesney's description was seen by a
woman near Lady Menzies' house. Still later, at 1:20 A.M., a
neighbour saw a man carrying a bag. Between these times, two

of the old people in the house had heard unusual noises. One heard water running; he glanced at his watch, which said 12:25. The other told Superintendent Daws that Lady Menzies had looked in at 12:35 to see if he was all right, and that a few minutes later he heard an exclamation, "Oh!" followed by a thud somewhere on the ground floor.

The events of the night were now becoming clearer, and very macabre they were. Eileen Thorpe had gone to bed at ten, and immediately afterwards heard Mrs. Chesney say good night to Lady Menzies and go upstairs. At ten past ten Mrs. Trull had left by the front door and heard Lady Menzies bolt it after her. About 10:30 the murderer must have entered the garden through a broken fence, pulled the french windows open, and gone upstairs to Mrs. Chesney's room. He plied her with drink, forced her into the bathroom with his hand over her mouth, and held her head under the water until she drowned. A small abrasion on her left cheek and some slight bruising on each elbow were the only signs of violence. When she was dead, the murderer had soaped her hair, wiped the bathroom clean of fingerprints with a towel and taken the towel to her room. Leaving the light on in her room, he then crept down the stairs.

Lady Menzies must have seen him—and he saw her. He realised that he would have to kill her too. He knocked her down, and she fell with a thud. She escaped into her room, but he followed and hit her with the coffeepot. She fought back fiercely, there was blood under her fingernails. Finally he strangled her.

He took the body into the back sitting room and covered it up. Then he tidied Lady Menzies' room, wiping away all his fingerprints, went upstairs and washed his hands, leaving traces of watery blood in the basin. He returned to Mrs. Chesney's room and made the bed look as though it had been slept in, and in doing so left faint blood smears on the sheets. He locked the bathroom door and took the key downstairs. Since her mother had so obviously been murdered, there was no longer any point in trying to make Mrs. Chesney's death look like an accident. His only concern now was to delay discovery of the bodies as long as possible.

Chesney, we learned, had lately been calling himself Milner; but, Chesney or Milner, he had disappeared. He must have read about himself in the papers, however, and decided that he had little hope of permanently evading capture. On February 15, at teatime, he telephoned his solicitor, a Mr. Clarke of Hastings, from Cologne, saying that he had just read of his wife's death and asking Clarke to obtain the settlement funds. Chesney agreed to send a letter of authority, and asked his solicitor to tell the police he would be returning to England in a day or two and would see them then.

Mr. Clarke passed this message on to the Hastings police, who immediately telephoned Scotland Yard. We communicated with the German police through Interpol. And next day Chesney was found in a wood near Cologne, shot dead with a revolver by his side—just as his mother had been twenty-seven years before.

This was the end of the hunt but not of the case. I sent Daws and another officer who spoke German to Cologne, to see the body and to collect Chesney's belongings. As well as hair and blood samples, he brought back Chesney's forearms, because they had bruises and scratch marks on them.

Following Clarke's advice, Chesney had written to the Public Trustee, authorising release of the settlement fund. He sent a covering letter to the solicitor: "On receipt please arrange to transfer the total amount, less £300 which I should like you to retain for me, to Miss Sonja Winnikes of Duren, Germany, in whose favour you already have a will. With regards to my wife's death, I need hardly tell you I am innocent but with my past record, things will probably be sticky for me. . . ."

The following day, he wrote a second letter:

Dear Clarke,

Since writing you yesterday, I have given the matter of my future much thought and I realise that although innocent, I haven't the chance of the proverbial snowball in Hades of getting out of the mess.

I have seen so much of prisons I have no wish to return there even for a day and the prospect of being hanged appeals to me even less.

I assure you that the way I shall have taken to get out of it all may seem cowardly—but it nevertheless *does* require some courage. I know too it will probably be taken to indicate my guilt. This is, however, *not* the case. I can only hope that the police eventually do find the doer of the deed.

I wish only to make sure that Miss Sonja Winnikes gets *everything* to which I am heir and which falls due to me i.e. the settlement money—some £10,000 and the carpets, silver and chest of drawers at 22, Montepelier Road, Ealing.

Please get in touch with her when you receive this letter and act for her in her best interests.

Despite all appearances to the contrary, I am in full possession of all my senses and do what I do after careful deliberation . . .

Yours truly,
John D. Milner

He evidently feared that his lady friend would not receive the settlement money if it were proved that he had murdered his wife: and he was quite right—it would be forfeited to the Crown. He seems to have thought that his protestation of innocence, followed by suicide, would render such proof impossible: but in this he was wrong. A coroner's jury would still have to decide whether it was he who had committed the murder, so Daws continued the investigation with as much zeal as though the principal suspect were still alive.

There was, in fact, no shortage of evidence. Statements were taken from six people who, at various times, had heard Chesney say that his wife would be worth more to him dead than alive. When he was in Wandsworth Prison he had told his cellmates that he would pay anyone £1000 to kill her. They thought it was a joke, but, after their release, Chesney repeated the offer and obviously meant business.

Laboriously, his alibi was broken down. His passport in the name of Milner had no record of any return to England at the time of the murder: but Daws eventually discovered that he had obtained another passport under another name. Chesney had apparently destroyed this telltale document before killing himself, but the Passport Office was able to produce the application form.

He had flown from Amsterdam to London on February 10, and returned on the morning of February 11—before the bodies of his victims had even been discovered. Witnesses were found who had seen him on the aeroplane and in the airport bus; they identified his photograph.

At Scotland Yard our scientists examined the specimens which Daws had brought back. Under Chesney's fingernails they found some fibres of bright pink wool, similar to the material of his wife's cardigan. But Chesney's own cardigan betrayed him even more conclusively; on it were dog hairs, similar to those of Lady Menzies' two Chows; a bloodstained white human hair, similar to Lady Menzies' own; a small tuft of blue wool, similar to her cardigan; and a little clump of blood-encrusted fibres similar to those in the tartan scarf round Lady Menzies' head.

At the inquest, Mr. Clarke gave evidence but claimed privilege on behalf of his client, Miss Sonja Winnikes, who, he said, had "inherited the privilege which formerly vested in Chesney"; a curious doctrine. She inherited little else. The jury found that Chesney had committed both murders, and the settlement fund went to the Crown.

Ronald Chesney, alias John Donald Merrett alias John D. Milner, was a classic example of the incorrigible criminal at his nastiest and most dangerous. Perhaps he loved Sonja Winnikes: but I find it difficult to believe he ever really loved anyone except himself. As he said, he was in full possession of all his senses, and did what he did after careful consideration. He has been described, quite rightly in my view, as one of the strongest arguments for retaining capital punishment.

CHAPTER 15

Ordeal of a Girl Guide

Chesney escaped the gallows, and so, for another reason, did an even more unpleasant and dangerous murderer a few years later.

The story began on Friday, September 9, 1960. An eleven-year-old girl had been to a Girl Guide meeting. Her mother had said goodbye to her at twenty past seven, when she set off on her bicycle for the Church Hall, about three miles away. She was supposed to be back by ten.

But she wasn't. Her mother became increasingly worried and, before long, told the police. A search party was organised: but in vain. The hours ticked by.

Then at 1:20 A.M. there was a sound at the back door. The girl's mother turned—and saw her daughter, face bloody, lips swollen, eyes full of fear and shock. The child was panting and gasping with terror. The mother very sensibly didn't try to question her; it was quite obvious—only too obvious indeed—that something very unpleasant had happened to her.

When the child had slept and some of the shock had worn off, a woman detective constable talked to her, very gently and patiently. And so the story emerged.

After the Guide meeting, the Patrol Leaders had stayed behind for a discussion, and the girl had waited for one of them so that they could cycle home together. A few more minutes were wasted in trying to mend a rear light which wouldn't work, but eventually they set off. The Patrol Leader took the turning which led to her home, leaving the younger girl to cycle the last mile alone.

She was stopped by a man who was standing beside a car. "I'm a police officer," he said. "There have been some bikes stolen round here and yours looks like one of them. Please get into the car and leave your bike over there behind that tree."

He then asked her where she lived and said he'd take her home before going on to the police station. He produced a revolver from his pocket, showed it to her and told her it was loaded.

They drove several miles and turned into a lane. There he attacked her, very savagely, and committed a series of sexual assaults. At one point, with his hands round her throat, he almost strangled her, only releasing his grip when she was on the point of losing consciousness. Afterwards he took her quite close to her home and allowed her to leave the car.

The policewoman pieced together a description, notably that the man had a scar on the side of his face. The girl remembered quite a lot about the car; beside the front seat, she said, there was a pocket with two packets of sweets in it. The man had offered her one. She ate it, and it had tasted of peppermint.

From the girl's description, the car seemed to be a black Vauxhall. The police took her to a secondhand car dealer's, where she identified the actual make; it was almost certainly a Vauxhall Velox or Wyvern. Details of the crime, of the man with the scarred face and of the car were circulated to every police force in the country.

The Sunday newspapers gave the story considerable publicity, and, as usual, the police received a flood of letters making suggestions and offering advice. One woman wrote to tell me that her husband, whom she described as a sexual maniac, had obviously committed this crime. He owned a Luger pistol, she said, drove a Vauxhall car and had convictions for just this type of offence. All of which proved on investigation to be absolutely true: but unfortunately he had a cast-iron alibi for the night in question.

Meanwhile, the girl was taken on a tour of the district, but, though her bicycle had been found just where she said it would be, and she was able to recognise several landmarks from her terrifying journey, she couldn't find the lane where the attack itself had occurred. She was shown photographs of known sexual criminals, but identified none of them.

House to house enquiries were made throughout the neighbourhood, and roads were watched over quite long periods. All to no avail. On November 10, Detective Chief Superintendent Lewis, who was in charge of the C.I.D. in No. 1 District, reported that every effort to find the man had so far proved fruitless.

But I'd already had even more disturbing news. Nearly a fortnight earlier, Deputy Commander Spooner told me that another Girl Guide had failed to come home after a Guide meeting. Her name was Brenda Nash, she was twelve years old and she lived at Heston in Middlesex, not far from the scene of the first rape. And she was still missing.

The facts were ominously similar. On that Friday evening there had been a Girl Guide Divisional First Aid Contest held at a school in Heston. The meeting was over at 9:20 P.M. Brenda Nash and two friends left together on foot. They bought a bag of chips at a fish-and-chip shop, and at five minutes past ten they parted at a place called Armytage Road. Brenda was only a quarter of a mile from her home.

When she didn't arrive, her parents went out and looked for her themselves, and they called at the homes of the other two Guides. At 1:20 they informed the police.

The duty officer organised a search which went on through the night. By seven o'clock next morning all available police officers in adjoining divisions had been brought into the hunt.

There were soon two hundred policemen actively looking for Brenda Nash, plus six dogs and their handlers, and fifty Scots and Irish guardsmen from nearby depots.

Parks, commons, farms, golf courses and gravel pits were searched. On Sunday two hundred civilian volunteers joined in, mostly from the estate where Brenda lived. A week later, 1650 members of the Middlesex Civil Defence Corps combed the Laleham, Shepperton, and Ashford districts. Officers of the Thames division dragged the appropriate parts of five rivers, four miles of the Grand Junction canal and all the gravel pits in the vicinity. Some of these were too deep for dragging, and on a bitterly cold November day 107 members of the British Sub-aqua Club searched several flooded gravel pits. The Chief Constable of Berkshire, who was proud of his frogmen, lent us a team of five. They worked every day between November 28 and December 9. Other officers, meanwhile, searched the lofts, drains, and sewers of more than six hundred houses.

There was no need to appeal for public co-operation. Everyone was anxious to help. During the house-to-house enquiries, a Mr. Kerr, who lived not far from Brenda Nash's home, said that, while he was standing at his garden gate on the night of her disappearance, he had glimpsed a dark-haired man come out of an alley and get into a black Vauxhall car. The car had gone into Cranford Lane and turned left: a few minutes later it had passed him again, again gone into Cranford Lane and again turned left. But he hadn't seen the man clearly enough to be able to identify him.

A couple of weeks later, a Mrs. Mary Barker told the detective who called on her that, at about 10:10 P.M. on the night of Brenda's disappearance, she had noticed a black Vauxhall (she recognised the make and year because her husband had one just like it) being driven slowly along Cranford Lane. It had stopped, she said, at the junction with Armytage Road; and it was still there when she passed by on her way home.

All she remembered about the driver was that he had dark hair.

Spooner came to my office and told me he thought we ought to trace and interview every owner of a black Vauxhall registered with the Middlesex and Surrey County Councils between 1951 and 1954.

"How many are there?" I asked.

"Five thousand, two hundred and seventy-seven," he replied.

"In that case," I said, "the sooner we get started the better."

Within a week, the County Councils had supplied a complete list. And the interviews began.

On November 24 it was the turn of a man named Arthur Albert Jones. His car matched the description—and he had a scar on the side of his face and was dark-haired. The detective who examined the car found a packet of peppermints in the glove compartment on the passenger side. Asked if he always carried peppermints in his car, Jones said "Yes."

He was asked to account for his movements on the two vital nights, September 9 and October 28. On both these dates, he said, he had been visiting his sister-in-law at Beckenham in Kent. His wife confirmed this statement, and so did the sister-in-law when she was interviewed the following day. Jones had been at her home, she insisted, on the two nights in question.

So, for the moment, Arthur Albert Jones was ruled out and no further enquiries were made about him.

On December 11, three little boys were playing on a common near the small village of Yateley in Hampshire. They wandered into a copse, and suddenly saw the body of a girl lying in the long grass. She was dressed in Guide uniform.

The body was carefully guarded but left untouched until late that afternoon when Detective Chief Superintendent Jones of the Hampshire Constabulary arrived, together with Detective Chief Superintendent Lewis and Superintendent Hixson of the Metropolitan Police. On the girl's blouse they saw the words *5th Heston*. It was Brenda Nash, and she had been strangled.

The murder investigation was now a matter for the Hampshire County Constabulary. The Chief Constable discussed the situation with me, and we agreed that Chief Superintendent Jones should be in charge, while Superintendent Hixson continued the enquiries in the Metropolitan area, and that Chief Superintendent Lewis would act as co-ordinating officer between the two forces. This arrangement worked well enough, but the necessity for it was undoubtedly awkward; a good example of the disadvantages entailed in not having a national detective force.

Detective Superintendent Salter of the Metropolitan Police Laboratory went down and made a detailed examination of the site. Just where the body had been lying, he found a small piece of gold coloured chain. It would have been under the girl's shoulders.

The day after the discovery of the body, a young woman named Lesley Carruthers walked into the West Hampstead Police Station. She said that about the time when Brenda Nash had disappeared she was working for a West End hairdresser. One morning another employee, a girl called Christine Eldridge, had remarked that her uncle fitted the description of the man the police were looking for. And she said that this uncle had been to see her mother and asked her to give him an alibi for the night of the twenty-eighth. He had been out with a woman that night, he said, not his wife, and he was afraid of having to tell the police about her. Christine's mother agreed to give him the alibi. His name was Arthur Albert Jones.

On December 28 Jones was taken to Twickenham Police Station for questioning, and his car was subjected to a thorough examination. A rug and a blanket were found in it, similar to those which had been described by the girl who had been raped as being in her assailant's car. The following day, Jones made a long statement. He insisted that on September 9 and October 28 he had been staying with his sister-in-law, Mrs. Eldridge, at Beckenham. On the former occasion he was accompanied by his wife and son, on the latter he had been alone. His memory wasn't very good, he said, but he remembered the date because he had gone specially to repair Mrs. Eldridge's vacuum cleaner. He denied having talked to her before she was interviewed by the police.

What he didn't know was that she had now been seen by the police again: and this time had said she wasn't certain any longer that her brother-in-law had been with her on those two dates. But he and his wife had come to see her, she said, the night before her first interview with the police. They had told her the police would be asking questions about his movements and would probably ask whether he sucked peppermints.

Clearly the investigation had now reached a critical point. None of us had any doubt that the two crimes had been committed by the same man. When we discussed the case, I agreed that there was sufficient evidence to charge Jones with the offence committed within the Metropolitan Police District. On December 30 he was charged with the rape of the Girl Guide.

His house was searched, and in his son's bedroom the police found a small box containing a length of yellow metal chain: and in a drawer there was another separate piece of the same chain.

Mrs. Eldridge made two more statements. She now admitted having agreed to a request by Mr. and Mrs. Jones that she should give her brother-in-law a false alibi, and that she had confided this to her daughter Christine. Christine was interviewed too, and confirmed what she had told her friend at the hairdresser's.

Jones then made another statement. He admitted that his former alibis were an invention. The truth was, he said, that on September 9 he had driven to Holland Park, met a prostitute, gone with her to her flat and afterwards to a club. When they got there, the girl told him that the man who "looked after her" had arrived and that Jones had better leave. He went back to his car and drove home, stopping at a restaurant on the way to have a meal. He got home at 12:30 A.M.

On October 28, he said, he had again driven to the West End, where he spent some time looking at the photographs exhibited outside various strip clubs. He then drove to Notting Hill Underground Station, picked up a prostitute and took her to a quiet cul-de-sac off the Bayswater Road. Afterwards he set off home, but the weather was foggy and his car broke down twice. He got home at 2 A.M.

The two alibis seemed curiously similar.

At Feltham Magistrate's Court Jones was remanded to Brixton Prison. He was taken back to Twickenham Police Station first, however, and there, within the hearing of a detective sergeant, he had a conversation with his wife. Mrs. Jones asked him what he had done with his revolver. He said he couldn't remember. She urged him to tell the truth to Mr. Matthissen, his solicitor, and he said he meant to but couldn't remember what had happened. Then he burst into tears.

When his wife had gone, he said to the sergeant: "These terrible things I've done are getting on my nerves. I want to tell somebody about it now, but I've promised my wife I will only tell Mr. Matthissen what happened when I see him next week in Brixton. I don't want to break that promise, because we've been married a long time."

Jones was tried at the Old Bailey on March 7. The jury took nearly three hours to find him guilty. Mr. Justice Hilbery sentenced him to fourteen years imprisonment. He appealed, and the appeal was dismissed. He began to serve his sentence at Wandsworth Prison.

But the story wasn't over. There was another prisoner there called Roberts. One day a prison officer overheard Roberts telling some of his fellow prisoners that he had met Jones before at Brixton, when they were both on remand: and that while he "walked round" with Jones they talked about their cases. Jones had said he was charged with rape but didn't think the police could make it stick. Roberts, who had heard about Brenda Nash, asked Jones if he was charged with the murder as well. Jones said he wasn't, and added that the police didn't have enough evidence. He then gave a peculiar smile and said "I did it."

The prison officer reported this conversation to the governor, and the police were immediately informed. Roberts made a statement, repeating in full what he had told the other prisoners.

At the same time, some more evidence had come to light. A Mr. Frederick Holloway came forward to say that Jones' photograph, which had appeared in the papers during the trial, strongly resembled a man whom he'd seen standing at a road junction about three hundred yards from Brenda Nash's home some twenty minutes before she parted from her friends that night. Mr. Holloway had made a statement on October 30 about seeing this man, but he hadn't then been able to identify the man.

With these new facts before him, the Director of Public Prosecutions ordered that an identification parade should be held. It was attended not only by Mr. Holloway but also Mr. Cuthbert Wakefield, who had seen a man in a Vauxhall not far from the spot where Brenda Nash disappeared and very close to the time.

Both witnesses picked out Arthur Albert Jones.

After a conference with the D.P.P., Chief Superintendent Jones of the Hampshire Constabulary went to Wandsworth Prison and there charged Jones with the murder of Brenda Nash.

The second trial took place at the Old Bailey on June 12.

It lasted a week, but this time the jury were out for only seven minutes before returning a verdict of guilty. Mr. Justice Sachs passed sentence.

"Arthur Albert Jones," he said, "you have been found guilty now of two crimes evil to a degree beyond all adjectives, and it is proper that you should serve your sentence for the first crime and that neither as a matter of fact nor of appearance should it cease to be operative. In those circumstances I pass upon you the sentence according to statute, that you be sentenced to imprisonment for life. And for the protection of the public, I think firstly that it should be a sentence to commence upon the expiration of your existing sentence, and secondly that it would be lamentable indeed if upon the second sentence you do not serve a far longer time than upon the first."

Jones appealed against conviction and against sentence.

The main ground of the appeal against conviction was that the Judge had misdirected the jury as to the degree of similarity between the piece of gold coloured chain found under Brenda Nash's body and the chains discovered by the police in Jones' home, and on the inferences which should be drawn from this evidence. The complaint about the sentence was that the Judge had failed to abide by Section 9(1) of the Homicide Act 1957 which provided that in cases of non-capital murder "the sentence should be one of imprisonment for life."

Neither ground of appeal found favour with the Court of Criminal Appeal, and the case went to the House of Lords, where it fared no better. Their Lordships said that there had been no misdirection over the exhibits. If the life sentence had been made concurrent rather than consecutive, they said, there would have been no practical difference. Since making the sentence consecutive had, therefore, no effect, it was undesirable: but since the result was the same in either event, they saw no reason to allow the appeal. So it was dismissed.

This whole affair of the second trial was oddly reminiscent

of a similar case which took place a quarter of a century before. In 1937 a ten-year-old girl by the name of Mona Tinsley disappeared on her way home from school. Frederick Nodder, a former lodger of the Tinsleys, was in due course arrested and charged with taking Mona away by fraud. When he appeared in the dock at Birmingham Assizes, there was still no trace of the girl, and he was sentenced to seven years' penal servitude. But the police, who were convinced that Nodder had murdered the child, continued to drag rivers and canals: and, a few weeks later, their determination was rewarded. The body of Mona Tinsley was retrieved from the River Idle. Nodder was brought from prison to Nottingham Assizes, charged with murder, found guilty and executed.

I cannot help feeling that the relationship of the two sentences was more just—more evidently just—in the case of Nodder than it could be in Jones' case, when the death penalty was no longer available.

CHAPTER 16

The Most Dangerous Animals

Once a month the Chief Superintendent in charge of the Flying Squad used to prepare a list of all the robberies which had taken place in the Metropolitan Police District: and I made sure it was put on my desk as soon as the figures were available. Robbery, housebreaking, and burglary—these are the crimes which really affect the public. Murder is more sensational but much less important; it touches only a handful of people, and, though there are exceptions—the Potters Bar case was one—murder tends to be a domestic crime and therefore, unlike theft, not something liable at any moment to hurt ordinary innocent citizens.

Robbery, however (which means theft accompanied by violence or the threat of violence), may itself involve a risk of murder: and this is a risk which does seriously endanger innocent citizens and policemen in the course of their duty. I've never heard of a detective being poisoned by a wife-murderer: but many policemen have been shot by robbers. This is why I thought the distinction drawn by the Homicide Act 1957 between capital and non-capital murders was a perfectly sensible one. Armed and violent thieves are the most dangerous animals in the metropolitan jungle. They are the criminals I wanted most of all to discourage.

Their activities tend to go in cycles; that is, they concentrate on one sort of theft until mounting opposition renders it too dangerous; whereupon they move on to something else;

and then to something else again, until their original victims have grown slack enough to invite another assault.

Banks have always been favourite targets. What could be more profitable to steal than cash? A few years ago, the fashion was for breaking into strong rooms during the weekend, usually by tunnelling through from adjoining premises. The safes and locks and alarms were often extraordinarily primitive, and most banks didn't regard it as worthwhile to employ watchmen. Bank security is far from perfect even today, but modern security devices have been widely installed and there's more awareness of vulnerability.

As the banks grew more worried and the profits from breaking into them correspondingly hazardous to earn, the fashionable technique switched to hold-ups during banking hours, and to wage-snatches as the money was carried from the banks on payday. A wage-snatch in the street may look to bystanders like a sudden act of spontaneous violence, but in fact it's usually the climax to weeks of careful preparation and observation; weeks in which the gang will have familiarised themselves with the faces and habits of the wage-collectors, with routes and vehicles customarily employed, and with avenues of escape for use after the assault.

In the spring of 1962 wage-snatches had become so frequent in one part of London that we mounted a massive counter-attack. Every Thursday and Friday between 9 A.M. and 6 P.M. all our available men, both uniformed and plain-clothes, on foot and in cars, were concentrated on the area. In particular, Aids-to-C.I.D.—that is, volunteers from the uniformed branch who are working temporarily in plain-clothes, usually because they hope to join the C.I.D. later—kept watch in the likeliest places. Within three months the number of wage-snatches had been halved: and after two more months the problem had ceased to be urgent. Of course, we couldn't keep it up; the strain on our resources of manpower was far too great.

The effectiveness of our tactics on that occasion shows what could be done if the police had all the men they need. In the foreseeable future, they are never, I suppose, likely to have enough men. The Commissioner, Sir Joseph Simpson, reckoned that the current strength of the Metropolitan Police is 5000 or 6000 below the minimum really required: and some people would put the figure considerably higher. Given a shortage of manpower, the question is: How to deploy the available men most effectively? This is a much argued subject. One school of thought would like a big increase in motor patrols: another wants more uniformed men on the streets: a third would increase the proportion of plain-clothes detectives. And to each argument there is a counterargument: prowl cars can't pick up information; an increase in men on the beat is only worthwhile if the streets can be flooded with them; plain-clothes officers don't have the same contact with the public. I won't attempt to adjudicate; bickering between the C.I.D. and the uniformed branch has too often been an unnecessary cause of friction in British police forces.

In our drive against wage-snatches we tried to educate, as well as protect, the businessmen whose money was at risk. We did a good deal of propaganda. We urged them to vary the time and route of collection, and, if possible, not to have large sums of money carried through the streets by an old man and a boy. These lessons were partially absorbed: but some people, of course, will never learn.

The crooks, meanwhile, switched techniques again, and began kidnapping managers of shops and stealing their keys. This, in turn, has led to better habits of key-security. And so the cycle continues.

Month by month, however, during my latter years at the Yard, I saw the total number of robberies increasing, and the arrogance and self-confidence of professional thieves growing too. Worse still, there was a small but significant increase in the use of guns.

What this can mean both to the police and to the public was spectacularly illustrated one autumn day in 1955.

Just before lunch, two men walked into a jeweller's shop in Earl's Court. The taller of the two wore a thick black false moustache: the other had a dark green scarf over the lower part of his face. Both produced revolvers.

"It's a stick-up," announced the taller man, while his companion shut and bolted the door.

The only other people in the shop were the proprietor, Mr. Drew, and two male assistants. The assistants were told to stand facing the wall. One of them, too surprised to move, was prompted with a blow on the head from a revolver.

Mr. Drew was made to open the safe at the back of the shop. While the taller man ransacked it, the other began looting the display counter and showcase.

At that moment, two customers tried to enter. Their names were Sheila Stewardson and Marion Ford, and they worked as ticket sorters in the nearby Underground station. One of them wanted a watch repaired.

"It must be shut for lunch," said Sheila, when the door wouldn't open. But Marion knew the shop was normally open at lunchtime, and thought the door must be stuck. So they banged and kicked it, and then peered through the curtains. They saw a man by the safe holding a gun.

Marion ran towards the butcher's shop next door to give the alarm, but one of the gunmen had noticed them. "Quick, we've been spotted," he said.

"Lie down on the floor, all of you," ordered the taller man. They obeyed. He scooped up some loose jewellery from a shelf, and then the two men backed out of the shop, turned and ran across the road to a Rover 90, which started up as soon as they appeared. They scrambled in and drove off—but not before

Sheila Stewardson and Marion Ford had made a note of the registration number, PXP 804.

Like the efficient and sensible girls they were, they telephoned Scotland Yard from a call box: and, within a minute or so, a message to all cars was being sent out from the Information Room.

It was heard by the occupants of another Rover, Detective Sergeants Chambers (the same one who four years later jumped on Podola) and Cooke of the Flying Squad and their driver, Police Constable Cameron, just as they were crossing the Serpentine. They had barely heard the message when they saw PXP 804 race past them, heading north. Cameron wrenched their car round and they set off in pursuit, other cars giving way to the clamour of the police gong.

They caught up with their quarry at one of the park gates, where the bandits had been stopped by a traffic jam. Chambers and Cooke jumped out and ran towards the bandit car, one on either side. The driver's window was open. Cooke reached through and grasped the steering wheel. Just then there was a break in the traffic. The driver accelerated. Cooke was knocked off his feet and into the path of oncoming traffic; he was lucky not to have been badly hurt.

Chambers ran back to the Flying Squad car and resumed the pursuit. Still in the park, PXP 804 feinted as though to go out at Marble Arch, and then swung round to the south. Traffic was heavy, but Cameron touched 70 m.p.h., and still couldn't catch the bandits up. They went out through Grosvenor Gate into Park Lane. Here the traffic slowed them to a crawl, and now the two cars were only ten or fifteen yards apart. One of the gunmen leant out of the front passenger window and fired at the Squad car. The bullet flew wide. Twenty or thirty yards on, he shot again, more carefully this time, and scored a hit in the middle of the windscreen. Cameron heard the bullet whizz past his head, and it narrowly missed Chambers who was sitting in the back. The windscreen had been frosted by the shot. Chambers climbed into the front and knocked out the broken glass. At the same time another gunman leant out of the Rover's back window, took deliberate aim and fired. They saw the flash and heard the bang, but the bullet flew wide.

The bandit car was now trying to force a passage through Curzon Street, which was packed with lunchtime traffic. After colliding with two taxis and a van, the gunmen and their driver abandoned the car and took to their heels. Chambers and Cameron jumped out and chased them. One gunman turned into a side street. Cameron followed him for about fifty yards, then lost sight of him and returned to the Squad car.

The other two had run on down Curzon Street. An officer on beat duty, P.C. Wood, saw one of them brandishing a gun and joined in the pursuit. Further down the street was a policeman on a motorcycle, P.C. Karn. He saw them coming and prepared to intercept them.

When they turned into a side street, he ran after them. The man with the gun turned and fired from only three yards away—but missed. Karn hurled his crash helmet, hitting him on the back of the head. They ran on, Karn leading the pursuit, Wood overtaking him and Sergeant Chambers pounding along behind.

They went into Shepherd Market, where Chambers lost the trail for a moment, but soon picked it up again from the noise. They doubled back into Curzon Street and across towards Charles Street. There they separated, and one got away in the crowd. So now there was only one left; one man, running and desperate, with a gun.

Charles Street was even more crowded than Curzon Street. In those days there were no parking meters in Mayfair, and cars were parked bumper to bumper along both sides of the road. Traffic could move only at a crawl, and the pavements were swarming with office workers out for lunch. A normal midday scene—and into it burst a gunman. Everything happened too fast and too confusedly for the eyewitnesses afterwards to give a clear picture. There were cries of "Stop him!" and "He's got a gun!" Someone threw a bottle of Scotch at the fugitive, but no one ever claimed credit for this unselfish act. A van driver, called Gerald McGhee, tried to stop the gunman, and had two shots fired at him over the roof of a stationary car. The fugitive then jumped on to the running board of a taxi.

"I'm engaged," said the cabby.

"Keep moving," snapped the gunman, pointing his pistol at the cabby's head.

A woman in the taxi screamed. The cabby stared blankly at the traffic ahead, unable to keep moving even if he wanted to.

The gunman jumped off and leaped aboard a van going in the opposite direction. He threatened the driver with his pistol, but, after only a few yards, the van too was jammed. The gunman darted through a break in the line of cars and raced along the pavement. P.C. Wood also veered on to the pavement and began closing on him. The gunman suddenly stopped, dodged behind a pillar box and fired. Wood was on him now, grabbing his lapel. The gunman fired again, point blank, and hit Wood in the groin. The policeman fell, and the gunman ran on.

Karn was level with him, but in the road, with no way through the line of parked cars. Karn again threw his crash helmet, which he had scooped up after his first throw, and struck the man's face. The gunman staggered but didn't stop. Chambers too was running parallel in the road. The gunman fired at him over the car tops. For thirty yards this strange pursuit continued, then Chambers saw a small gap between two cars and dashed through it. He dived at the gunman's legs and brought him down. The gunman fired again, wounding Chambers in the wrist. But Chambers clung on, fighting him for the weapon, and wrenched it from him just as Karn arrived, and together they overpowered the man.

Their prisoner was called John Cohen. The other gunman, Ronald Parsons, was arrested later that same day, violently resisting. The third member of the gang, John Cotten, who had been the driver, was captured two days afterwards; he didn't resist. I was in Court when all three were tried at the Old Bailey before Lord Goddard, the Lord Chief Justice. Cohen, who was charged among other things with trying to murder Sergeant Chambers, got twenty years, Parsons twelve and Cotten ten. Lord Goddard thanked the officers for their gallantry. "It takes courage of no mean order," he said, "to run up and tackle desperate criminals who are in possession of firearms." I recommended them all for the Commissioner's High Commendation. Sergeant Chambers received the George Medal as well.

Policemen are not called upon to show such courage every day, but they never know when they may be: and, for the Flying Squad in particular, physical battle with criminals is an occupational risk. Sometimes, far from being unexpected, it can be the culmination of a long period of patient waiting: and danger has then to be faced in cold blood.

The Flying Squad had a tip-off, in March 1961, that a mail-van holdup was being planned. The ambush would probably occur, we were told, in a small cul-de-sac called Maple Place, near the Tottenham Court Road. But who was involved we couldn't discover.

A watch was kept on Maple Place, but nothing unusual seemed to be happening. A further tip came down the grapevine that two members of the gang were known as Jeff and Tony. Then on May 3, two Flying Squad officers, who were still keeping a protective eye on the collection of mail from a number of business premises in Maple Place, spotted a couple of men who got out of a Thames van and seemed to be making a reconnaissance of the area.

The men returned to their van just before 6:45, when the mail was due to be collected from Matthew Hall & Co., a firm of building contractors. The G.P.O. van pulled out and drove along Maple Street, the Thames van following and behind it the Flying Squad officers in their nondescript car. The mail van called at Maple Place for a further collection, then drove away to its depot in Wimpole Street. The Thames van followed it to the depot, and afterwards returned to the Maple Place area. The men alighted and made another reconnaissance on foot. Nothing else happened.

We checked the registration number of the van. It belonged to a man named Henry Edward Jeffery, who had recently completed a six-year sentence for office-breaking. And he had been associating with a man called Anthony Terroni. So it all fitted.

Matthew Hall, we learned, employed a large number of men all over the country, and on Wednesdays their wage packets were dispatched by registered post. Next Wednesday Flying Squad officers were hidden in various buildings round Maple Place, and two unmarked vans patrolled nearby.

At about six o'clock the Thames van drew up and parked in front of a Rover. Jeffery and Terroni both got out, and were immediately joined on the pavement by five men. Jeffery, Terroni and one of the others walked to the Tottenham Court Road and back. Then one man got into the driver's seat of the Rover, Jeffery and Terroni returned to the van and the other four climbed in behind them. Both vehicles drove off.

When the mail van appeared, the two Flying Squad vans slipped in behind it, so that the three vehicles were travelling in convoy when they reached Maple Place. There was no sign of the Thames van or of the Rover. The mail van paid its usual call and drove on unmolested. It looked as though the robbery had been called off for the day.

The two police vehicles continued to follow the mail van, however, as it turned into Duchess Street. The Thames van was waiting there. It pulled in front of the mail van; the post office driver (who had not been warned, because we wanted him to behave naturally) jammed on the brakes. Immediately the leading police van swung out and forward, and rammed the Thames van. One of the Flying Squad officers, Sergeant Jones, was thrown forward by the collision and half-stunned. His companion in the van, Sergeant Mitchell, jumped out— but the bandits had already gone into action.

There were five men in the back of the Thames van, as well as Jeffery, who was driving. All five wore identical cloth masks and were armed with pickaxe handles, bound in black tape for a better grip. One of them struck Mitchell a heavy blow on the shoulder, and then ran to the driver's cabin of the mail van and tried to wrench it open.

Meanwhile, Sergeant Firth and Sergeant Burdett were sprinting up from the second police vehicle. At the sight of them, the Thames van began to move off with its back doors open and two of the bandits still inside. Another scrambled aboard. Firth grabbed hold of him, but was knocked into the road. Burdett tackled the third man, but was also kicked away. The first bandit left the mail van, hotly pursued by Sergeant Mitchell, and was pulled by his friends into the back of the Thames van.

Burdett, still lying on the ground, suddenly saw the Rover, held up by traffic, a little way ahead. "Get the driver of that Rover!" he shouted.

Mitchell and Jones, who had now recovered, ran to the car and seized the driver. But the Thames van, with Jeffery and the five masked bandits, was clear away.

The weeks of preparation had told us where to look. The homes and known haunts of Jeffery and Terroni were immediately visited, but without success. Later that same day, however, two men were arrested; we were pretty sure they had been at least involved in the affair. One of these men had in his pocket a fragment of a cigarette packet with a telephone number scribbled on it. The number was traced and a watch kept on the house.

Five weeks later, at 12:30 P.M. on June 17, Jeffery, Terroni, and another man were seen entering the house. At 2:30 P.M. the police raided it. Expecting violent resistance, they went in at a rush. Two officers burst into the front room, three others into a back room, and two more ran upstairs.

Jeffery, who was in the back room, gave up without a struggle. Terroni, in the front room, fought savagely. When the police broke in, he was lying on a sofa. He grabbed for something under his pillow. It was a fully loaded Webley automatic. The two detectives prevented him from reaching it, but weren't able to overpower him until Sergeant McFadzean came in from the back room to help.

Upstairs a similar struggle was taking place. A man, who turned out to be the brother of the one arrested in the Rover, was lying on a bunk. Like Terroni, he promptly thrust his hand under the pillow, reaching for another fully loaded Webley. But they too were on to him before he could use it.

The three prisoners were taken away. A little later, a man drove up in a car. Detective Inspector Groombridge opened the door to him.

"Police—we want you," announced Groombridge. The man, whose name was John Walker, turned and ran: but they soon caught him.

All seven were tried at the Old Bailey, convicted and sent to prison for terms adding up to a total of forty-six years. One of the officers testified that Terroni's first remark after his arrest was: "Another two seconds, and I'd have blown your heads off."

CHAPTER 17
Violent Generation

Many of my senior officers, men with long experience of London's criminals, held that a chief cause of the increase in violence was the employment by the underworld planners of younger, and therefore more reckless, thugs to do the rough stuff. In normal economic theory, more planning should mean fewer personnel required for the job. The development of crime in recent years has shown just the opposite pattern. The teams which attacked mail vans, raided banks, and rammed cars carrying wages no longer consisted, as they might have done before, of only two or three men. Between five and eight now became usual. These larger teams were more effective because they were more terrifying. Eight men, uniformly masked and armed, moving fast and purposefully, exercising deliberate violence, are a spectacle frightening enough to paralyse opposition. The planners use violence scientifically, like a tool.

Almost more shocking, however, is the violence which hasn't been planned at all; which is mere senseless brutality. The young thugs who perpetrate it are often not, in the accepted sense, professional criminals, though they provide the pool of ruthlessness from which professional criminals are recruited.

One such case occurred on a summer night in 1960. A young engineer, called Allan Jee, was walking home along a footpath in Isleworth, after spending the evening with his fiancée, to whom he had become engaged only the previous day. He was waylaid, knocked down and kicked on the head again and again. He was found, at 11:30, lying on the towpath unconscious.

He died in hospital without having recovered consciousness. Nothing seemed to have been stolen from him, and it looked as though we were dealing with a motiveless murder.

The footpath, we learned, was lonely at the best of times, and on the night of the murder it had been dark too. A mechanical fault had prevented the lamps from being lit.

Isleworth is in "T" Division, but four neighbouring Divisions and detectives from Scotland Yard joined in the hunt. They went from house to house, and asked questions in cafes, pubs, dance halls, and youth clubs. The first lead they turned up was a man who had walked along the path shortly before the estimated time of the attack—11:20 P.M.—and had noticed four youths loitering there. His story was confirmed by another man, who said, quite independently, that he had seen four young men near the footpath at 11:15. Unfortunately, the failure of the lights prevented either of these witnesses from giving more than the sketchiest description of the youths.

They were traced, however, quite quickly, because of the vanity of one of them, an eighteen-year-old called Forsyth and known among his friends as "Floss." He boasted to a girl that he had been in a fight. As soon as they heard it, the local police knew his name. He was notorious, they said, for his vicious temper; he would start a fight on the least provocation, and it was his agreeable habit to kick his opponents in the face, once he had got them down. Further enquiries produced the names of three other young men with whom he was associated—all known to the police: Norman Harris and Christopher Darby, both aged twenty-three, and Terence Lutt, who, though he was only seventeen, weighed about 240 pounds and was strong in proportion.

All four were brought to Hounslow Police Station and interrogated. They admitted having been together on the night of the murder but put forward an alibi. It couldn't be immediately disproved, and they were released.

This murder had made me very angry, so I kept in close touch with the investigation. I was pleased, three weeks later, to hear that enough facts had now been unearthed to make it worthwhile questioning the four youths again. They were brought back to the police station and interrogated separately. Harris, who was questioned first, began by repeating his previous story but eventually made a statement admitting his involvement. But he insisted that he had taken no part in the actual violence. Lutt had knocked Jee down and Forsyth had done the kicking.

The other three were then interviewed in turn. Each abandoned the pretence of innocence but tried to shift the major blame on to the others. Darby said he had acted only as a look-out. Lutt admitted having knocked Jee down but said he hadn't kicked him. Forsyth confessed to having kicked Jee in the head, but only, he said, "to quieten him down a bit." None of them showed the slightest remorse; neither then nor later. Indeed, Forsyth seems not to have regarded Jee's death as a particularly serious crime, or perhaps he thought (with some justification) that in our society the young can get away with anything. "I reckon we'll get five years each," he was heard to say in the Magistrates' Court. "Anyway I should be out by the time I'm twenty-four."

The four statements didn't really contradict each other. With differences only on emphasis, they fitted together to make a chronicle as savage as anything in the old Newgate Calendar. Harris, Forsyth, and Lutt, after consuming a good deal of beer, had decided to go out and rob someone. Their first thought was to break into a shop or a house. Then they decided instead to "jump" the first suitable victim who came by. They lay in wait by the footpath, while Darby, who had joined them, kept watch. The first two passers-by were the witnesses who had described the four youths; they were luckier than they knew. One had been spared because they thought someone else was approaching from the opposite direction, the other because he looked too big. The third person to pass that way was Allan Jee. Like the woman in the Potters Bar murder, he had done nothing to deserve or invite his fate: he was just the one to whom the black card was dealt.

Lutt knocked him down with a single blow of his huge fist. Harris fumbled inside Jee's jacket, looking for a wallet, while Forsyth started to kick the fallen man with his sharply pointed "winkle-picker" shoes. Harris continued searching Jee's pockets until he saw blood on his hands. Then he became frightened and ran away. He had missed the small amount of money Jee was carrying, so the robbery was a complete failure. Darby and Lutt ran away too, leaving Forsyth still kicking Jee either for personal amusement or out of irritation because there was no loot.

They were tried at the Old Bailey for murder in the furtherance of theft, a capital offence. Harris, Forsyth, and Lutt were found guilty of capital murder, and Darby of simple murder. Darby was sent to prison for life: Lutt, being under eighteen, was ordered to be detained during Her Majesty's pleasure: Harris and Forsyth were sentenced to death.

That there should be the usual outcry from the opponents of all capital punishment was natural: but there was also, really for no good reason, a certain amount of public sympathy for Forsyth, partly on account of his youth and partly because of some flowery letters to his girl friend, which he wrote from prison and which were published in the newspapers. The letters he might have written he didn't write—no word of regret was received by the fiancée or the parents of Allan Jee.

Harris and Forsyth were executed on November 10, 1960.

The murder of Allan Jee came close to being the result of violence for violence's sake, but not quite: the original attack was made for gain. London, like all big cities, has its share of young hooligans who will assault people and destroy property for no reason at all, other than the fun of brutality and destruction. In the past, society's opinion of such behaviour was made painfully clear to them if they were caught. Now excuse after implausible excuse is trotted out on their behalf. They appear on television, staring vacantly into the camera and answering leading questions in sullen monosyllables. They are said to be bored—as though that were some excuse for beating up a harmless stranger or terrorising a seaside resort.

One sort of thuggery, however, produced quite a different reaction because it couched another, and even more sensitive, nerve in the tightly knit bundle of ready-made liberal responses.

At two in the morning, on Sunday, August 24, 1958, a young West Indian, named MacDonald Waldron, was walking along Ladbroke Grove with a white girl. A white youth, called Paddy, crossed the road towards them: and, though they were complete strangers to each other, Paddy and Waldron exchanged angry words and then came to blows.

Paddy won. He knocked Waldron to the ground. Immediately, four more youths, armed with sticks and iron bars, rushed across the road and began beating the prostrate Waldron. He struggled to his feet, ran a few paces, but was brought down and belaboured again. Eventually they left him lying in the street, where he was found and taken to St. Charles' Hospital, suffering from concussion.

At 2:45 A.M. John Pirmal and Matthew Lucien, both coloured, were walking along Lancaster Road, near the junction with Ladbroke Grove, when they saw a small black car stop near them. Nine youths poured out of that one small vehicle. Brandishing sticks, iron bars, a table leg, a starting handle, and at least one knife, they hurled themselves on to the two inoffensive West Indians. Lucien managed to escape. Pirmal was not so lucky; he was beaten to the ground and then stabbed in the back. When the thugs had gone, Lucien returned and took his friend to St. Charles' Hospital. Pirmal's condition was serious, and remained so for several weeks.

At about 5 A.M. another West Indian, Joseph Welsh, was walking along the south side of Shepherd's Bush Green when he noticed a small black car pull up a short distance away. A few moments later a man (he was afterwards identified as Paddy) jumped over the fence surrounding the green and struck Welsh in the face. Welsh was tougher than Waldron, and fought back strongly. Nine other men piled out of the black car and attacked him with sticks and bars. He managed to keep his feet, and finally broke loose and ran away. At St. Charles' Hospital, he was treated for concussion, multiple bruises, and lacerations.

At about 5 A.M. two maintenance workers on the Underground, James Sylvester Etienne and another coloured man, were coming off night duty when they saw the small black car. A moment later, Etienne received a blow on the head from behind. Turning, he saw several youths armed with sticks and bars. Etienne's companion ran away.

Etienne spotted a crate of empty milk bottles, ran to it and began hurling bottles at the youths. They retreated out of range. At that moment, a trolley-bus stopped nearby. Etienne sprinted to it and jumped aboard. Some of the youths rushed forward in pursuit. One of them had a knife. They reached the platform of the bus and told the conductress to put Etienne off. She refused. The driver saw what was happening and drove quickly away. The youths followed in their car until the driver stopped at a police box to phone for help. The black car then vanished, and Etienne, suffering only from slight injuries, was taken to Hammersmith Hospital.

The local police were now thoroughly alerted. They took statements from those of the victims who were fit to be interviewed, but none of them was able to give much of a description of his attackers or had noted the number of the car.

However, a general description of the car and of the youths was at once circulated to all officers on duty.

At 5:40 A.M. Constables Wilding and Knight saw a small black Singer, crammed with youths, driving along the Uxbridge Road. Wilding ran after it on foot, while Knight phoned the Information Room at Scotland Yard. Wilding was lucky. A cruising taxi appeared. He hailed it and followed the Singer to Loftus Road, where the youths got out. When they saw a uniformed constable alighting from the taxi, they ran away, leaving their weapons in the car. They disappeared, before Wilding could catch any of them, into the maze of buildings on the vast White City housing estate. The car and its contents, however, were taken to Shepherd's Bush Police Station.

Detective Sergeant Walters, who was acting head of the C.I.D. at Notting Hill, was told of the night's doings at 6:30 A.M. He rapidly assembled and briefed a small team—two detective sergeants, one detective constable, and one Aid-to-C.I.D. He warned them to be very careful in their questioning. If a suspect was interrogated and then had to be released, all the culprits would know that the police were having difficulty over identification.

The only real clue was the car. The registration number was traced to a car dealer, who had sold the vehicle to a seventeen-year-old youth named John O'Brien, living on the White City estate. Whether or not he was involved, the police assumed that O'Brien would shortly be reporting his car as stolen. Officers in the local police station were warned not to question him or show any particular interest. At lunchtime that day, he duly arrived at Shepherd's Bush Police Station and reported the theft. The station sergeant wrote down the details, asked no questions and allowed him to leave.

Walters' team, meanwhile, had been making discreet enquiries throughout the Notting Hill area. The result gave them several names, including O'Brien's. At 5 P.M. they held a conference, and Walters decided to interrogate the suspects. During the evening, eight youths were interviewed. The first of these interrogations began at 5:30 P.M., the last ended at four the next morning. By that time, eight youths had been arrested. They all made statements which amounted to complete confessions.

It was a nasty enough story. These eight and another had been milling aimlessly around when one of them suggested a "spade-hunting" expedition. They all agreed. Some of them proceeded to arm themselves by breaking off iron railings from in front of a row of houses.

While O'Brien was filling his car with petrol, four of the youths strolled into Ladbroke Grove and saw Waldron fighting with the man whom they later knew as Paddy. When Waldron was knocked down, they rushed to help not the victim but the aggressor. Their comrades then joined them in the car, and they all drove off to look for further victims. At a late stage during the night's work, Paddy faded away; we never found him.

Walters' team had been on duty continuously for more than twenty hours. When the eight youths had been safely locked up, they snatched about three hours' sleep: then resumed work at nine the next morning. At 12:30 P.M. they arrested the ninth youth, who also admitted his part in the affair.

At 1:45 P.M. all nine appeared before the West London Magistrate. They were remanded until the following Saturday, which allowed the prosecution very little time to prepare the case. But the matter was urgent. A smouldering race antagonism had been fanned into flame. There were several more incidents. The whole situation was getting very rough.

The trial took place at the Old Bailey early in September, amid a good deal of public speculation about the sentences likely to be passed. The oldest of the youths was only twenty, six of them were seventeen years old. Only one had a previous conviction. Their crime was not merely vicious but, at that place and time, constituted a special public danger. People wondered what compromise there could be between the need to deter such offences once and for all, and the leniency which the hooligans' youth and technical good character might normally have earned.

There was no compromise. Mr. Justice Salmon sent them all to prison for four years, and his remarks from the Bench made front page news:

"Everyone, irrespective of the colour of their skin, is entitled to walk through our streets in peace, with their heads erect, and free from fear. That is the right which these courts will unfailingly uphold.

"As far as the law is concerned, you are entitled to think what you like, however foul your thoughts; to feel what you like, however brutal and debased your emotions; to say what you like, providing you do not infringe the rights of others or imperil the Queen's peace, but once you translate your dark thoughts and brutal feelings into savage acts such as these, the law will be swift to punish you and to protect your victims.

"I bear in mind what has been said on your behalf: you are young and have no previous convictions. Your victims, though grievously injured, after two or three weeks in hospital have sufficiently recovered to be allowed to return home and it is unlikely that they will suffer any permanent physical ill effects from your savage attacks. But for those facts I would have imposed much longer sentences. As it is, I am determined that you and anyone anywhere who may be tempted to follow your example shall clearly understand that crimes such as this will not be tolerated in this country, but will meet in these courts with the stern punishment which they deserve."

The effect of these stiff sentences was immediate, salutory, and apparently conclusive. Race violence between white men and black in Notting Hill came to an abrupt end, and has not yet been resumed. For once, no liberal voice was raised against the harsh treatment of these young criminals. No complaints were made about the severity of the sentences. Everybody, it seems, thought that justice had been done.

It would be pleasant to record that one result of this affair was the creation of confidence and mutual esteem between the West Indian community and the police. Alas, the world isn't like that. The West Indians are still profoundly, and quite unfairly, suspicious of the police. A state of tension exists which, since it is not based on reason, cannot be dissipated by reasoned argument. It is, I suppose, only a domestic reflection of those greater tensions, jealousies, and suspicions between black and white which are among the chief plagues of our time.

CHAPTER 18
Unfair Ladies

Crime is one sphere of activity in which women have neither claimed nor secured equal rights. Women become "gangsters' molls," of course, but I've never myself come across a female gang leader—though there was a Chicago grandmother who ran an arson ring in the 1930s. Young hooligans are sometimes egged on by their girl friends, but the Teddy Girl on her own, or in an all-girl group, is a very rare phenomenon. The most celebrated female criminals were, I suppose, the great women pirates: and, if their pictures are to be believed, they looked like men.

Certainly there are far fewer women than men in British prisons. Perhaps women are too sensible, more concerned than men with the building and preservation of a home. Perhaps they are deterred from the risks of crime by being more imaginative.

Women can kill as ruthlessly as any man, and, once embarked on a crime, can be just as cool and resolute. My professional world has been peopled chiefly by men—policemen, lawyers, and crooks: but there were exceptions.

One case haunts me because of its macabre opening scene.

On the night of July 28, 1954, a certain Mr. Young went into his garden in Hampstead and saw flames leaping up at the back of the house next door but one. After calling out several times, he jumped the fence and walked across the intervening garden towards the blaze. He was then able to look over a wall into an area or yard, some fifteen feet below. There, lying on the ground, he saw what he took to be the wax model of a woman, completely surrounded by flames. He was reassured by the sight. He knew that his neighbours in that house did have tailor's dummies. The flames were not particularly fierce and didn't seem to be accidental; there was a strong smell of paraffin and also what he later described as "a waxy kind of smell."

The figure lay just outside a pair of french windows leading into the kitchen, where there was an electric light burning and a woman moving about. While Young watched, she came out into the yard and bent over the burning figure. There was nothing hesitant about her movements. She walked firmly and purposefully, and stooped over the now dying fire, not as if she wanted to put it out, but as though she were going to stir it up.

Satisfied that everything was all right and his neighbour was merely burning rubbish, Young withdrew as silently as he had come. He returned to his own house in time to hear the midnight weather forecast and news summary.

About an hour and a half later, the woman dashed into the street and stopped the first car which came along. "Please come—fire—three children sleeping," she cried in broken English.

The driver was a Mr. Burstoff, a restaurateur on his way home with his wife. Before he could reply, the woman was already running back towards her house. He followed her. The front door was open, and there was no sign of smoke or flames. "Shsh—the children are asleep," the woman said. "Please come, please come."

She led them through to the back of the house and showed them the figure lying in the area. The fire was out, and it no longer looked at all like a wax model. Mrs. Burstoff screamed.

"Shsh—children sleeping," repeated the woman angrily.

The body was completely naked, the face covered in blood.

Mrs. Burstoff, somewhat shakily, asked the woman what had happened.

"I went to bed and smelled burning," she replied in her halting English. "I came down. Threw water. No good. She was dead."

Mr. Burstoff asked if he could use her telephone. At that moment, all the lights went out. By striking matches, he found the instrument and dialled 999. A police car, he was told, would be on its way.

"Girl sewing, sewing. Plenty shoes, plenty dress," the woman said to Mrs. Burstoff while they were waiting. "German girl going to Germany with children. I went to bed and smelled burning. I went down in my pyjamas. Throw water, but girl was dead."

When the police arrived, they briefly examined the body by the light of their torches, and then phoned for the Divisional Surgeon. When they tried to question the woman, she replied "I no understand" or "No speak." All these preliminary investigations took place in the dark, illumined only by flashlight, until the woman gave one of the officers a shilling to put in the meter, and the lights went on again.

Sergeant Welch arrived from Hampstead Police Station. He got no further with the woman, but he noticed damp floor cloths on the kitchen step, apparently laid out to dry, and that the woman's bed had not been slept in. This, he decided, was a case for the C.I.D.: and the Divisional Surgeon suggested that the body ought to be seen by Dr. Camps, the pathologist, before it was moved. In the midst of this grim bustle, a boy of about twelve came down the stairs and asked what was going on. He was the dead woman's eldest child.

At 2:35 A.M. Detective Inspector Fenwick arrived. He looked round, noted some pieces of charred material beside the body and that the floor of the kitchen was very clean. He managed to extract a few more words from the woman.

"I wake up," she said. "Smell burning. Go downstairs. Hella burning. Throw water. Touch her face. Not move. Run out. Get help."

At 3:30 A.M. a dark-haired man of about thirty-five let himself into the house. He was startled to find it full of policemen, and appalled by the spectacle of his dead wife. The other woman, the police now learned, was his mother. They were Greek Cypriots, named Christofi. And the whole bitter story began to come out.

Stavros, the son, worked as a waiter in the West End. During the war he had married a German refugee called Hella, and they had three children. Twelve months before, his mother had arrived from Cyprus, hoping to earn some money in England with which to pay off a mortgage on the family farm. The two women got on badly from the start. The elder Mrs. Christofi had never been to school and was completely illiterate. She resented her more sophisticated daughter-in-law, and begrudged her the money she spent on clothes and on the home. Hella equally disliked her mother-in-law, and was afraid she might infect the children with germs or teach them primitive habits. They quarrelled continually, until Stavros finally told his mother that it would be better for them all if she went back to Cyprus.

The matter seemed to have been settled quite amicably. Hella was due to begin her annual holiday soon. She would take the children to visit her parents in Germany, and, when she returned, Mrs. Christofi would leave. Hella had been in unusually high spirits at the prospect.

But now she was dead, her body charred, her head battered. These, however, were not the injuries which had caused her death. Dr. Camps found a white band of almost unburned skin around her neck, and the marks of a knot and of a weave pattern.

In a dustbin the police discovered some pieces of charred

236

and bloodstained cloth with a weave that matched the marks; these were the remains of a scarf belonging to the boy. It wasn't a difficult case to solve. There was no lack of physical clues. A bloodstained ashplate, which had been replaced on the kitchen stove, had evidently been used to knock Hella down: then she had been strangled with her son's scarf, and undressed by someone who cut her stockings away with scissors or a knife, probably because the murderer didn't know how to unfasten suspenders. Her clothes were found, still damp from recent washing, in a bucket by the sink. The funeral pyre in the yard revealed traces not only of paraffin (an empty gallon can lay nearby) but also of paper and wood. The kitchen floor had evidently been scrubbed, but there were bloodstains in the outflow pipe of the sink and bloodstained towels in the bathroom upstairs.

With her son acting as interpreter—it must have been a most harrowing duty—Mrs. Christofi made a statement. She had woken up, she said, smelled burning, seen the front door open and gone down to find Hella on fire in the yard.

Mrs. Christofi's shoes were bloodstained and stank of paraffin. In her bedroom the police found the dead woman's wedding ring, wrapped in cellophane and hidden behind a china ornament, and inside the ornament a screwed-up soap carton which contained some charred fragments of wood and paper and gave a positive reaction for blood.

Mrs. Christofi was charged with murder. I asked the Commissioner of Police in Cyprus for any information about her past history. He replied at once. She had been charged in 1924 with the murder of her mother-in-law by ramming a piece of burning wood down her throat: but, for some reason, she had been acquitted and had continued to live with her husband. "Girls will be girls" was perhaps the view taken; she came from a rough part of Cyprus.

At the Old Bailey she refused to allow her counsel to plead

insanity; in which she was supported by three doctors who subsequently examined her in prison and declared her sane. She was executed on December 15, and there were no protests even from the most vociferous opponents of capital punishment. The execution not long afterwards of Ruth Ellis, who had shot her lover in the street, followed him round the car, and shot him twice more as he lay on the ground, caused much public indignation because of her sex. But public indignation and sympathy are highly selective. Mrs. Christofi had less appeal.

Let us turn, with some relief, to lighter things; to a woman called Margaret Dowse. After eluding the police forces of England for four years, she was finally betrayed by her boy friend.

Margaret Dowse was born in 1932. After marrying at the age of seventeen and parting from her husband four years later, she contracted a less formal alliance with a certain Stanley Trinder. Trinder was a sporty character, fond of a flutter on the horses or the dogs. Money was therefore chronically short in the Trinder-Dowse household. In April 1956 Margaret stole a Post Office Savings Book, forged the owner's signature and withdrew £5. The pair then set out on their travels.

Though she had left school at fourteen and received no subsequent training, Margaret was an exceptionally good clerk, quick at figures, adept at handling money, and with a most engaging personality. She soon established a regular *modus operandi*. Having arrived in a new town and taken rooms in a respectable neighbourhood, she and Trinder would consult the Situations Vacant column of the local paper. A job in a shop or a sub-post office was what they wanted; somewhere which would have cash on the premises. Margaret's charm and glib tongue usually got her the job, and she would start work at once. In no time the proprietor or manager would be trusting her implicitly.

She kept the books in immaculate style, and, before long,

was taking the day's cash to the night safe at the bank every evening. Every evening except the last one. Then she took the money to her rooms instead, collected Stanley and caught the next train to somewhere else.

Stanley Trinder took no part in acquiring the money. He simply helped her spend it, or, to be more precise, usually passed it on to the bookies. After some half-dozen of these offences had been reported to the Criminal Record Office, we had a full description of Margaret, but no clues to her real identity or where we could find her: nor did we know, at first, about Stanley Trinder.

When doing a job, she always tried to keep her local address secret from the people she was working with: but it slipped out at Birmingham one day, and the police were able to trace her to her lodgings. The birds had flown, but now we had a description of Stanley Trinder as well. Records were able to identify him. He had been convicted of minor offences several times in the past. His photograph was immediately published in the *Police Gazette*, and every force in the country was warned to be on the look-out. But in vain. Margaret continued her career undisturbed.

By October 1960 she was officially "wanted" in forty-one different towns, and her total haul now exceeded £12,000. She had been employed as cashier to a grocer, a butcher, a radio dealer, a baker, and a ladies' outfitter. She had worked in the box office of a cinema and as a counter clerk in a Post Office. We plotted her movements from Worthing to Newcastle-on-Tyne, from Bristol to Poole, from Wood Green to Brixton. In police circles she had become almost a standing joke. At Selection Boards I used to ask candidates for the C.I.D., "What would you do about Margaret Trinder?"

The man who finally did something found the opportunity to do it—as often happens in police work—by chance. In October 1960 Stanley and Margaret were living in West London.

It was a lovely mild autumn morning, and Stanley announced that he was going down to Fontwell Park to see if he could recover some of their money from the bookmakers.

Police Constable Goddard, an Aid-to-C.I.D. at Bow Street, had similar thoughts. It happened to be his day off, so he took a train to Barnham and boarded a bus for Fontwell Park racecourse. He was sitting on the top deck, idly watching other race-goers getting on the bus, when he noticed a face which seemed familiar. Was it Trinder? Could it be Trinder? He had only seen that one photograph in the *Police Gazette* but it looked very like him. Goddard went down to the lower deck where he could study the man's face more closely. Yes, surely this was Trinder.

They both alighted at the racecourse, and Goddard approached his man from behind. He tapped him on the shoulder. "Hello, Stanley," he said. "Do you remember me? We were at school together."

The man spun round. "I've never seen you before," he blustered. This was quite true: but Goddard was now so confident that he revealed his own identity and said he was going to arrest him. Trinder started to escape, but was overpowered after a fierce struggle; which no doubt relieved Goddard's mind of any lingering doubts. He was taken first to the racecourse lock-up and then to Chichester Police Station, where he was questioned by the local detectives.

He cut no very heroic figure. Collapsing at once, he offered to lead them to Margaret: and he was as good—or as bad—as his word. A Flying Squad car met the Sussex police car at Putney Bridge, and Trinder guided Detective Inspector Groombridge to the house where they were staying. Margaret's feelings when she saw Stanley must have been poignant: or perhaps she knew him well enough not to be surprised.

She was tried at Lewes and convicted on five charges of larceny, forgery and falsification of accounts; and she asked for another thirty-seven cases to be taken into consideration. Both she and Stanley were sentenced to five years' imprisonment.

Margaret Dowse (or Margaret Trinder, which is the name she used) wasn't really the sort of criminal I can very much dislike. She was scarcely an ornament to her sex, but Stanley Trinder was surely the more deplorable character. So perhaps the moral even of this story is that men are more scoundrelly than women. It makes a nice point for moral argument.

CHAPTER 19

The Glamorous Visitor

A few months later we found ourselves hunting another equally elusive and rather more ambitious lady whose connections with the bookmaking profession were a good deal more direct than Margaret Dowse's had been. I must confess that I have never fully shared the British passion for horses, and until I went to Cambridge I wasn't particularly interested in racing. But as most of my friends there were keen racing men and Newmarket was only thirteen miles away, I came to take an interest and now I enjoy a day at the races, provided I can go in comfort.

The corollary is that I have been interested too in the crimes that affect racing. Criminals tend to infest the Turf, chiefly I suppose because there is a lot of easy money on a racecourse, and partly because the mentality which takes readily to crime is apt also to be attracted by gambling. Members of the Flying Squad have for years attended all the big race meetings within striking distance of London, and their presence has certainly decreased the number of pickpockets and other criminal types very considerably.

The razor-wielding race gangs of the 1930s were stamped out by tough police action, and have not yet returned. But the "nobbling" of horses—particularly doping—has remained an endemic disease of British racing. The dope itself is easy to obtain and hard to detect and identify—but a bucket of water, administered by a stable lad shortly before the race, will stop a horse just as effectively. Doping to win, giving the horse stimulants, which was a common practice in the last century, seems to have become much rarer. The effect of stimulant drugs is too variable and uncertain for guaranteed success.

Modern doping, therefore, is almost entirely doping to stop. And who benefits from preventing a horse from winning? Not, on the whole, other owners or trainers or punters; rarely, if ever, could they be sure that by stopping one rival they would enable their own horse to win. The people who benefit are bookies. If they know that a heavily backed horse is not going to win, they can save a great deal of money by not laying-off as they would otherwise have to do. The only really effective way to prevent "nobbling," it seems, would be to abolish bookmakers and give the tote a monopoly, as in many other countries. This solution has been considered but is apparently not acceptable. It smacks too much of blowing up the house to get rid of the rats.

Doping, like other crimes, goes in cycles. When it gets too bad, precautions are tightened, and it dies down again: but it never dies out. During my first years as A.C.C., there were several major racing cases—including the sensational Francasal affair, in which horses were swapped during the night and the telephone line to London cut.

Since 1954, Colonel Blair, who headed the small body of ex-policemen which then constituted the security department of the Jockey Club, had been calling on me regularly to discuss his problems. And these problems became steadily more acute. The Jockey Club was worried not only by the fact of doping but by the bad publicity which it brought to the whole business of racing.

The matter finally became so serious that I was consulted by Mr. W. E. Weatherby and shortly afterwards by Sir Randle Feilden, Senior Steward of the Jockey Club. I had to point out that racecourse security wasn't really a police job, but that if there were evidence of crime, I would of course take action.

244

I added that most racecourses were outside the Metropolitan Police area and fell within the jurisdiction of a large number of different police forces—but these forces would certainly co-operate with each other and with us. I promised that C9 would do everything possible to make this co-operation effective. I also suggested that it might be helpful if the Jockey Club retained a private investigator. On my recommendation they hired an ex-C.I.D. man, Robert Hill who had been practising as a private detective since his retirement. I discussed all this with Chief Superintendent Davis, the head of C9, and detailed an officer of the Branch, Chief Inspector Barnett, to be in charge of the Metropolitan enquiries.

The trail first became clear at Kelso races. Two horses, Irish Honour and Bronze Warrior, owned by Major Bewicke, had been entered for steeplechases on October 21, 1961, and were expected to start as favourites. At 6 a.m. on the morning of the race Irish Honour was found to be unsteady on his legs. The vet was promptly called, and he issued a certificate saying that the horse was unfit and should be withdrawn. Bronze Warrior ran, but, after taking only three jumps, collapsed on level ground. Both horses were then examined further, and they were found to have been doped with Phenobarbitone.

The Northumberland Police went to Shawdon Hall, where Major Bewicke lived, and learned that a woman had visited the stables on October 14. She had arrived in a Ford Zephyr, and had announced herself to the head lad as an owner from Paris, where she had a string in training. She would soon be bringing some of her horses to England, she said, and she wanted to inspect Major Bewicke's stables as a possible place to train them. She was then conducted round the stables, and told the names of the various horses and shown where their boxes were sited. She made notes in shorthand. Major Bewicke was away at Ayr Races, but she promised to get in touch with him very soon to discuss terms.

The woman was described as being about twenty-five years old, with a French accent, a slim figure and dark hair. One of the stable boys said that he had seen a woman very like her at Kelso; she had been taking a close look at Bronze Warrior during the parade in the paddock. He remembered her because her interest had been so apparent.

The Northumberland Police sent a report to Chief Inspector Barnett, who realised at once that the description of this mysterious woman ought to be checked with all the stables where doping had been suspected—and, indeed, with other stables as well, because trainers are often not in a hurry to report their suspicions. (Conversely, some trainers, when they have been disappointed by a horse's performance, are apt to cry "Dope!" though they have no real reason for suspecting it.)

So Barnett dredged his net through a large number of stables, and the results were spectacular.

Between the beginning of October and November 20 the elegant visitor from Paris had inspected stables in fifteen different counties of England and Scotland, sometimes alone, sometimes accompanied by a man and once by another woman. She always told the same story about wanting to bring horses over to be trained.

On November 18 she had called at W. A. Stephenson's stables in Bishop Auckland, where the head lad had been bright enough to note the number of her car. Barnett checked the number and found that the car was owned by one William Roper, bookmaker. And a day or so later the head lad at Shawdon Hall saw a photograph in *Sporting Life* which he recognised as the Frenchwoman. Her name, we now learned, was Micheline Lugeon.

Barnett began building up a file on her. She had visited twenty-one stables so far, and many of them had suffered from doping quite soon afterwards. A photograph of Roper was shown around, and we established that he had been the man with her on several occasions. Sometimes he accompanied her to the stables, sometimes he waited at the local hotel.

Mlle. Lugeon, we discovered, was in fact a Swiss. She had come to England in 1955 as a mother's help to Mrs. Roper. After periods of domestic work for one or two other employers, she had set up in business as a beauty specialist with an office in the West End. Roper was a man in his late fifties. Between 1954 and 1959 he had been employed as a bookmaker's clerk, and had then become a bookmaker himself under a different name. We felt pretty sure that it was Roper who had organised the recent spate of doping, but we still had no direct evidence. What we needed was to find the link, witnesses who would testify to the actual administration of the drugs.

The breakthrough came in Sussex. A horse named Scarron, from Captain Ryan Price's stable, had been doped after a visit by Micheline Lugeon. While they were investigating, the West Sussex police received a tip that a certain Mrs. Santus, a former stable girl, could help them. And so indeed she could: and did. She told them that her husband, from whom she was separated, had been hired, together with two men called Bob Herd and Darkie Steward, to dope horses at £80 a time.

At first this trail too seemed to peter out. Fifteen police forces searched in vain for Herd and Steward. Then came another tip. On August 8 a man and a woman (who were careful throughout to preserve their anonymity) spent the day at Brighton races. They struck up a conversation—so they told Inspector Simpson of the Brighton Police—with a complete stranger, who happened to remark, during this casual chat, that he had come to the races to deliver some dope which was to be used on one of that day's runners. They took Simpson and Chief Inspector Dunstan to a bar in Tattersall's, and there pointed out a man who was having a quiet drink. When Dunstan spoke to him, he tried to conceal something in one of his pockets. It was a small bottle containing a white powder.

247

At the police station he was searched and a white capsule, wrapped in a dirty sweet paper, was found among his possessions. He said he was supposed to give both the powder and the capsule to a man he was to meet outside the Metropole Hotel.

His own name, he said, was Edward Smith and he lived in Surbiton. The police immediately took him there, searched his house and found quite a large quantity of drugs. At Surbiton Police Station Chief Inspector Barnett joined them. He asked the name of the man who was to have received the dope at the Metropole rendezvous. Smith hesitated, then asked: "Do the names Roper, Mitchell, and Steward mean anything to you?" Barnett said he'd heard them. "Give me time to think," said Smith. "I'll come and see you tomorrow."

Barnett took a risk. He let him go. And the risk paid off. Smith came to the Yard next day and unfolded a remarkable tale. For the past ten years he had been engaged, one way or another, in doping horses.

He worked for a firm of manufacturing chemists, and in 1952 had become friendly with the tablet manager, Richard McGhee. At about the same time, he met a stable boy named Darkie Steward. One day, Steward asked Smith if he knew of any drug which would make a horse go faster. Smith in turn asked McGhee, pretending that he was interested, not in horses, but in greyhounds: and McGhee suggested a tonic. Smith passed this suggestion on to Steward, and it was, at least ostensibly, tried on a horse—and didn't work. Steward told Smith about the failure of the experiment, and asked instead for a drug which would have the opposite effect.

Steward got in touch with McGhee, who had now moved to the north of England, telling him bluntly that he wanted drugs to stop a horse. McGhee sent them. Two other racing men were introduced to Smith by Steward—Joseph Lowry and Edward Dyer: and the four of them formed a syndicate.

This arrangement worked well enough until 1960, when Dyer brought William Roper in. Roper knew all about drugs, convinced the others that they needed something more powerful, and told Smith what to ask for. Obediently McGhee supplied it. Soon afterwards, Dyer left the syndicate and was replaced by Roper's friend and bodyguard, Charles Mitchell, a dangerous man well known to the police.

Smith's story was a long one, with all sorts of ins and outs. He told how McGhee grew restive and announced, on one occasion, that the supply of drugs was exhausted; they had already had enough dope, McGhee said petulantly, to stop an army of horses. On another occasion, Steward had gone to Catterick with Harry Field and Bob Herd, and they had doped the wrong horse.

A lot of people were involved in Smith's story, and statements had to be taken from them all. For months Barnett, the officers of C9, more than a dozen provincial police forces and the Jockey Club's security department, especially my nominee, Robert Hill, were occupied in building up the long chain of evidence. One short cut had been denied them right at the beginning. They lay in wait outside the Metropole Hotel, but no one came to the rendezvous; Smith's contact had been warned, it seems, by an enterprising, if premature, story in that day's evening paper. And at the very end of the trail they suffered a much worse setback. Edward Smith threw himself from the second-floor landing in Lewes Prison, and died six weeks later from his injuries.

Micheline Lugeon, on the other hand, gave herself up. She simply arrived at a London police station with her solicitor.

Finally they all came to trial. The prosecution called 112 witnesses, who travelled to Brighton from thirteen English, three Scottish and three Irish counties, and from Jersey, arriving at the peak of the holiday season and needing accommodation for three weeks. "You know, Joe," grumbled the

Chief Constable to me, "it was only a confounded accident that I got landed with the case. If Smith hadn't gone to Brighton that day, I'd never have come into it."

"But think what fun you'd have missed," I replied. He made it clear that he was not convinced.

The end of the case was that all the prisoners were found guilty. Micheline Lugeon went to prison for twelve months, and the men for periods ranging from one to four years. The end of the case was not, of course, the end of doping; but it did have a very salutary effect. Not only did it remove one particular gang of dopers and act as a deterrent to others, but, what was almost more important, it convinced people who had been inclined to be sceptical that the risk of doping is a very real one. Racecourse and stable security have been greatly improved: random tests for doping are now made at every race: and the Jockey Club's security department has grown bigger and tautened its methods. And new arrangements have been made for the security of racecourse stables.

As I said, wherever there's gambling, there will always be a danger of crime. Racing remains popular with crooks both as a pastime and as a target for their activities: but, during the past few years, other forms of gambling have enjoyed a mushroom growth in Britain. The betting shops and casinos and one-arm bandits have attracted gangsters more professional and vicious by far than mere dopers. I am sufficiently English, however, to be glad that these gangsters at least do no harm to innocent horses.

CHAPTER 20

The Ringers

The motorcar, all true Englishmen feel, is only a horse manque, or, to be more precise, a carriage unhappily horseless, with its notional steeds in front and its vestigial box for oats behind (only the unfeeling Germans have reversed the natural order of things). It seems appropriate, therefore, that one of the basic crimes connected with motorcars should be known as "ringing," a term borrowed from the Turf.

In 1844 the Derby was won by a "ringer"; the horse which was entered as Running Rein was later discovered to be a four-year-old named Maccabaeus, owned by an Epsom corn merchant. The Francasal case, which I mentioned in the last chapter, is perhaps the most famous modern instance of race horse "ringing." But the "ringing" of stolen motorcars goes on all the time, this being the oldest and simplest way of turning them into cash.

Motorcars have, of course, been stolen ever since they were first made, but the problem only became acute after the last war. The mass ownership of cars had far outstripped any possibility of garaging them, with the result that millions of pounds' worth of valuable and easily transportable machinery stood temptingly unprotected. In the streets and open spaces of the Metropolitan Police District alone, some 250,000 cars are left out every night: and the unattended car parks which commuters are urged to use present a rich harvest for thieves by day.

Nearly a thousand cars disappear from the streets of London

each week. About 85 percent of them are afterwards abandoned, and restored to their owners within a month; most of these were taken simply for joyriding or for a journey home after the last train had gone; a few—Jaguars, Dormobiles, Zodiacs—will have been used in the commission of some other crime. Of the remaining 15 percent, perhaps a third are ultimately recovered by the police.

The number of cars being stolen has increased even more rapidly than the crime figures as a whole. In 1965 there was a jump of 35 percent over the previous year: 7284 cars were stolen, and only 15 percent of these cases were officially cleared up.

The list of missing cars is probably swollen by a few which ought not to be there. They are the result of a trick slightly more complicated than plain theft. The crook buys a wrecked car, removes the identification tabs and plates, and destroys the rest. Then he goes out and steals another car of the same make, type and colour: and swaps the tabs and plates: and advertises the allegedly rebuilt car for sale. He sells it, if possible for cash and to a private buyer, and then, after a week or so, steals it back again, removes and destroys the false tabs and plates, restores the genuine ones, and abandons it. In due course it's found and restored to the original owner. Meanwhile, the purchaser of the apparently rebuilt car has reported the theft of a vehicle which never existed.

In a rather different type of case, a man reported the loss in the West End, of his recently purchased car. He produced the registration book, and the theft was duly recorded. After the usual waiting period, the insurance company paid up. The satisfied client insured his next car with the same firm. Which was unwise of him. His next car also disappeared shortly after purchase, and the insurance company sent one of its investigators to interview this twice-bereaved motorist. The man wasn't at home, but a neighbour was. "Car? He's never owned a car," said the neighbour. What the man had done, both times, was to forge a bill of sale for a non-existent car, obtain insurance cover, fill up the appropriate form with fictitious details and pay the tax. He was then issued with an index number and a registration book for the phantom vehicle.

A receipt from H.M. Customs and Excise is also worth a good deal more to a car thief than the amount of tax it costs. The thief brings into the country some old car from the Continent, paying a relatively small import duty. Then he sends the Customs receipt to the taxation authority together with details, including the engine and chassis numbers, of a car he has either stolen or intends to steal: and in return he gets a fresh index number and registration book with which to authenticate the stolen car. Sometimes he doesn't even bother to import a car in the first place; he just forges a Customs receipt.

Merely attaching false number plates to a stolen vehicle (or indeed to a legitimately owned vehicle which is being used in a crime) isn't "ringing" in the true sense. Proper "ringing" entails a complete swap of identities between two vehicles: and, to achieve this, professional car thieves need their own workshops and yards.

Road accidents are very helpful. They provide a steady supply of wrecked vehicles of every type and make. Insurance companies sell them to salvage brokers, who rebuild the less damaged cars and sell the remainder for what they can get. Those which were thoroughly mangled or burned out may be worth very little even as scrap metal: but the registration book is valuable.

The thief buys the wreck, removes the index plates and the tabs bearing the engine and chassis numbers, and destroys the rest of the vehicle so completely that it disappears for ever. He waits long enough to cover the time needed for a genuine rebuild, then steals a similar car, swaps the identifying plates, and sells it as a rebuilt car with the registration book from the wreck.

A change in the regulations a few years ago has made this form of "ringing" at least more difficult. Insurance companies are now obliged to inform the taxation authorities whenever they write off a vehicle as a total loss, and the taxation authorities inform the police whenever such a vehicle is relicenced. Cars which rise phoenix-like from the ashes of a severe wreck are therefore automatically objects of suspicion.

If the wrecked vehicle had only third-party cover, this system doesn't apply, because the insurance company is interested in the damage it caused but not in the damage it suffered. In such cases, the policeman called to the accident has to assess and report the severity of damage, and, if it looks like a write-off, the station officer will notify the taxation authority on a form similar to that used by the insurance companies.

With the possibility of "ringing" so much in the mind of any suspicious policeman, the thief who wants to pass a stolen vehicle off as a rebuild needs to do rather more than merely swap the tabs and plates and respray the body. To add verisimilitude he may hammer some dents into the panels and then beat them out again. He may remove and clean the front suspension unit. One thief went so far as to cut through the roof and floor on an Austin A30 to give the impression that a new front quarter had been welded in as a replacement for a damaged section.

If a policeman really knows about cars, there are dozens of clues he can look for. The suspect vehicle may, for example, have been registered as new in 1959. He thinks it may really be older: so he starts by looking at the windscreen. If it's made of Triplex safety glass, he will see the trade mark, in which the words "Triplex" and "toughened" form a small circle. Under one letter of "toughened" he will observe a small dot. If the dot happens to be under, say, the letter "n," he knows that the car was made in 1957 or possibly in 1947, but certainly not in 1959; for the Triplex company record the year of manufacture by marking one of the nine letters, t-o-u-g-h-e-n-e-d, to correspond with the last figure of the date.

Electrical equipment is usually stamped with a date-code which gives the month as well as the year. This serial number can generally be found on the windscreen-wiper motors, the dynamos, junction and fuse boxes, coils, distributors, flashing indicator units and starter motors. To remove the numbers from all these points would be extraordinarily laborious and, if the deletion were noticed, would scarcely tend to allay suspicion.

The ingenuity of car thieves goes much further than this, however. The "double-ring" is an elaboration unknown in the simpler world of racing. The thief buys a wreck, removes the identification tabs and plates in the usual way, and destroys the remains. Then he buys a secondhand car of the same type and make, and substitutes the tabs and plates. Finally, he steals a third car of the same type and make, removes its tabs and plates and destroys them, and substitutes the tabs and plates from the second car. He then sells the second car as a rebuilt version of the wreck. The police, if they ever examine it, may suspect it to be a ringer but cannot identify it as stolen, for the simple reason that it wasn't stolen but bought. The thief, meanwhile, also sells the third car, which really was stolen—but the police have no reason to examine this one, because its registration number comes, not from a suspect wreck, but from the blameless second car, which the thief acquired by legitimate purchase.

The "double ring" can be turned into a "triple" or "quadruple ring" by the interposition of further cars between the wreck and the stolen vehicle: and the thief can make detection still more difficult by stealing back one or two of the cars he sells, thus creating a break in the chain. Even the most determined policeman is apt to lose so complex a trail. But we discovered that, in practice, there was often a bright side to the problem: thieves attempting so intricate a plan frequently ended up by confusing themselves.

Almost ludicrously straightforward by comparison is the simple method of re-registration; the only disadvantage, from the thief's point of view, is that the stolen car must be in more or less mint condition. To register a new car the buyer has only to fill up Form R/F 1/1, obtainable from any post office, and take it or send it to the local taxation authority, together with an invoice or bill of sale, a certificate of insurance or cover note, and the appropriate fee. An invoice can easily be forged with the innocent help of a jobbing printer, and insurance can then be obtained without difficulty.

Some professional car thieves go through this process before they even steal the car. All the thief has to do is pick the car he means to steal; surreptitiously open the bonnet and copy out the engine and chassis numbers, which have to be entered on Form R/F 1/1; wait until he is allotted a virgin index number and receives the registration book; steal the car, fix the new plates and sell it. Since the registration book is dated, the car has to look new; so, for this ploy, the thief generally picks a car with not more than a thousand miles on the clock.

A more specialised version of this method was practised by a North London car-hire firm. They began by having a quantity of chassis tabs, replicas of those used by Austin's, made for them by an outside firm: and, at the same time, they acquired some Austin cylinder block units, each bearing an engine-number tab. They then stole A55 and A40 cars from the streets, changed the tabs and the cylinder block units, and removed the index plates. They invoiced the cars to an associate company, which registered them as new vehicles, producing the invoice from the parent company as proof of purchase.

They were caught in the end because they had another trick in their repertoire, a variation of the "double ring." They bought, in the name of the parent company, seven new Austins from a London distributor. They stripped from each of these the engine, index plates, chassis tabs and road fund licence, which they proceeded to exchange for those on similar cars stolen from the street. The stolen cars were then sold into the motor trade with registration books matching their identifying marks. The thieves now had seven new cars without engines or identification plates and tabs. To these they fitted replacement engine units, which they had bought legitimately, and welded on the false chassis tabs from their stock. They invoiced the cars to their associate company, which proceeded to register them as new vehicles.

Though we became suspicious of these cars, we found we couldn't identify them. On the assumption that they had probably been stolen, we showed them to losers of similar cars: but nobody recognised them, because in fact the bodies and the engines had been bought legitimately. It was only when the bodies were traced back to the distributor who had supplied them, complete with engines, that we began to realise what had happened. The index numbers of the seven cars sold by the distributor were traced, and the cars to which they had been transferred were examined with a rigour going well beyond a mere check of the engines and chassis tab.

Car thieves, like other professional crooks, have to find and cultivate a sales-channel for their loot. Disposing of stolen cars abroad was easiest when honest motoring had been made most difficult, trammelled by the need to produce such formidable-sounding documents as the *triptyques* and *carnet de passage en douane*; documents which are blessedly no longer required by most European countries. A *carnet*, issued in England by the A.A. or R.A.C., is an undertaking to pay customs duty to the country to which the car is being "temporarily exported" (in the revolting official phrase), if it has not been brought out again within a specified period of time. The export-minded car thief assiduously fills up a large form requiring every conceivable detail about the car. How could anyone doubt that the car so lovingly described is his own? But in fact it is very likely a car which he has merely marked for future theft; a car which the owner helpfully parks in the same place every day. A quick look under the bonnet will have given him the engine and chassis numbers, a squint through a telephoto lens will have told him the number on the ignition lock. He submits the application form, and back comes an official document which will be his title to the vehicle.

If he collects the car from a railway station car park early in the morning, he can change the index plates on some quiet road on the way to the coast, stop for a comfortable lunch, and still be in France before the theft has been discovered. Once there, he will probably head for Spain. But he won't go quite so far. Since a British car cannot be sold in Spain without an import licence, he will take it to Andorra instead, where smugglers and receivers of cars abound. The vehicle can then be registered with the Automobile Club of Andorra, fitted with local index plates which are quite valid in Spain, and slipped across the frontier by people highly skilled in that art.

The only disadvantage for the British car thief is that this disposal route is inevitably seasonal. Unlike a holiday-maker, he cannot book his cross-Channel passage months in advance, so he has to go in the off-peak seasons when he can be sure of getting a passage at once. The whole of the winter is excluded because the mountain roads in the Pyrenees are snowed up, and the car-smuggling trade closes down, between late October and early spring. Autumn and spring are therefore the peak periods, and indeed the only satisfactory seasons, for the export of stolen cars. Which, from the police point of view, is fortunate for once a car crosses the Channel any hope of recovering it must be reckoned negligible.

A much simpler, but physically laborious, method of disposal is to take the stolen car to bits, blend the parts inextricably with those of other vehicles, and rebuild the whole thing into a body bought from the manufacturer. Or the stolen car can be disposed of piecemeal through the spare-parts trade. The country is full of "hot-rodders" and do-it-yourself mechanics who scour the car-breakers for good spares, which they can build into Fibreglas bodies. When the police find the abandoned body shell of a car, bereft of engine, wheels, suspension, and axis, they have a shrewd idea what's happened: but there's very little they can do about it.

Many car thieves have connections with the motor trade, and can conveniently dispose of stolen vehicles through one of the sixty or more motor-vehicle auctions which are held every week. In August 1959 a car which had been stolen at Stoke Newington in London was auctioned at Tunbridge Wells: and this was the beginning of a case which occupied a number of detectives for more than a year.

It was an unusual case in many ways, and its initial peculiarity was that the system which the thieves were using, though almost foolproof in itself, rendered detection of the stolen car virtually inevitable; for when it was sold and the new owner sent the registration book to the taxation authority, the fact that two cars with different engine and chassis numbers had the same registration number became painfully apparent. And from there it was only a short step to discovering that all the numbers in the registration book were forged.

Having realised this, the police worked back to find how the thieves had acquired the registration book. In this case the thieves had not been buying up wrecks: they preferred burglary. One of them would visit a secondhand car dealer and, pretending to be interested in some car, ask to see the registration book. What he really wanted was to see where the registration books were kept: and the dealer usually invited him into the office and obligingly showed him. Next night the thieves would break in and steal the entire stock of registration books. The details recorded in the books were removed with some domestic bleach, such as Milton or Parazone, and the paper would be ironed to replace the shine.

The thieves then proceeded to tour the streets and car parks of London, noting the registration numbers, vintage, and color of likely vehicles. When they found one similar to a car on the list which they had already prepared, they ascertained the number of the ignition lock by peering at it through an instrument made from half a pair of binoculars, and chose the appropriate key from the complete set which they possessed: and they constructed new index plates. Since ignition keys invariably fit the car doors too, they had no difficulty in entering the vehicle and driving it away.

They took it to a small lock-up garage, where the index plates were changed. The engine and chassis numbers and other particulars were then entered in the bleached registration book, and the stolen car's Road Fund Licence was bleached and altered to match the new index plates (identical with those of a legitimate car of similar make and size) and registration book.

The car, with all its particulars in apple-pie matching order, was driven off to an auction sale. The altered documents were so well forged that auctioneers and dealers never raised an eyebrow, and the original entries were invisible even under the ultraviolet lamps with which shrewd motor dealers make a routine check.

One of the gang, meanwhile, would have booked lodgings somewhere near the auction, and, giving a false name and the address of these lodgings, opened a deposit account at the local bank; no references being required for deposit accounts.

The car was always sold quite easily, because its reserve price, though plausible, would be low. Cash is never paid out immediately after an auction. The auctioneers allow six days to elapse and then send their cheque to the vendor at the address shown on his entry form. The thief, who would not in fact have been staying at his lodgings, though he would have paid a deposit, went there on the seventh day, made some excuse for not being able to use the room after all, gave the landlady another week's rent in lieu of notice, collected the letter from the auctioneers and quietly faded away.

Off he went to the local bank, where he paid the cheque into his account, telling the clerk that he had sold his car; a fact borne out by the auctioneer's name printed on the cheque. After a few days, he would come back and withdraw almost the entire sum from his account—clear profit except for his expenses.

Motor auctions, generally speaking, are the preserve of the trade. The cars bought there go into a showroom or are resold to another trader. A convenient cushion of time was therefore interposed before the stolen cars were bought by private customers and the changes of registration notified. The auctioneers are themselves always on the look-out for stolen vehicles, but the thieves in their jugglery with the identification numbers had anticipated all the ordinary checks. Perhaps the most professional of their precautions was the care they took to avoid using the number of any car which was the subject of a hire-purchase agreement.

Before a sale, the auctioneers normally check with Hire Purchase Information Ltd, to make sure the cars are free of lien. So the thieves did the same thing. Calling themselves "Mason Motors," they enrolled as subscribers with Hire Purchase Information, and, as they compiled their list of cars suitable for impersonation, they telephoned the numbers for checking. They also rented a small office, to which Hire Purchase Information could post written confirmation. Cars which were found to be subject to a hire-purchase agreement, were promptly dropped from the list.

All we had at the beginning were a few forged registration books. These revealed certain similarities; several of them seemed to be in the same handwriting. Two detectives went to the head office of Southern Counties Car Auctions, Ltd, at Farnham in Surrey, which handles thousands of vehicles every year. They began sifting a great pile of entry forms, and in due course were rewarded. They found first one, then another, and then another, in the same handwriting as some of the registration books: and on each form the vendor had given a different name and address.

The addresses proved to be lodging houses. The landladies were questioned, and gave descriptions of the men who had booked rooms but never used them. These descriptions were passed to selected officers throughout the Home Counties and to trustworthy people in the motor trade. And that was as far as we dared to go. If we had circulated a more general warning, it would almost certainly have scared off the thieves: and it was clear that our only chance of catching them would be after the sale and before they collected the cheque from their temporary lodgings. The situation was rendered trickier because there are people in the secondhand motor trade who would do anything rather than co-operate with the police.

Our two detectives continued to collect information about stolen registration books, and to accumulate landladies' descriptions: but we still had no authentic names. Then other police forces were now helping us. In February 1960 the Birmingham police heard that a suspected car had been spotted in the weekly auction at Birmingham Racecourse. Investigating, they discovered that two other stolen cars had been sold at the same auction. They checked the addresses on the entry forms, set a watch on the house and actually saw one of the team as he went in to collect his cheque. He came out again, got into a car which was waiting for him, and drove off with a girl and another man. The detectives followed, but lost him in the traffic.

A description of the two men and the girl and of their car was transmitted at once to Scotland Yard. It tallied with the descriptions we had been getting from the landladies. The car was traced to a motor trader called Harry Jacobs, who lived in Stoke Newington: and the other man seemed to be an associate of his by the name of John Goodall. The evidence linking them not only to the sale, but to the theft, of the stolen cars was thin, however, and we decided not to arrest them yet.

A couple of months later, a firm of auctioneers at Measham in Leicestershire informed the local police that they were suspicious about a car which had just been sold to a Nottingham dealer. The police checked the car and found that it matched one which had been stolen, shortly before the sale, at Whetstone in North London. The vendor had given an address in Northampton.

Twenty-four hours before the cheque was due to arrive, two detectives from Northampton Borough Police took up their positions in the house. The cheque came promptly by the first post next morning. At nine o'clock the telephone rang.

"This is Chief Inspector Halliday of Scotland Yard," said the caller. "I wish to speak to one of the officers who are keeping observation."

The telephone was passed silently to one of the detectives. He knew that the Yard had been kept in touch with what was going on, but this call somehow smelled wrong.

"There are no policemen in this house," he said. "I suggest you phone the local police station."

The caller insisted that there were officers in the house, but the detective continued to deny it, and the man finally rang off. Three minutes later the new lodger entered the house to collect his cheque. He was promptly arrested. His real name proved to be Terence Mackey of Stepney in London.

Meanwhile, out in the street, another plain-clothes detective was watching a car which had been parked about a hundred yards away. There was a girl in it. Eventually she grew restive, and moved from the back of the car into the driver's seat. As she started the engine, he put his hand through the window, switched it off again and removed the ignition key. After asking her a few questions, he arrested her and took her to Northampton Police Station.

The two Scotland Yard men came hurrying up from London to collect both her and Mackey.

The time had now come for swift action. A watch was set on Jacobs' house at Stoke Newington and on a number of other houses, including one at East Barnet where Jacobs' car had been seen parked. Detectives entered this house, searched it and settled down to wait in the hope that Jacobs might turn up. Presently the telephone rang.

"This is Sergeant Halliday of 'H' Division," said the caller. "I wish to speak to one of the officers."

He was told there were no police in the house. He rang off, but called again a few minutes later. And then twice more. Eventually Jacobs was seen walking towards his car. He halted, studied the house, got into the car and drove away. The police, resisting the temptation to go after him, remained concealed in the house. Five minutes later he returned, let himself in, and was arrested. Only four hours had elapsed since the arrests in Northampton.

The third man, John Goodall, was caught after being on the run for several weeks. All four of them came up for trial together in September 1960. The larceny of fifteen vehicles was proved. Jacobs went to prison for three years, Mackey and Goodall for eighteen months, and the girl was put on probation.

In that same month we formed a separate Stolen Vehicle Investigation Branch of the C.I.D., staffed initially by twelve detectives including those Flying Squad men who had been specialising in the investigation of car thefts. This Branch—C10 —is now considerably larger: and needs to be. It was designed from the beginning, like the Fraud Squad and the Fingerprint Branch, to be helpful to police forces throughout the country; for professional car thieves are essentially mobile, and their apprehension needs expert knowledge.

The list of ostensibly stolen cars has been somewhat reduced by lengthening the qualifying period from twenty-four hours to a matter of months. It would be reduced in a more valuable sense if more motorists would fit their cars with an anti-theft device; no such device will baffle a really determined thief, but several are quite adequate to deter casual driving away. On the other hand, the list, not of missing, but of stolen, cars would be lengthened if the law were changed, as it ought to be and probably soon will be, so that taking a car and afterwards abandoning it was punished as severely as theft. This type of offence has been increasing by seven percent a year. It causes a lot of inconvenience and worry, and cars are often damaged in the process. There seems to me no reason why the dishonest and selfish people who commit it should be exempt from serious punishment.

I can speak on this subject with Olympian impartiality. I've never driven a car and don't propose to start now.

CHAPTER 21

Picture a Murderer

"If this paper remains blue," Sherlock Holmes told Watson, "all is well. If it turns red, it means a man's life." He dipped the litmus paper into a test tube and it flushed into a dull, dirty crimson . . .

Conan Doyle's stories may have had some influence in showing the police how science can be used as an aid to detection, and even more influence in leading the public to think of forensic science as a kind of magic. It is a very useful aid: it isn't a kind of magic. Criminals are caught by men, not by gadgets.

Forensic science has, of course, tremendously advanced since Sherlock Holmes' day, particularly in its ability to show, by matching minute particles of soil or dust or thread or cellulose, that a suspect must have been at the scene of the crime. As well as the laboratory techniques which support them, as it were, behind the lines, the police have acquired a number of gadgets to help both in their preventive and in their investigative work. Rapidly coming into use now are personal two-way radios carried by constables on the beat, hidden television cameras to keep a watch on vulnerable streets and markets and car parks, and an infrared spotlight for use at night.

One device which we acquired during my period at the Yard caught the public imagination more than any other: the Identikit.

I first heard about it on July 30, 1959. At a lunch that day in the Cafe Royal I met a huge genial giant of a man, called Pete Pitchess. He had been in the FBI and was now Sheriff of

Los Angeles County. After lunch, he came back to the Yard to see the Black Museum and the Information Room. When we were having a drink in my room afterwards, with a few senior officers whom I'd invited to meet him, he showed us a piece of equipment which had been invented by his Deputy, Hugh McDonald. It was a book of interchangeable transparent flaps, each with a drawing of some part of a face—eyes, eyebrows, hairline, nose, mouth, and so on; rather like those books in which children put the head of a giraffe on to the body of a lion and the legs of an ostrich. With this range of possible parts, Pitchess said, a useful picture of a wanted man could be built up from the selection made by a witness who had seen him.

There was nothing new, of course, about constructing pictures from eyewitnesses' descriptions. As long ago as 1935, when I was prosecuting in the Grierson case, I was struck by what a good likeness the police drawing had been of the man who eventually appeared in the dock; it was a profile, I remember, with a hooked nose and glasses. But in Britain (contrary to the practice in some other countries) the artist didn't normally work with the witness; he merely followed a description which was handed to him. And a witness who is shown a completed drawing is too apt to accept it, whereas an Identikit picture can be continually altered until the witness really does feel satisfied that it represents the face he saw.

I showed the Identikit to the Commissioner, and we both expressed interest in the possibility of acquiring it. A week or so later, I received a letter from the American company which manufactured the equipment. (If the company had been British, I dare say I should never have heard any more about it, not for months or years anyway.) Pitchess had told them of our interest, they said; they were willing to consider leasing it to us, and they invited us to send an officer to California for a course of training. I replied that I couldn't spare a man. There was further correspondence, during which they asked me, among other things, for a list of every police force in Britain with more than a hundred officers. I sent it to them. They pondered on the size of the potential market, and, the following spring, offered to send their representative to Scotland Yard, to run a course of instruction here.

After clearing this proposal with the Commissioner, the Receiver, and the Home Office I circulated it to all provincial forces through the Chief Officers Association and the Chief Constables of Scotland Association. The response was gratifying. We finally arranged a three-day course for the beginning of March 1961.

The class consisted of thirty-one officers—ten detective sergeants from the Metropolitan Police, twenty provincial officers, and one officer from the United States Air Force. Superintendent Du Rose of C1 was in charge, and the instruction was given by Deputy Sheriff Hugh McDonald himself, who proved to be extremely good.

The course ended on Friday, March 3. A detective sergeant from "H" Division went back to his duties next day, and, using the Identikit, was immediately able to catch three men who had committed a robbery. But a more serious crime had been reported in "E" Division.

At 12:15 P.M. that Friday, before the Identikit course was even ended, I heard that a woman had been found stabbed to death in an antique shop in Cecil Court, off the Charing Cross Road. The body had been discovered by the proprietor, Louis Meier. A wireless car from Bow Street arrived, and the officers found the dead woman lying on her back with an antique dagger stuck in her breast and another in her neck.

She was Mrs. Elsie May Batten, and she had been an assistant in the shop. The daggers, which had evidently been taken from the stock, still had their price tickets on them.

At 12:30 Detective Superintendent Pollard arrived. In those

269

first few hours, his chances of success seemed steadily to dwindle. There was no reason to suppose—and, since the weapons were clearly impromptu, it seemed unlikely—that Mrs. Batten had been killed by a personal enemy: nor had she been sexually assaulted. Robbery was the likeliest motive, but her handbag and the box used as a till both appeared to be untouched; Mr. Meier couldn't say if anything had been removed from his stock. Local enquiries elicited nothing. A hairdresser opposite had seen Mrs. Batten open the shop at 9:15, but, since then, nobody had been observed going in or out. The only clue Pollard found was a piece of wood under the dead woman's legs, bearing the impression of a heel and faint sole marks.

When the pathologist, Dr. Keith Simpson, arrived half way through the afternoon, he found a third dagger underneath the body and a third stab wound in the back. He said the woman had also been struck on the head with a heavy stone ornament, and he confirmed that there had been no sexual interference.

Then things began to move. A fifteen-year-old boy, an apprentice sign-writer, was brought to the police by his uncle. The boy had told his uncle, and now told us, that he had gone into Meier's shop at about 11:30 that morning to buy a billiard cue, and had seen what he thought was a dummy lying on the floor at the back. When he realised it was a woman he assumed she had fainted—and promptly left the shop. Which doesn't seem a very chivalrous act. Perhaps he was a timid boy.

Meanwhile, Meier recalled that a young man who said he was half-Indian and half-English had been in the shop during Mrs. Batten's lunch hour on the previous day. This Eurasian had spent some time examining the antique daggers, but had left without buying anything. He had returned later, accompanied by a girl, and asked the price of a dress sword. Mrs. Batten had remarked to Meier afterwards that it was odd for a man so poorly dressed to be interested in a sword costing

£15. Meier gave us a description of the young man, and said he thought that he would be able to recognise him. All he could remember about the girl was that she looked somewhere between seventeen and twenty, and was fair-haired. There were several dress swords in the shop, and he couldn't say if any of them were missing.

A team of twenty detectives, working under Superintendent Pollard, began working their way through all the other antique shops and jewellers. But they found what they wanted, next morning, only a few yards away.

Opposite Meier's shop was a gunmaker. His nineteen-year-old son had been alone there on the morning of the murder, when, soon after ten a young Indian walked in and tried to sell him a dress sword. The sword had been wrapped in a sheet of brown paper. When he was asked how much he wanted for it, the Indian replied: "I paid fifteen pounds but I'll take ten." The gunmaker's son rightly thought this a suspicious remark. He asked the Indian to come back at 11:15, when his father would be in. The Indian agreed and left the sword, but never returned.

The gunmaker himself now added a piece of information. A dark young man—he couldn't remember much else about his looks—had called at the shop on the previous afternoon, and asked "Do you buy swords?" The gunmaker said he might, but would need to see the article. The young man replied that this sword had an engraving on it, and he promised to bring it in.

So we now had the sword. It was immediately identified by another woman who worked part-time in Meier's shop, and who remembered having shown it to a customer the week before. The brown paper had gone, having been used to wrap up a pair of gun barrels, but Pollard's men traced it to a customer in Kilburn, and sent it, together with the sword, to the Fingerprint Department at the Yard.

Meier and the gunmaker's son were each able to give a clear and detailed description of the young Eurasian: so, less than twenty-four hours after the course had ended, we had an ideal opportunity for giving Identikit a trial run. On March 4, one of the officers who had been on the course, Detective Sergeant Dagg, interviewed Meier and the gunmaker's son—separately —and built up pictures matching the descriptions they gave him. The two pictures proved strikingly similar, except for one detail: the hair style was quite different.

I was shown photographs of these two Identikit reconstructions. They looked good enough to be useful and close enough to each other not to cause confusion. I decided that not only should they both be circulated to all police forces but that they should also be published in the Press and shown on television. At the same time, we released Meier's much vaguer description of the girl.

Four days later, at 1:40 P.M., a certain P.C. Cole was on duty in Old Compton Street, Soho, when he spotted a young man who seemed to match the picture. And the young man was accompanied by a girl of about seventeen with blond hair. Cole stopped them, and told the man that he fitted the description of someone wanted for questioning in connection with the Cecil Court murder.

"Yes, I saw the photo in the paper," said the young man casually. "It did look a bit like me."

The accent—Cockney, not Peter Sellers-type Indian—also matched the police circulation. Cole asked them both to come with him to the police station.

"I'd rather not," said the man. "We're going to buy a ring."

Cole insisted, and, since this was a murder case, he took no chances. He searched the man, there and then. Finding no weapons, he marched the couple off towards a police telephone box in Cambridge Circus. An off-duty constable in civilian clothes saw what was happening and telephoned for a police car while Cole stood guard over his prisoners. Both the man and the girl repeatedly asked to be allowed to go; they were in a hurry, they said. Which merely intensified Cole's suspicions. Then a car arrived and whisked them away to Bow Street.

The young man was half-Indian, half-English, and gave his name as Edwin Bush. He was just twenty-four years old. As soon as he arrived at Bow Street, impressions were taken of the soles and heels of his shoes. While these were being compared with the marks found under the body, Pollard questioned the girl.

She was seventeen, and had known Bush for about two months, and had come into the West End with him that day to choose an engagement ring. As it was also his birthday, they were going to have a double celebration at an Indian restaurant.

She denied ever having been to the antique shop in Cecil Court, and, oddly enough, she was telling the truth. As we discovered later, the girl who had accompanied Bush was his sister, aged eighteen, who was not a blonde at all but very dark. It was sheer luck, that because Meier wrongly thought she had been fair, the description happened to fit the couple whom Cole picked out from the crowd in Old Compton Street.

While Pollard questioned the girl, detectives called at Bush's home. His mother said he had left the house at 7:30 A.M. on March 3, presumably for work. When in due course Pollard asked him about his movements on March 3, he immediately said that he had spent the whole of that morning at home with his mother. The shoe prints matched.

Pollard told the duty officer at Bow Street that he wanted to hold an identification parade. This was easier said than done, since it involved collecting nine men of similar age and colour who could speak English without a foreign accent. Eventually a group was assembled, and the parade was held at

10:25 P.M. Meier walked down the line first. He stood for some time in front of Bush, then said: "I'm not positive but I think this is the man." The gunmaker's son was brought in. He picked Bush with no hesitation at all.

Pollard then charged Edwin Bush with the murder of Mrs. Batten. After a moment's silence, Bush said: "The girl is nothing to do with it. I did it alone." And he went on to make a statement admitting that he had killed Mrs. Batten in order to steal the sword. Just to clinch matters, there was blood on some of his clothes, and his palmprint and two of his fingerprints were found on the brown paper in which the sword had been wrapped.

When he came up for trial at the Old Bailey in May, he pleaded not guilty to capital murder. He now said that he killed Mrs. Batten, not to get the sword, but after she had made an offensive remark about the colour of his skin. Cross-examined by Mervyn Griffith-Jones, Bush didn't deny that he had in fact stolen the sword.

"You admit that you went into the shop in order to steal it, and admit that having stolen it you killed the lady with these three daggers?"

"Yes, sir."

"You lost your temper simply because she passed the remark, 'You niggers are all the same, you come in and never buy anything'?"

"Yes, sir."

In his summing up, the Judge instructed the jury that, if they believed this was the true cause of Bush's attack on Mrs. Batten, they ought not to convict him of capital murder. They didn't believe it. After two hours' deliberation, they found him guilty; which, the Judge said afterwards, was the only possible verdict. Bush was hanged.

The result was a great deal of publicity for Identikit. The newspapers hailed it as a marvellous new aid to criminal investigation: and, sure as a Pavlovian reflex, some people expressed alarm at this new danger to civil liberties. How risky it would be, they said, to use composite pictures as evidence against an accused man. No one, of course, had ever suggested using them as evidence. If an arrest was made as a result of circulating an Identikit picture, the witnesses would then have to identify the suspect in the ordinary way. "If hopes were dupes, fears may be liars"—and vice versa. The apprehensions about Identikit were wholly unjustified, and the enthusiasm too was exaggerated. Identikit is simply a way—one way among several—of fixing, illustrating, and making permanent a witness's recollection, so as to help in the hunt for a wanted man when no photograph is available.

Its spectacular success in the Batten case proved a considerable embarrassment. Too much was then expected of it. As people saw more Identikit pictures, enthusiasm turned to ridicule. How odd, they said, that all wanted men should look just the same. But to policemen they don't look just the same; Identikit puts into visible form what a police description is supposed to provide—a catalogue of the few distinguishing marks which divide the wanted face from all the other human faces.

In his report to me after the course Superintendent Du Rose pointed out that one of the advantages, if Identikit were widely adopted, would be that a telephone call to a Central Index, the Criminal Record Office perhaps, could by using a code of numbers and figures pass a likeness to other forces without any need to transmit the actual picture. It could be useful internationally, he suggested: and he arranged a demonstration for the Chief Superintendents of C1, which includes the Interpol Office, C9 and the Criminal Record Office. Identikit requires trained operators, and he recommended that a phased scheme for its introduction should be adopted as soon as possible.

The arrangement we eventually made was that the apparatus

itself remained the property of the American company, which would lease the sets to the forces which wanted them. The Receiver of the Metropolitan Police District agreed to act as the hiring agent for all British forces. Whereupon we immediately ran into a bureaucratic snag. We became liable for import dues, assessed by the Customs at an exorbitant figure. Not without difficulty, we obtained special exemption.

The possibility of using Identikit internationally was debated at length during the Interpol General Assembly in 1962. I realised then for the first time how many comparable systems were already in use. The Canadians, for example, had been using cut-up photographs of their own criminals for years: and there were several rival systems in the States. Advocates of these other systems objected to the use of the word "Identikit" as though it were a generic, instead of a brand, name. The Assembly did not, in the end, recommend its international adoption, chiefly because it wasn't applicable at the moment to non-Caucasian faces.

That anyone could genuinely have objected, on principle, to the use of Identikit remains, to me, a great puzzle—or, at least, an example of the attitude of mind which is incorrigibly and irrationally suspicious of the police. British Courts and our rules of evidence provide the most scrupulous protection for the accused. To extend this proper care and start complaining that the police weren't "sporting" in the way they acquired the evidence is to tilt the whole balance of the law in favour of criminals, who aren't "sporting" at all. In some ways, the Americans have gone even further in this direction than we have, declaring inadmissible any evidence, however damning, which wasn't acquired in strict accordance with the rules; with the ludicrous result that confessed murderers have had to be released because their confessions weren't taken in quite the proper form.

Telephone-tapping is another example. On both sides of the

Atlantic this aid to investigation has roused strongly hostile feelings and has now been forbidden except in very special circumstances. The Metropolitan Police are allowed to intercept telephone calls only on the signed authority of the Secretary of State after application has been made by the Assistant Commissioner. Such nice regard for privacy no doubt does us credit, but is it really necessary? Innocent people have much more to fear from the unimpeded activities of criminals than from the remote possibility that the privacy of their telephone calls might one day be unobtrusively infringed by the police—an infringement far less embarrassing to their domestic secrets than the crossed lines which our beloved telephone system is forever mischievously providing.

CHAPTER 22

How Tall Must a Detective Be?

"There is," said H. L. Mencken, "a simple solution to every human problem—neat, plausible, and wrong."

This sapient observation certainly applies to the problems of crime and police organisation. The problems themselves, I suppose, really can be expressed very simply: too much crime, too few police. But the solutions are not so simple, though tens of thousands of earnest words have been devoted to these subjects in recent years.

Some of the arguments commonly advanced seem to suggest not merely that we haven't enough policemen, but that our policemen aren't good enough. This I would strongly deny. The reputation of Scotland Yard—I have to talk principally about the London police, because the Metropolitan Force is the only one of which I have personal experience—is still tremendously high throughout the world. I know, from talking to senior policemen in many other countries, that we enjoy in full measure their professional respect and admiration: and this, surely, is the most valuable sort of testimonial.

The quality of our police recruits has always seemed to me excellent. There is, it's true, some difficulty in attracting men whose educational and intellectual qualifications clearly suit them for the higher administrative ranks. The Bramshill Police College for potential senior officers has not, apparently, been able to fill all its places—though I wonder whether they couldn't have been filled if rather more imaginative selection processes had been used. The police are not getting graduates.

But this failure to attract the highly educated is perhaps less important than some people make out. The FBI is made up entirely of graduates, and a splendid force it is: but the crime figures go on rising in the United States just as fast as they rise here. Similarly, there are police forces, notably in the United States, with far more scientific aids than we possess: but I've never heard that their clear-up rate is significantly better than ours. Hard work, experience of criminals, knowledge of human nature, skill at interrogation and at taking statements—these are the essentials of detective work, and they haven't much to do with academic education or with technical devices.

Having made this point, however, I do, of course, recognise that the recruiting, organisation, and tactical disposition of the police are, in the long run, vitally important factors in the whole war against crime. The reorganisation of the Chicago police, for example, and their new technique of "aggressive patrolling" have had a dramatic effect on that city's notoriously bad crime figures. It is entirely proper that these subjects should be fully and even passionately discussed—as they have been, increasingly, during the past few years.

The central question in this debate is whether or not we ought to have a nationally organised police force, or at least a nationally organised C.I.D.

The most distinguished proponent of a national police force is Dr. A. L. Goodhart, who argued very cogently for it in a minority report of the 1962 Royal Commission on the Police. Many of the arguments against it are mere prejudice or nonsense, as, for example, the professed fear that a state police would lead to a police state. It is politicians, not policemen, we have to be frightened of in that direction. Any government with a fancy for exercising dictatorial powers would certainly not be deterred by details of police organisation. Prejudices, however, are no less real for being irrational. There are complicated human difficulties to be overcome before we can easily reorganise all the police forces of England and Wales into a single body. They will be overcome, I think, by sheer necessity: we shall eventually have a national police force: but not yet.

The possibility of a national C.I.D., or at any rate of some much closer linking of detective branches, is perhaps more urgent and more interesting, because it entails secondary—but also very important—considerations about the recruiting and status of detectives.

The position of the Detective Branch in the Metropolitan Police is not, in my view, wholly satisfactory. The blame for this goes right back to the origins of Scotland Yard, to the first Commissioner, Sir Richard Mayne himself. He was greatly concerned, as he had to be in the context of the times, to soothe public fears that the new police force would be a body of spies. He laid the emphasis, therefore, on crime prevention rather than on detection, and he refused to have a separate Detective Branch at all. When the Criminal Investigation Department was eventually formed in 1878, Howard Vincent's report, based on what he had seen in Paris, recommended a quite distinct organisation on the lines of the Police Judiciaire. The members of this organisation would receive higher pay than uniformed men. This idea failed to commend itself to the authorities, and the department of which Vincent became director remained firmly subordinate to the established hierarchy. And this is still, to some extent, the situation today. Detectives attached to the divisions, though responsible to their own senior officers, still have to submit their reports through the uniformed Chief Superintendent in charge of the division. A detective constable or a detective sergeant in no way outranks a uniformed constable or sergeant, though the detective's responsibilities are apt to be much wider. If we had a national C.I.D., the lowest rank would probably be sergeant, as it is in the Army's Special Investigation Branch. I would regard this as a useful step towards realism and the improvement of morale. Most countries do give their detectives some measure of higher status.

The Royal Commission—Dr. Goodhart and some other members dissenting—came down against the idea of a national C.I.D. But they made a proviso: "We think that this is a matter which should be kept constantly under review; and Government should not hesitate, by reason of pressure from interested parties or consideration of economy, to establish a separate C.I.D. if our present recommendations prove inadequate to meet the needs of the time." Many people would say that this condition had in fact occurred, that the crime figures speak for themselves.

My predecessor at the Yard, Sir Ronald Howe, has always been a keen advocate of a separately recruited national C.I.D. How absurd, he says, that men of average height or below, however brilliant, are prevented from becoming detectives, merely because they don't measure up to the physical requirements of the uniformed branch. How ludicrous that the investigation of a mail train robbery should involve at least three different detective departments—that of the city from which the train came, that of the city to which it was going, and that of the county where the robbery took place—as well as detectives from the railway police.

I used not to agree with him. I thought the arguments against a national C.I.D. were more persuasive than the administrative advantages such a reorganisation might bring. I knew that a great many, perhaps most, policemen were against it. "The time may come," I once wrote, "when a national C.I.D. will be necessary, but I agree with those who think the time has not yet arrived."

I have changed my mind. I think the time has now arrived. The crime figures do speak for themselves. Howe's belief that a separate C.I.D. is both practicable and desirable sprang from, or at least was confirmed by, his wide knowledge of Continental police forces. Now that my own experience has been broadened, as his was, by working in Interpol with colleagues from a dozen national forces, I am driven to the same conclusion.

The arguments against a national C.I.D. are perfectly valid as far as they go. If it was separately recruited, the effect on recruiting for the uniformed branch might be bad, because most aspiring policemen think (until they know more about the job, which often changes their minds) that they would like to be detectives. The antagonism which sometimes exists already between the C.I.D. and the uniformed branch might be exacerbated. There are considerable advantages in the fact that every detective began his career by walking a beat in uniform, and is thus accustomed to dealing with the public and familiar with the daily problems of ordinary policemen. It is true, also, that 80 percent of all crime is local, and is best handled by local police who know about local conditions and the local criminals. On the senior detective training courses for which I was responsible, uniformed officers from County forces (where there is much more interchange between the C.I.D. and uniformed branches than there has been in London) generally did conspicuously well; so why exclude them from detective work or compel them to make a choice at the outset of their careers?

But to each of these arguments there is a reply. Not a complete reply, of course. As Mencken implied, the solutions to human problems are rarely both simple and right.

If, as Howe envisages, a national C.I.D. had been able to draft 1500 men to the scene of the Great Train Robbery, the end result might not have been different, but at least the scale of the investigation would more quickly have matched the scale of the problem. Brigadier Cheney, the Chief Constable of Buckinghamshire, did, in fact, enlist the aid of the Metropolitan Police on that occasion with admirable promptness. Indeed, co-operation between adjacent forces has been quite good for a long time, allowing now and then for touches of personal

283

jealousy, and lately has been developing fast; senior officers meet regularly to discuss common problems, and men and equipment are freely loaned. However, the very existence of police boundaries clearly is a disadvantage, even if common sense and goodwill can minimise the handicap. It seems, for example, silly and a waste of time that the security officer of a tobacco firm, seeking to arrange protection for a vulnerable lorry-load of cigarettes, should have to discuss the problem with half-a-dozen different police forces along the route. Some duplication of effort, some delay in the exchange of information, are inevitable. Co-ordination should be automatic, not a question of special arrangements—and that means a unified command structure.

There are two sides, also, to the argument about physical standards, but I think, on the whole, Howe's point must be admitted. For a uniformed officer controlling crowds or walking along the pavement, sheer height is a distinct asset. The minimum requirement for the Metropolitan Police is now five foot eight inches, just above average for the male population. City of London policemen have to be five foot ten, and fine fellows they look with their height increased still further by tall crested helmets. But that the same stipulation should apply to detectives does seem hard to justify. It means that anyone of even slightly less than average height (or who, for example, wears spectacles) is excluded from a job for which, in all other respects, he might be admirably suited. The Police Federation has been very keen to preserve the physical qualifications. The Federation argues, quite truly, that detectives may find themselves in situations where they need to be at least as tough as any uniformed constable. But, even in such perilous situations, being above average height isn't an indispensable criterion of toughness. At a time when the police are suffering from an acute manpower shortage, and when the detective branches need all the talent they can find, this artifical restriction ought surely to be removed: but, if the physical standards of the uniformed branch are to be maintained, as I think they should be, the only solution is to have a separate entry for the C.I.D.

Similarly, it is of course an advantage for detectives to have some experience of uniformed work, but not an overwhelming advantage. Detective work may not require a Great Detective, a master logician in the storybook sense, but it does call for a special attitude of mind, an alertness to people, a fondness, if you like, for sticking one's nose into somebody else's business. The qualities which make a good detective are not identical with those of a good uniformed officer. A separate C.I.D. would attract men—valuable men—who won't join the police force now: and, provided it was still possible for uniformed officers to transfer to the C.I.D., I don't see why normal recruiting should be seriously handicapped.

Some senior officers stress the value of transferability, and perhaps of regular transfers, at all levels. What they have in mind usually is the ease and success with which members of rural forces can move between the C.I.D. and the uniformed branch: but rural crime is very different from the problem in London or in any other large city. A Scotland Yard detective is dealing with an essentially anonymous community. His expertise should be about crime and criminals rather than about local factors.

Admittedly, most crime though not the most serious, is local. No one is suggesting, however, that the tradition of local police and local detectives should be abandoned. A separate C.I.D. would be nationally organised and capable of drafting men all over the country in an emergency, but its infrastructure could and should remain local, rooted in each community.

There are, I repeat, perfectly sensible arguments on both

sides. But I'm now quite satisfied in my own mind that the balance of advantage indicates a national C.I.D.

The development of Regional Crime Squads and the compulsory merging of small forces constitute substantial and accelerating steps in the right direction. But even these comparatively modest moves have aroused fierce opposition. In this era of big crime there are still advocates of the small police unit.

Police reform is a currently fashionable subject, but too often, since the war, the Home Office, acting sometimes under pressure from the Police Federation, and moved sometimes by its own good intentions, had imposed rules and brandished red tape which prevent the best use of the talent available. For instance, a rule has been adopted which says that Chief Constables must have served in some force other than the one which they are now to command. This is a perfectly sound principle: but when it is applied with such rigidity that the admirable Acting Chief Constable of Liverpool, after slashing the city's crime figures, could not be confirmed in his appointment because he had never served elsewhere, it becomes ludicrous and damaging. There is another rule which says that nobody can be recruited to a senior rank who hasn't pounded an English beat. This has meant wasting the entire supply of high-calibre ex-colonial police who became available during the retreat from Empire. Whatever reforms and whatever kinds of reorganisation may be attempted during the next few years, the most important thing is that the resulting force should be flexible and adaptable, free to recruit wherever talent can be found and free to use it in whatever direction seems most effective. In the words of the Royal Commission, neither "pressure from interested parties" nor "consideration of economy" should be allowed to stand in the way.

CHAPTER 23
The Man from Interpol

I've no doubt that a national C.I.D. must, and will, come sooner or later—which, unless something extraordinary happens to Whitehall's normal pace, probably means later. But, even before I was convinced of this necessity, I felt it absurd that British police forces should not at least be exchanging information among themselves as effectively as the police forces of different countries exchange it through Interpol.

This is to ask for a high standard. Interpol ranks with the Rhodes Scholarships at Oxford as one of the very few international arrangements to have been an almost complete success; in which it differs conspicuously from certain more pretentious efforts to make many nations work together.

Interpol brought me an appointment which was, in some ways, the climax of my whole official career. It opened new horizons and gave me many new friends. It would have been fascinating at any time, but the period during which I was connected with Interpol happened also to be a crucial one; a time of rapid development both in the organisation itself and in general awareness of it.

When I was Secretary of the Metropolitan Police, the limit of my official interest in Interpol was that I had periodically to sign a green form certifying that Assistant Commissioner Ronald Howe's trips abroad were on authorised business. Unofficially, however, through his introductions I met a number of his colleagues in Interpol. On one holiday, for example, Mary and I were entertained in Brussels by Florent Louwage, who was for ten years president of Interpol and—equally important to us then—a considerable gastronome; on another, we stayed at the two-hundred-year-old farm of Harry Soderman, the director of the Swedish Institute of Criminal Technology. Soderman in his youth had travelled from India to Baluchistan on a camel; but, before driving us down to the farm, he refused even one drink for fear of being arrested. The Draconian Swedish law about drivers who drink when in charge of cars has been an effective deterrent.

Normally I should have become the British representative at Interpol as soon as I was appointed A.C.C. But in 1953 it was decided, quite rightly, that Howe, who was staying at the Yard as Deputy Commissioner, should continue to represent us at Interpol until he retired. He had played a major part in its revival after the war, and, since 1946, had been on the Executive Committee, which, in those days, was still small and intimate enough for all its members to be able to go out to lunch together and discuss their problems informally.

Before the Second World War, the International Criminal Police Commission, as it was then called, was surprisingly little known. I can't remember any thriller in which it was even mentioned. The situation is very different now. "Interpol"—this abbreviated title was originally the telegraphic address of the Italian bureau—has become world famous. Not even Scotland Yard has been subjected to such relentlessly inaccurate publicity. A few years ago, two television series were running simultaneously in both of which a Man from Interpol, equipped with wide powers and a slightly sinister glamour, roamed the world frustrating master criminals in country after country. Alas, Interpol has no such peripatetic agents, and its permanent staff, though they would probably recognise a master criminal if they saw him (for identities are their business), are most unlikely ever to meet one. The Interpol Conference in 1961 debated whether there might not be some way of copyrighting or otherwise protecting the name "Interpol" to prevent its unauthorised use: but in most countries there was no legal machinery for doing so.

Interpol's new fame, like that of the Yard and the FBI, may have the advantage that it does, to some extent, deter criminals. When Donald Hume was arrested in Zurich for murder, he was also wanted by the Yard in connection with two armed robberies. He told the Swiss police that he had come there because he thought, wrongly, that, since Switzerland was not a member of the United Nations, she would not be a member of Interpol either.

Some of Interpol's "clients" are like Hume, men who have fled abroad after committing serious crimes in their own country—murder, robbery or, most commonly, large-scale fraud; others are international criminals in the full sense—gold and diamond smugglers, drug traffickers, travelling confidence tricksters or white slavers (the "white slave traffic" isn't really white nor does it involve slavery nor is it properly a traffic, but it does exist); others again, like the skilled forgers of pound notes and dollar bills, may never travel themselves but their work does.

Interpol doesn't put armies into the field against them. It circulates information and alerts the local forces.

Its headquarters are in Paris, where they have just been re-housed in an impressive new building erected for the purpose. Custom and convenience dictate—and it is now laid down in the constitution—that the Secretary General and his staff should be nationals of the country where the headquarters are situated. The staff is not large, only about sixty people even today, some civilians, some seconded from the Sûreté or the Préfecture of Police—and including one officer from Scotland Yard. They maintain a Criminal Record Office, a fingerprint collection and case files.

They are in constant communication, by letter, telephone, Telex, and a special radio network, which has its own central control station and transmitters, with the police forces of the member nations.

Each nation sets up its own National Central Bureau to deal with Interpol business. These bureaus maintain contact not only with headquarters but with each other. Britain's N.C.B. is a branch of the Central Office in "C" Department at Scotland Yard. When I became Assistant Commissioner, it was manned by a sergeant and a constable. When I retired, ten years later, the establishment was a Chief Inspector, three sergeants, three constables and one clerical officer.

Information submitted by the N.C.B.s is distributed by the International Bureau in Paris through a system of confidential "circulations," with different coloured corners to indicate the subject matter. A "red-corner circulation" is a description of somebody "wanted" by a member police force and states that extradition will be applied for. A "green-corner circulation" gives details about some international crook, known to commit a certain type of crime, who ought to be watched wherever he turns up. A "blue-corner circulation" asks for information—real name, aliases, convictions, known activities—on some crook about whom either the International Bureau itself or one of the member forces feels it ought to learn more. There are also circulations with black corners. These are much sketchier documents. They contain the scanty particulars of unidentified bodies and ask if any member can help.

Most of these circulations are issued at the request or suggestion of one of the member forces. But Interpol Headquarters is no mere post office. Always eager to enlarge their files, the Paris staff themselves originate many requests for information. More could, and should, be done still, just as it should be between different police forces in England. I remember, for example, mentioning quite casually at an Interpol meeting that a number of foreigners, mostly Italians, had come to Britain lately, trying to sell what purported to be (but was not) a kind of non-flammable cloth to petrol stations—and I learned that the same fraud had been reported in several other European countries. If we had circulated the facts when we first heard about them, it might have been possible to stamp out this little racket much sooner, perhaps merely by a discreet refusal of entry visas, which is one of Interpol's simplest weapons.

The Secretary General's report to the annual conference provides a conspectus of Interpol's work. Between June 1960 and June 1961, for example, the Secretariat dealt with 3117 police cases, made up of 13 homicides or attempted homicides, 212 thefts, 883 cases of fraud, 1049 of counterfeiting or forgery, 498 of drug trafficking, 71 sexual crimes, 153 identifications, and 238 miscellaneous. These figures, the Secretary General announced, showed a 17 percent increase over the previous year, and a 45 percent increase during the previous five years, the biggest growth being in theft, fraud and counterfeiting. In the same year 375 descriptions had been circulated throughout the world. Action co-ordinated by the Secretariat had resulted in 231 arrests and 53 identifications in countries other than that where the person concerned was wanted. On June 1, 1961, Interpol Headquarters had 494,000 general information cards on about 175,000 persons, 37,000 fingerprint cards and 4800 photographs of specialist criminals. In that same year, the Secretariat had begun issuing regional circulations on the principal drug traffickers of the Middle East; 46 had so far been described in three loose-leaf books.

Since then, of course, all those figures have greatly increased, as has the membership of Interpol, which now stands at ninety-five.

This expansion would have gratified the farsighted criminologists who met at a conference in Hamburg in 1905. They drew attention to the dangers of "an international form of crime which has appeared as a consequence of the increase in travelling," and suggested that the police in all capital cities should have a duty to exchange information about these peripatetic criminals. Of course nothing came of the suggestion. It would have cost money.

The problem was discussed again in 1914 by a conference of magistrates, lawyers, and police, organised by Prince Albert I of Monaco. Once again, nothing came of it. The consequences of the murder at Sarajevo overwhelmed lesser crimes. The aftermath of war, however, threw up all the familiar elements—deserters, refugees, black markets, a taste for violence: and, to make matters worse, the old structure of Europe had disintegrated. The problem of international crime reached new dimensions.

One of the first people to realise the urgency of this postwar situation was Dr. Johann Schober, the head of the Vienna police. He was a remarkable man, who later became Chancellor of the Republic, and the force he commanded was the inheritor of a fine tradition. The police, in a sense, *were* the Austro-Hungarian Empire; they held it together. The dissolution of the Empire left the Austrian police with their responsibilities diminished but their skill unimpaired. At Schober's suggestion, an international congress of criminal police was held at Vienna in 1923. Twenty countries sent representatives, and, before the conference was over, they had formed the International Criminal Police Commission. Its headquarters were to be in Vienna and Schober was its first president.

For the next fifteen years Austria remained the dominating element, for the Viennese police had the advantage, not only of their professional expertise, but, more tangibly, of extensive dossiers on criminals in all the countries which had been part of the Austro-Hungarian Empire. The files, which are the lifeblood of such an organisation, and the membership increased steadily until, by 1938, there were thirty-four member countries. Britain was among them, but not particularly enthusiastic; our interests were still imperial rather than European, and the

I.C.P.C., unlike Interpol today, was orientated primarily towards the concerns of Europe.

And, before long, the concerns of Europe overwhelmed it. The Germans annexed Austria. The 1938 Assembly was held at Bucharest in mid-June; it was hot, and the delegates were glad to learn that their meeting place would be a river steamer on the Danube. Very agreeable it must have been. The new president was a German, Herr Steinhause. He, and indeed the whole German delegation, went out of their way to be conciliatory. As the session closed, the Commission was invited to hold its next Assembly in September 1939 at the new police building in Berlin. Early in 1939, the I.C.P.C. secretariat with all its records was moved to Germany, and shortly afterwards there was a new, self-appointed, president—Reinhard Heydrich, Himmler's second-in-command. And that, for all practical purposes, was the end of international, non-political, police work for the next six years.

But the six years passed, and, as the war drew to an end, Florent Louwage, the Belgian Inspector-General of Police, foreseeing that the familiar pattern would soon start to repeat itself and that the shores of peace would be promptly lapped by a record tide of international crime, got in touch with as many as he could find of his old colleagues from the I.C.P.C. In June 1946, the representatives of nineteen nations met at Brussels and brought Interpol back to life. Louwage was to be president, Louis Ducloux of the Sûreté would be Secretary General, and there would be two other members of the Executive Committee, Wernher Muller, Chief of the Swiss Federal Police, and Ronald Howe.

A return to Vienna, then under four-power occupation, was clearly impossible. Paris seemed the best choice for a new headquarters; the French government provided offices and a small staff. At first, the staff consisted of Ducloux and two others, both of whom were still with Interpol in my time. One of them, Jean Nepote, became a close friend of mine. No one has worked harder for Interpol or shown more unfailing tact. In 1963 at Helsinki he was elected Secretary General. He well deserved it.

The files which had been taken to Berlin were lost or destroyed during the war, so Ducloux and his minute staff were faced with the laborious task of building up the essential records again from scratch; which they did by importuning the members to submit material. In other ways, the climate was favourable. International co-operation was, at least theoretically, in fashion, and the new nations which have proliferated since the war, were faced, just as the fragments of the Austro-Hungarian Empire had been faced, with criminal problems of which they had little experience.

By 1955, when the General Assembly met in Istanbul, the nineteen nations of 1946 had increased to fifty-five: and they were no longer exclusively, or even predominantly, European. The Istanbul meeting—it took place during the Turkish revolution, the sounds of which Ronald Howe is said to have mistaken for fireworks—was a kind of watershed. Rather sadly, the old intimacy and informality of the early postwar years had finally disappeared. A new constitution was adopted, under which the president would be elected for a four-year term (Louwage had held the chair for ten years), and there would be only two vice-presidents (instead of vice-presidencies being an honour which could be awarded quite lavishly to deserving people); and, in practice, these three principal offices would be held, for equity's sake, by a European, an African or Asian, and someone from the Americas. Even the name was changed. The International Criminal Police Commission became the International Criminal Police Organisation, on the grounds that an "organisation" sounds more permanent than a "commission."

The new constitution reaffirmed the principles which had

guided the old commission from its beginning. The co-operation between members must be within the limits of the laws in the different countries. The organisation could concern itself only with "ordinary" crimes—those universally recognised as such. Political offences were strictly excluded. Indeed any kind of religious, racial, or political activity was expressly forbidden. This was, and is, a vital condition. Interpol depends on there being confidence between members. If once they began to suspect political motives behind requests for information, that confidence would disappear, and the usefulness of the whole organisation would start to crumble. Because the members of Interpol are police forces which recognise this fact, it has been possible so far to keep politics out: but this hasn't been easy and needs constant vigilance.

There are notable gaps in the enlarged membership. The Soviet Union never joined: but Czechoslovakia was one of the nations represented at the original Brussels meeting and Poland, Hungary and Rumania all joined soon afterwards. Ironically, the General Assembly was held at Prague in 1948, which was the year of the Communist *coup*. In 1950 and 1951, the four satellite countries resigned, one by one, without giving any reason. Yugoslavia is now the only Communist country in Interpol. South Africa has also resigned.

More surprising, perhaps, is the absence of America's FBI. When Interpol was reconstituted after the war, J. Edgar Hoover sent representatives but in 1952 decided to withdraw. The United States is now represented by the bureaus of Narcotics, Customs, Internal Revenue, and the Secret Service, and in 1961 the then Attorney General, Robert F. Kennedy, nominated the Treasury Department to act as the National Central Bureau.

Interpol has never claimed a monopoly of relations between its members, however, or between a member and outside police forces. Normal inter-police communications continue, and the

FBI always provides admirable co-operation. The same cannot be said for the police forces of Communist countries, but, in their case, the need for co-operation is slight. Soviet criminals find it no easier than honest men to escape through the Iron Curtain: and no Western crook in his right mind would go the other way, and, if he did, the police of his own country would hardly think it worth trying to get him back.

The General Assembly of Interpol meets in a different capital city each year. The first General Assembly I attended was at Lisbon in 1957. The British delegation was small—just Ivo Stourton, who was Inspector-General of Colonial Police, and I. The following year, however, the Assembly was held in London. Since no travelling expenses were involved, the British delegation was increased to the magnificent total of twelve, including the only woman delegate, the late Miss Denis de Vitre, a remarkable lady who was then Assistant Inspector of Constabulary and had once worked with Russell Pasha in Egypt.

Other nations have usually been more generous in their supply of delegates. The French never sent less than eight or nine; and in the American contingent the agents of the Treasury Department's bureaus were generally reinforced by government lawyers and high-ranking officers from the investigation branches of the armed forces.

For the London meeting I provided a special staff from C1 to help the Secretary General's staff, who had come over from Paris. The Lord Mayor gave a luncheon for all the delegates and their wives. One delegate was so impressed by the Sword Bearer's fur hat and long robes that he shook him warmly by the hand, assuming that so splendid a figure must certainly be the Lord Mayor in person.

During this Assembly I was elected to the Executive Committee, which meets twice a year; one of these meetings being in Paris in the spring, which is not disagreeable. It was an immensely enlarging experience. Our duties were to exercise a measure of control over Interpol's administrative and financial affairs, to prepare an agenda for the General Assembly, to supervise the carrying out of the Assembly's decisions and to keep a general eye on what was happening. These functions required a good deal of diplomacy. Different police forces have different interests. The Americans, for example, have always thought that Britain takes the narcotics problem too lightly; addicts from Canada and the United States have been known to come to Britain because they can get drugs more easily here. The Indians think other countries give them too little help in the prevention of gold smuggling; but to export gold from France, or indeed from many countries, is no offence. If policemen sometimes think that other police forces are less co-operative than they might be, this complaint is rare and mild compared with the almost universal belief of policemen that governments are letting them down. Many of the Assembly's resolutions amounted to a decision that pressure ought to be put on governments to achieve some end which seems desirable to policemen—such as the compulsory hospitalization of drug addicts.

But it was the serpent of politics which tried most persistently to slither in and which had to be most rigorously expelled.

Feeling that the time had come for a General Assembly to be held outside Europe, the London conference accepted an invitation from Pakistan to meet in Lahore in 1959. It sounded an excellent and, particularly for me with my old attachment to India, an attractive idea. Then suddenly, not very long before the meeting was due, we were informed that Pakistan, the host country, not only refused to invite a delegation from Israel but would not even be willing to issue visas to Israeli delegates if they were invited by the Secretary General.

The Executive Committee held a hasty and anxious meeting, the upshot of which was that the Secretary General was instructed to inform the host country, that, unless Israeli delegates were accepted, the Assembly might not be held in Pakistan. They weren't and it wasn't. The original meeting was cancelled and an Extraordinary Meeting of the General Assembly held in Paris instead.

Tempers soon fell, however, and the incident was forgotten (except, I hope, as a salutary lesson). Indeed a Pakistani officer was elected to the Executive Committee the following year, and eventually became a vice-president.

The 1960 General Assembly was held in Washington. The cost of so long a journey to so expensive a country naturally failed to arouse the enthusiasm of the Treasury, and the Home Office had to make out a strong case before I was allowed to travel first class.

I welcomed the trip not least because it would give me a long-sought opportunity to meet J. Edgar Hoover, with whom I had often corresponded and who by any standards must rank as one of the world's great policemen. His achievement has not only been the forging of the FBI into the magnificent crime-fighting weapon it is but that he has managed also to sell the idea of law-enforcement to the American people, who are not the most docile supporters of authority in any form. This propaganda success was no mere accident. It was done deliberately. And, as we have seen to our cost in Britain, getting the public on to the side of law and order is one of the hardest and yet most important tasks for any police force.

Meeting people about whom one has heard a lot and whom one admires is often a disappointment. Meeting Hoover wasn't. On my first, and indeed my only, free afternoon in Washington, I presented myself at the FBI's headquarters, and was conducted by a coloured major-domo, who had been with Hoover for years, through a large anteroom into the great man's office, with the Stars and Stripes behind his chair. We talked about crime in our respective countries, the differences and the rather similar causes which, we agreed, underlay its recent increase—notably a softening of the law. We saw eye to eye on many of these matters. His singlemindedness, his uncompromising dislike of criminals, his dedication, were as impressive in person as they had been by reputation.

He had recently launched a campaign to reduce overweight among his officers: and he had set them an example by shedding many surplus pounds himself. He must have looked on me as a hideous warning. When I came out, a group of FBI men were waiting in the anteroom. "I've done you boys a very good turn," I told them. "The Director will never be able to take *your* weight problems seriously again."

I called, that same afternoon, on Allen Dulles, the head of the Central Intelligence Agency, whom I'd met before in London. He made an interesting contrast with Hoover. Quieter and less forceful, he was much more like an Englishman in manner and appearance—a comparison which Mr. Hoover wouldn't in the least resent, for he has never wanted, I'm sure, to be anything but American to his fingertips.

For me October 15 was the big day. I spent the morning at General Assembly, but left early to make a speech at a National Press Club luncheon. I returned in the afternoon and was elected president of Interpol. After dining with the Washington correspondent of *The Times* I finished the evening playing poker with some Canadian and American friends. I lost consistently until, in the last hand but one, I was dealt three aces and two queens, and won back everything I had lost, with a little bit over. A good omen, I felt; an auspicious launching in my new post.

Among the letters of congratulations I received was one from Hoover. He was delighted, he said, to hear that I had been elected president of Interpol, an honour which he knew I would value very much. Whether he valued it very much he was careful not to say. Another came from my old friend Sebag Shaw, the Recorder of Ipswich, who used to do a lot of work for the Metropolitan Police. It was in rhyme, more or less:

Reductio ad Magnum

How amply doth he fill the role
Of President of Interpol.
Confounding logic rigmarole,
The part *is* greater than the whole!

I've read more elegant poems, but it's the thought that counts. And I treasure it nostalgically beside that other rhyming tribute, written so many years before, and presented to "Tiger" Jackson by his colleagues at the Calcutta Bar.

Such honorific posts as the presidency of Interpol are almost always rendered either pleasant and easy or intolerably difficult by someone else, some permanent official, who really does the work. I couldn't have had anyone more helpful than Marcel Sicot, who had succeeded Ducloux in 1951. Sicot had been a fine detective officer and was later Inspector General of Training for the Sûreté. He was white-haired and dignified, a good speaker and a tireless administrator: and his courtesy was unfailing. He spoke to me always in English, though he suspected me of knowing more French than I admitted to—and, indeed, once caught me listening to a committee, which was talking in French, without my earphones on. Perhaps he gave me the benefit of the doubt and thought I was merely behaving like Evelyn Waugh, who, when bored, would ostentatiously switch off his ear trumpet.

The fact of an Englishman's becoming president did, I believe, help to make the British authorities more Interpol-conscious. It was no longer what jealous colleagues at the Yard called "Ronnie Howe's club for having fun on the Continent." It had to be taken seriously. The British delegations grew larger. Local authorities began to feel that the expense of sending provincial Chief Constables might be justified.

As a curtain raiser to the General Assembly in Copenhagen in 1961, we held a special conference on forgery and counterfeiting. For the first time Interpol invited representatives of commercial firms to attend. Britain sent a very strong team. Apart from the police delegates there were representatives of the Mint, the Bank of England, and the Treasury Solicitor. The firms which sent observers were Portals, which for more than two hundred years have made paper for the Bank of England notes; Thomas de la Rue & Co., and Bradbury Wilkinson & Co., manufacturers of bank notes for many nations.

Sir Francis Portal addressed the Conference and presented every delegate with a book made up of blank pages, each with a different watermark—the last being the arms of Interpol. There was plenty to talk about. Since the previous Conference on this subject, which had been held at The Hague in 1950, no fewer than 1300 different sources of counterfeit money had been discovered, two hundred clandestine printing shops had been raided and forty-six countries had reported false currency in circulation.

The following year the Assembly met in Madrid, and I went to a football match: Real Madrid v. Manchester United. With me were my wife, my daughter Virginia, and the crime reporters of the *Daily Express* and the *Daily Mirror*, Percy Hoskins and Tom Tullett, both old friends of mine. As a vastly outnumbered block of British supporters, we tried to make up for our lack of numbers by the loudness of our cheers. That Assembly was spoiled for me by illness. I retired to bed for a day, and, though I managed to attend the official dinner, I couldn't face anything more than dry bread and Perrior water. Despite these handicaps, my speech was rather good, as I remember. Manchester United having won, I complimented our hosts on the courtesy of the Spanish crowds, who had loudly applauded when Manchester United scored their two goals. I wish I could believe that a British crowd would have done the same in reverse.

Hoskins and Tullett had, hitherto, been the only London

newspapermen who regularly attended Interpol conferences. But as Interpol grew in fame, fashion and prestige, it attracted more reporters as well as more delegates and observers: a number of well known crime reporters from the British national newspapers turned up. I made sure they were invited to the parties, given by various member countries. Furthermore, in order to get maximum coverage in the London papers, I arranged for the daily press bulletin to be issued at noon instead of 5 P.M.

The 1963 Assembly, my last, took place in Helsinki. We stayed at the Torni Hotel, which surprisingly has not only an excellent Spanish restaurant, supervised by a chef from Madrid, but perhaps the best Chinese restaurant in Europe, with a chef who flies in from Hong Kong for the season. There were many distinguished delegates but fewer British pressmen. As far as criminological publicity was concerned, we were hopelessly outclassed—for the Great Train Robbery had occurred just two weeks before and the hunt was still in full cry. Inevitably it was the chief topic of conversation.*

* So much has been written about the Train Robbery that it would be superfluous for me to tell the story again. There are only two really interesting things about it; one is a mystery, the other a moral.

The mystery is this. Why should criminals who were capable of planning and organising a robbery on so large a scale have been such idiots as to leave the deadly fingerprint evidence in the farm just waiting for the police? There was plenty of time to burn or wipe it away. The robbery took place on August 8. The thieves almost certainly left the farm on August 10, and the police didn't arrive there until August 13.

I don't know the answer. It was said, at one stage, that somebody had been paid £30,000 to "wipe" the farm, but, through fear, negligence or malice, had left the job undone and was now in grave danger of reprisals. When Edwards surrendered to the police in 1966, he claimed that he was the culprit and had simply panicked. But this may not be the truth.

The moral is that the police were very lucky and can hardly expect such luck again. In this type of case, quick police action on the widest scale is vital: and this would be greatly facilitated if there were a central controlling body, such as a national C.I.D. should provide, which, recognising the magnitude and extent of the crime, could organise all branches of the investigation on an appropriate basis from the beginning. I think it's desirable, too, that the public should be given brief details through press, radio and

Most of the European police officers I talked to expressed a touching faith that Scotland Yard would soon track down those miscreants who remained at large. Two—Bell and Cordery—had already been caught, Wilson and Biggs were arrested while I was in Helsinki. Leatherslade Farm, with its rich supply of fingerprints and other clues, had been found a few days earlier. Over £200,000 had been recovered—£100,000 of it abandoned in a plastic hold-all, presumably jettisoned by a robber who panicked. Our European colleagues assumed that clearing up the rest of the case would be only a matter of time, and I was fairly confident that they were right. I was rather sorry to be away from London and missing the excitement.

At the end of this Assembly I submitted my resignation. My term of office still had a year to run, but I was due to retire from Scotland Yard, and I had always taken the view that the president of Interpol, and indeed the members of the Executive Committee, ought to be serving officers in daily contact with the National Central Bureaus of their respective countries. My predecessor, Agostinho Lourenco, had retired from the Portuguese police force after his first year in office but remained as president for another three. This didn't seem to me a good precedent. I was therefore pleased to hand the chair over to my friend Fjalar Jarva, Finland's Chief of Police, a big, tough, jovial man, typical of his courageous and resilient country. He has since been succeeded by another good friend Firmin Fransseu of Belgium who always ended his letters to me with the handwritten words "bye bye."

Earlier that year I had taken some accumulated leave and gone cruising in the Aegean on Stan Joel's yacht, which Mary and I joined at Istanbul. Very flatteringly, the Chief of the

television as soon as they are known to the police. The perpetrators of large-scale crimes are most vulnerable, most likely to behave in suspicious ways, during the hours immediately following the robbery, and it can be very helpful to have the public alerted.

Turkish police flew there from Ankara to greet us. Before we left Turkey, the head of the National Central Bureau said he would signal his opposite number in Athens to expect us when we arrived at Peiraeus. When we reached Greece, however, nobody paid the slightest attention. At Helsinki I learned why.

The Turkish N.C.B. had duly sent the message saying that Mr. Jackson was coming and suggesting the Greek police might care to meet him. The Greeks seem to have found this message puzzling, and signalled Interpol Headquarters in Paris asking for further details of the man Jackson and what offence, or offences, he had committed. Paris presumably was baffled, since I was neither arrested nor warned off, nor, to the best of my knowledge, even followed on my short journey from Peiraeus to the airport.

It was, no doubt, a salutary lesson. The largest president of Interpol is small beer in the great global battlefield where the cops and robbers struggle unendingly.

For me, however, at least in my official capacity, the struggle was ending. I am particularly glad that, in those last years, I got to know the police of many different countries. Policemen everywhere, I discovered, have much in common. Some forces have special skills, some are tougher than others, some more scientifically inclined: but I honestly believe that the Metropolitan Police are as good as any, and better than most. Our strong suit lies not in any special expertise, and certainly not in ruthlessness, but in sheer efficiency at getting things done. Nor am I alone in this opinion. If Britain's reputation stood as high in other fields as it does for Police work, our position in the world today would be a great deal better than it is.

CHAPTER 24
Another Room Beside the Thames

Going to the races, as I've said, is an entertainment I enjoy only when everything is laid on in a civilised way. At Goodwood in 1962 the circumstances were admirably civilised; our host provided an excellent luncheon after which we strolled over to the racetrack, lost a little money and returned to refresh ourselves again.

En route I met Sir Philip Margetson, who had been A.C.A. at the Yard and a friend of mine since my arrival there as Secretary. Before we parted he said, "You'll be retiring next year, Joe, why don't you come to us?"

One of the comforting things about my career with the Metropolitan Police was the prospect of a reasonably good pension at the end of it; but in a period of inflation and exorbitant taxes no pension is good enough. So I thought seriously about what Philip had said.

Both he and Ronald Howe had retired in 1957 and both had joined the boards of industrial security companies. Philip was chairman and Joint Managing Director of Securicor, the biggest security company in Britain.

Before the war industrial security companies were almost unknown in this country but they have existed elsewhere for generations. Pinkerton's in the United States is over a hundred years old and there are several European companies with a history nearly as long. Securicor, the oldest in Britain, originated as a small affair supplying uniformed guards to patrol at night outside private houses. It did quite well, until the outbreak of war in 1939 brought its business to a standstill. Like Interpol, however, it was revived soon after the war ended.

The rise in crime which began in the 1950s provided new scope for commercial security firms, and, as the years passed, their numbers rapidly increased. Securicor began to expand and no longer confined itself to providing uniformed patrols for private houses. By 1960 it had three branches and a staff of more than six hundred.

In that year the firm was bought by Kensington Palace Hotels, Ltd., and Keith Erskine, the chairman of that company, became Joint Managing Director. Under the spur of his imagination, energy, and enthusiasm, Securicor expanded so rapidly that by 1963, the three branches of 1960 had proliferated to close on seventy and the staff of six hundred had become more than four thousand.

I decided I could do much worse than follow the example of my two friends. I took Philip Margetson up on his suggestion and, when I left Scotland Yard in the autumn of 1963, a new job was waiting for me. I became a director and Joint Vice-Chairman of Securicor.

Thus the continuity of my life was agreeably maintained. If a corpse with a strangely curved Oriental dagger in its back were thrown into the Thames in front of my new office on Chelsea Embankment it would, unless fished out by the River Police, float in due course, past my old office now occupied by the new A.C.C., "Rasher" Bacon. It caused me no distress to think that finding the murderer would now be his responsibility, not mine; but it was satisfactory to know that the frustration of criminals, and especially of violent criminals, was still part of my work as well as his.

In their early days private security firms had to overcome a certain amount of police suspicion, but that time is long past. The undermanned, overworked police of today are glad of anything which makes crime more difficult, and they welcome an organisation, provided it's honest and well run, which can guard the inside of buildings where they could only enter when specially sent for. Conversely, no security company could do its job properly if it didn't have a good understanding with the police.

Securicor's ranks are filled mostly with ex-servicemen rather than ex-policemen, but besides Sir Philip Margetson and myself there are some notable recruits from the Yard. Sir Ranulph Bacon also became a director when he retired in October 1966.

A couple of months after I came to Securicor, I was joined by former Chief Superintendent George Davis, who had done so very well as head of C9; former Chief Superintendent James Miller of the Uniformed Branch came in 1964 and took charge of Securicor's training programme; and, when my old friend Deputy Commander Colin MacDougall retired in 1966, he too joined the company.

George Davis had been the Scotland Yard Officer chiefly responsible for the horse doping enquiries a few years earlier. I knew from some of my friends who owned racehorses that the problem of doping was still a real one. Philip Margetson, himself a racing man, was well acquainted with many of the principal figures in the Jockey Club. Here then was a chance to pick up some old threads and for Securicor to acquire an important and valuable assignment.

After a year's negotiation the contract was signed. Before that, however, Davis took part in an extensive survey of the precautions which the racecourse stables were currently taking, the arrangement of gates, the adequacy of perimeter fences and so on. When this survey was complete and agreement had been reached, we accepted responsibility for the security of all the horses at racecourse stables from twenty-four hours before the first race until the last race of the meeting had been run. We covered every racecourse except a few where the structural precautions seemed inadequate. Most of these have since been brought up to standard, and there has, so far, been noticeably less doping. The presence of our guards is doubtless not the only reason for this but we like to think it is a material one.

Racecourse security is, of course, only one of Securicor's rapidly proliferating interests. In the three years since I retired, I have come to realise that industrial security is to some extent a specialised art and even long experience of police work does not make one an expert. Apart from the purely commercial side, there are technical questions to do with locks and safes and alarms; and there is the need to guard against an enemy even more destructive than the professional criminal— fire.

I found a lot to learn. But it was fun, and the very fact that working for a commercial firm is so different from anything I'd done before has kept me constantly interested. But the most important thing, from my point of view, is that I am still occupied in the business of preventing crime, which has been the object of my whole career, just as it was the principal objective laid down by Sir Richard Mayne when the Metropolitan Police were founded. To prevent a crime, he held, was far more desirable than merely catching the criminal after a crime has been committed. The overwhelming emphasis originally laid on their preventive role may actually have done some harm in the development of London's police, because it delayed the introduction of a proper detective department: but the emphasis itself was right.

I believe that crime—especially planned professional crime —is evil and cruel, and that all police work, all law enforcement, all penal institutions, must be directed to preventing its occurrence. This is the true criterion by which to judge every proposed reform in these fields.

Reformers, unhappily, are apt to become so enthusiastic about their own pet theories that they forget about the end altogether. And this leads them, since they are then obliged to defend their reforms on a false premise and often in the teeth of common sense, into a dangerous intellectual dishonesty. As the famous English philosopher and statesman, A. J. Balfour, once observed: "It is unfortunate, considering that enthusiasm moves the world, that so few enthusiasts can be trusted to speak the truth."

I have found this warning very applicable to the enthusiastic liberal reformers who are now so influential. They base their theories about crime on a doctrinaire belief that no criminal is personally to blame for what he does. Instead, they blame "society" or poverty or boredom or mental disturbance, never the man himself: and they hold this belief unshakeably, often in complete defiance of the obvious facts. Their principal aim, therefore, becomes, or seems to become, the treatment of the criminal, in the hope of educating him into a good (which, to them, means liberal) citizen, rather than the prevention of crime and the protection of other citizens. My own belief is that a penal system which cannot, or does not, bite when justice demands it simply breeds criminals.

I am a keen advocate of certain reforms—the stiffening of the penalties for violent crime, for example, and the integration of the country's detective forces—because these measures would, I think, contribute materially to the prevention of crime. But I am not an enthusiast in the sense of imagining that these or any other organisational reforms would solve the problem. "Can you influence a tortoise by rapping on its shell?" asked Sydney Smith. "You might as soon hope to influence the Dean and Chapter by rapping on the dome of St. Paul's." If crime is ever to be substantially reduced, we must get through the dome and influence the minds of ordinary people.

They must be convinced that crime is wrong, that violence and callous disrespect for property are wrong, that professional criminals maim and kill as ruthlessly as the germs of some foul disease and that policemen are therefore as worthy of respect and as deserving of public gratitude as doctors. They must come to recognise that the rule of law is a prerequisite of civilisation, and that criminals who deliberately defy it are enemies, undermining the fabric on which all civilised life depends.